Caviar and Cabbage

Melvin B. Tolson

Caviar and Cabbage

Selected Columns by Melvin B. Tolson from the *Washington Tribune*, 1937–1944

Edited, with an Introduction, by Robert M. Farnsworth

University of Missouri Press
Columbia & London
1982

To the memory of
V. F. Calverton and
Oliver Cromwell Cox

Copyright © 1982 by
The Curators of the University of Missouri
University of Missouri Press, Columbia, Missouri 65211
Library of Congress Catalog Card Number 81–10480
Printed and bound in the United States of America
All rights reserved

Library of Congress Cataloging in Publication Data

Tolson, Melvin Beaunorus.
    Caviar and cabbage.

    Essays, originally published Nov. 1937–June 1944
as a column in the Washington Tribune.
    I. Farnsworth, Robert M.   II. Title.
PS3539.0334C3   814'.52   81–10480
ISBN 0–8262–0348–5   AACR2

Acknowledgments

As part of my project for a 1979 summer grant as a Senior Humanist Fellow from the National Endowment for the Humanities, I planned to review all of Melvin B. Tolson's "Caviar *and* Cabbage" columns as necessary research for writing his biography. The columns proved sufficiently revealing and fascinating to suggest that at least a selection of them once again deserved a public audience. Hence the origin of this book.

Since the only copies of these columns publicly available are in the microfilmed records of the *Washington Tribune* at the Moorland-Spingarn Research Center at Howard University, there were a great many problems in creating a workable transcript of the columns. The task could not have been done without much help from many professionally talented people who generously supported my project.

Therefore, I wish to thank particularly the National Endowment for the Humanities and the Faculty Research Council of the Graduate School of the University of Missouri–Kansas City for the financial resources that made the research for this book possible. Cornelia R. Stokes and her staff at the Moorland-Spingarn Research Center were consistently gracious and generous with their help, particularly when I belatedly discovered that I had missed some of the columns on my original review.

Making a typescript from often dim and blurred copies was an especially onerous task. I am grateful to the typing staffs of the University of Missouri–Kansas City English Department, the College of Arts and Sciences, and particularly to Robert Dean for their persistence and skill.

And, throughout my research for the introduction to this book as well as for a new Tolson biography, I have been deeply grateful for the constant support and help of Melvin B. Tolson's wife, Ruth S. Tolson, his three sons, Drs. Melvin, Jr., Arthur, and Wiley Wilson Tolson, and his sister, Mrs. Helen Tolson Wilson.

A Note on the Text

While the columns in this volume are nearly exact reproductions of the "Caviar and Cabbage" columns that appeared in the

Washington Tribune, the reader should be aware of the few changes that have been made. First of all, I have corrected typographical errors, misspellings, and inconsistencies that appeared in the original columns, except of course where Tolson was intentionally misspelling a word to make a point or a pun. Second, for the convenience of the reader, I have consistently used italic type for the titles of books, newspapers, and magazines, although in the original columns a wide variety of typographical devices were used to set apart the titles of works. In one instance (2 November 1940), I added words in brackets to complete a sentence omitted from the column by a printing error. Finally, columns occasionally included two or more unrelated topics, and in such instances I did not use the entire column, although the majority of the columns that appear here are complete.

From 9 October 1937 to 24 June 1944, assuming that the *Washington Tribune* appeared once a week, there would have been 350 issues. There are 217 "Caviar and Cabbage" columns on microfilm. I have selected 101 for this collection. The microfilm records of the *Tribune* during this period have significant gaps, but there are copies of the *Tribune* in which "Caviar and Cabbage" did not appear. For two years, 1939 and 1940, there are copies of fifty columns each year, indicating that for at least those two years a column appeared practically every week.

R.M.F.
Kansas City, Mo.
October 1981

Contents

Introduction, 1

III. World War II

IV. Random Shots

V. Writers and Readings

VI. Reminiscences

Introduction

Melvin B. Tolson was an engaging man, and known to be so by a large number of colleagues, students, and friends during his lifetime. For those who know him today only through his published poetry, it may require diligent reading to catch the unexpected dimensions, the human surprise of the man. He was too various to pigeonhole. As a platform performer he used his voice and gestures with the dramatic flair of an old-style preacher. Yet for the last fifteen years of his life he was a jealous spokesman for avant-garde modernist poetry. Identifying himself publicly as a radical and, occasionally, to close friends as a Marxist, he would argue passionately for a social reawakening to the message of a caring Christ. At professional meetings and at intimate social gatherings, friends and acquaintances marveled at his capacity to sip an impressive amount of whiskey and remain eloquently coherent. Although a devoted family man, he seemed to be forever traveling, crisscrossing the United States with his Wiley College debaters, lecturing on all kinds of platforms, speaking his mind fervently, but also listening and watching acutely, always seeking the electrical touch that Whitman celebrated almost a century earlier.

Attempting to write a new biography of this man whom I had never met, yet whose personality constantly changed and grew the more I worked with his writings and the more I talked to his friends and relatives about him, I sought copies of the weekly columns that Tolson had written under the title *"Caviar and Cabbage,"* which appeared in the *Washington Tribune* from October 9, 1937, to June 24, 1944. I quickly realized that these columns were an even richer biographical resource than I had hoped, and the more I read the more strongly I felt that they were more than a biographical resource. They are also a very vivid commentary on an important period of American history. Hence, this collection of *"Caviar and Cabbage"* is intended both to introduce readers to many of Tolson's most strongly held beliefs in a much more direct and simple form than one is likely to find them in his poetry, particularly his later poetry, and to reveal these beliefs, shaped and challenged by the social experiences of the Great Depression and the events of World War II, as a commentary on an important period in American cultural history.

Tolson's career as a published writer began in the 1930s, a period in which widespread hunger, joblessness, and thwarted hopes caused many to believe that they were witnessing the convulsive deaththroes of American capitalism. Born February 6, 1898, Tolson was thirty-three years old when he took academic leave from Wiley College to live for a year in Harlem and enroll in a master's program in comparative literature at Columbia University. His wife and four children went to Kansas City to live with his parents for the year.

He had aspired to write poetry from early childhood. His first published poem appeared in an Oskaloosa, Iowa, newspaper when Tolson was fourteen. Its subject was the sinking of the Titanic. He was the class poet of his Lincoln High School graduating class in Kansas City in 1918 and wrote both poems and stories for the 1917 and 1918 yearbooks. He attended Lincoln University in Oxford, Pennsylvania, from 1919 to 1923, and in the 1923 yearbook, *The Paw*, his predilection for poetry is recognized and humorously mocked: " 'Cap' arrived on campus with a suitcase and basket in 1920 [*sic*]; the basket carried his clothes and the suitcase his poems in manuscript. A country paper once published one of them and that ruined 'Cap.'"

Tolson married during his sophomore year at Lincoln, and two years later he became a father during the same month that he received his bachelor's degree. His early family responsibilities made it imperative that he find a job. Thus, while other aspiring writers of his age were finding their way to glamorous Harlem, the emerging new cultural capital of the black world, Tolson accepted a teaching position in the English department at Wiley College in faraway Marshall, Texas. Tolson's father, a Methodist minister for many years, appealed to his bishop and successfully arranged the position at the Methodist-sponsored school.

Little evidence remains of Tolson's writing during those early years at Wiley. Tolson told Joy Flasch, his first biographer, that he wrote a novel, *Beyond the Zareto,* in 1924, but no manuscript remains. In 1926, however, his story "The Tragedy of Yarr Karr" was published in the Wiley *Wild Cat,* the school yearbook. It is the story of a young man "born in Greenwich Village [not Harlem], the Bohemian center of New York City," who travels through a series of exotic and melodramatic adventures. The child of an enigmatic, artistic, but lecherous father and of a refined actress from a patrician New England family, the protagonist linked his fortune with that of a classmate, Marcus Dewey. "In pursuit of the red grape of existence" they wander through Europe and Asia, stopping for several months of "productive toil" with the radical Russian Nihilists, until interrupted by the czar's "assassins." Marcus dies in

Liverpool, and the narrator goes to North Africa with the British Expeditionary Force. Captured by the fierce Antar Abrahim, the narrator escapes with the ravishing Bellah, Abrahim's daughter. Bellah dances the "dance of love" and mysteriously disappears after her usual nocturnal swim in the Yarr Karr. The narrator concludes his tale:

> Years have passed. I have attempted to forget. I am now a mission worker in the slums of an Eastern city of my native land. I am ministering to the broken souls of men who, like myself, have suffered from "soul-shock." But ever there flows through the vast expanse of consciousness the yellow waters of the fateful Yarr Karr; and ever, in my dreams, I see the bizarre and lovely figure of Bellah, my Bellah, dancing the "dance of love"—there in the golden moonlight on the sands of Northern Africa.

It is possible that this story is an intentional "collegiate" parody, but, whether parody or not, as a literary fantasy it is, in subject matter and style, about as far removed as possible from the life Tolson must have been living in Marshall, Texas. It lends credence to a later judgment that Tolson himself made about the state of his literary imagination prior to the effective beginning of his poetic career. In 1938, having failed to find a publisher for his first book of poems, *A Gallery of Harlem Portraits,* Tolson tried to make literary capital out of his failure by writing an article about it. In this article, "The Odyssey of a Manuscript," referring to his year at Columbia University, he wrote: "In 1932 I was a Negro poet writing Anglo-Saxon sonnets as a graduate student in an Eastern university. I moved in a world of twilight haunted by the ghosts of a dead classicism."

For his master's thesis at Columbia, Tolson chose to study the writers of the Harlem Renaissance. That year away from his family, living in Harlem, becoming personally acquainted with published writers, many of whom were of his own generation, and critically examining their writing and how collectively they became part of a cultural movement, gave Tolson's own writing career a new vigor and a clearer sense of direction. In 1932 he very deliberately laid "the ghosts of a dead classicism to rest" by beginning to write the brashly vivid poetic sketches of *A Gallery of Harlem Portraits.*

In December 1932, after Tolson had returned to Wiley, an event occurred that was to indicate the new direction of his literary career. It was the publication of Langston Hughes's poem "Good-

Bye Christ.'' In his master's thesis, at the beginning of his chapter on Hughes, Tolson observed: "Countee Cullen and Langston Hughes represent the antipodes of the Harlem Renaissance. The former is a classicist and conservative; the latter, an experimentalist and a radical." Tolson's frequent comments on radicalism in "Caviar and Cabbage" indicate to which of these two antipodes he is drawn. Tolson also describes Hughes's life in terms that echo the romantic adventurism of "The Tragedy of Yarr Karr": "With a biography that reads like a page from the *Arabian Nights,* Langston Hughes, the idealistic wanderer and defender of the proletariat, is the most glamorous figure in Negro literature."

Tolson prefaced his thesis with quotes from five different poets. From Hughes he chose these lines:

> Strange
> That in this nigger place
> I should meet life face to face;
> When for years, I have been seeking
> Life in places gentler—speaking
> Until I came to this vile street
> And found life stepping on my feet.

In "Caviar and Cabbage," June 29, 1940, Tolson remembers a taxicab ride with Hughes that probably took place in 1931, just before Hughes set sail for Russia. In Tolson's account, Hughes is passionately concerned with the Scottsboro boys. Tolson is preoccupied with a previous engagement, and even years later feels guilty that he declined Hughes's invitation to lend his support to a rally that he ironically observes is closed out of a Christian "House of God" because of concern with the rally's association with the Communist party. During his year's residence in Harlem, Tolson found Langston Hughes both adventurously bold and challengingly realistic. In the early stages of Tolson's career, Langston Hughes became his model of the engaged poet.

Thus, when late in 1932 the publication of "Good-Bye Christ" triggered righteous attacks from clergymen and anti-Communists, Tolson jumped to Hughes's defense, particularly since Hughes, traveling in Russia, was not able to defend himself. Tolson chose to reply to an attack on both Hughes and his poem made by the Reverend J. Raymond Henderson in the *Pittsburgh Courier*. Tolson's reply, his first significant literary statement to be published, appeared in two parts in the January 26 and February 2, 1933, issues of the *Courier*. Tolson defended Hughes's sincerity of purpose in the poem: "He has always stood for the man lowest down and has sought to show his essential fineness of soul to those who were too high up—by the accident of fortune—to understand." Then Tolson insisted that the efficacy of contemporary Christianity was the real issue:

> Christianity must come down from the pulpit and solve the problems of today. Men will no longer listen to the echo of that beautiful, but illogical, spiritual language of long ago:
> "You may have all this world,
> Give me Jesus."
> In fact, Jesus Christ would not have sung a song like that. He was a radical, a Socialist, if you will. His guns were turned on Big Business and religionists. He heralded the dawn of a new economic, social, and political order. That is the challenge to all.

Tolson's view of Christ as a radical heralding the dawn of a new order probably preceded his year in Harlem and almost certainly did not stem simply from his reading of Hughes. Such a view of Christ had been common for some time. Art Young had depicted Jesus as an outlawed agitator in a cartoon in *Masses* as far back as 1913. His caption read, "He Stirreth up the People." When Angelo Herndon was arrested in Atlanta in 1932 on the charge of inciting insurrection, a charge that was to lead to his becoming, next in fame only to the Scottsboro boys, a cause célèbre of the early thirties, one of the "incriminating" documents found in his room was a pamphlet by a Bishop Brown entitled "Christianism and Communism." And the view would have been familiar to Tolson, since his father was a Methodist minister, Wiley College was a Methodist school, and both harbored a mix of patrician rules and social challenge. In "Caviar and Cabbage," June 4, 1938, Tolson described a sermon by Dr. James Leonard Farmer, the father of the man who was to lead the Freedom Riders in the early 1960s. The column suggests the socially bold theology that apparently was readily acceptable at Wiley in the thirties. There were also many other influential voices scathingly critical of the church's role during these times of hardship. W. E. B. Du Bois in *The Crisis* had been acerbically critical for years. But Tolson's defense of Hughes also reveals how his zeal for a relevant church in times of desperate economic hardship caused him to syncretize the teachings of Marx with the Christian prophetic tradition. Christ led a revolution of the poor and the powerless. Marxism, with its promise of wresting power from the bourgeoisie in favor of the deserving proletariat, seemed to follow in this prophetic tradition.

The mouth-Christians had grown conservative and complacent. The present-day Marxists often seemed more responsive to social injustice, ironically even more Christian, than nominal Christians.

Wilson Record, in his detailed study *The Negro and the Communist Party,* writes of "the deepening crisis in all areas of Negro life emanating from the debacle of 1929": "For literally millions of Negroes in the United States the pressing problem was not securing the franchise, justice in the courts, or admission to the colleges on an equal basis. It was one of sheer physical survival. Men did not live by bread alone, but it was hard to survive in Harlem on a dissenting opinion of Mr. Justice Brandeis."[1]

Langston Hughes had accepted the presidency of the Communist-sponsored League of Struggle for Negro Rights in 1930. For Hughes it was a nominal position in an organization that regrettably sputtered ineffectually before lapsing into obscurity. Near the end of Tolson's stay in Harlem, Hughes and a group of enthusiastic young actors, writers, and film technicians sailed on the *Bremen* at the invitation of Meschrabpom Films of Moscow to make a film in Russia about black life in America. In "Caviar and Cabbage," September 25, 1943, Tolson reminisced about the decision that his friend Wayland Rudd, an actor, made before joining this group. In the early thirties dramatic choices seemed possible, yet Tolson, because of his family and professional responsibilities, was principally an observer.

By 1932 he had begun writing *A Gallery of Harlem Portraits,* a collection of approximately two hundred poetic portraits, which by their great variety give an epic cross section of the city of Harlem. *A Gallery* is a celebration of Tolson's discovery of Harlem, the community that in the 1920s made the dreams and dilemmas of black Americans vivid. The Harlem of the Renaissance is recognizable in the bold humor and gusto of *A Gallery,* but the work is also heavily marked by the bitter economic depression that followed the stock-market crash of 1929. Much of the exotic glitter, as a fashionable playground for wealthy and sophisticated whites and as a promise of a quick and glamorous entry into the American dream for blacks, is gone from this Harlem. It is a Harlem with the proletarian blues, an angry, sturdy Harlem, proud of the achievements of its people, but ready to reach out to the underdogs of the world and realize the promise of a new order that it believes justly inevitable. According to Tolson's own account in "Odyssey of a Manuscript," he showed Langston Hughes a complete manuscript

---

1. *The Negro and the Communist Party* (Chapel Hill, 1951), p. 93.

of *A Gallery* in Los Angeles in 1935, but Hughes was too preoccupied with the illness of his mother to be of much help or even much encouragement.

While Tolson was writing the poems of *A Gallery,* the NAACP was involved in a frustrating conflict with the Communist-sponsored International Labor Defense over how best to defend the Scottsboro boys. To the public, distanced from the calculated infighting of the ILD that Wilson Record later described convincingly,[2] the ILD appeared as the stout defender of the victims of jim-crow justice while the NAACP seemed ineptly indecisive and abstemious. But the Scottsboro case and the later celebrated case of Angelo Herndon were only the tip of the iceberg. The catastrophic consequences of the economic depression were causing almost all established institutions to reassess their programs. For example, in 1933 the NAACP called the second Amenia conference at the Hudson River estate of Joel Spingarn, white philanthropist and staunch NAACP supporter. Invitations were sent principally to the young and the intellectually elite. Such participants as Ralph Bunche, E. Franklin Frazier, Abram Harris, and Sterling Brown were in the beginning stages of what were to become notable careers. These young leaders denounced

> the tactics and ideologies of their elders. They charged that the ideas of long-time leaders like W. E. B. Du Bois and James Weldon Johnson were irrelevant. They were "race men"—men who looked at all problems with a racial perspective. . . . While their elders had generally continued to place their faith in the struggle for civil rights within the capitalistic system, many of the young men, like so many other intellectuals during the 1930's, were convinced that industrial capitalism had failed. Hence the primary problem for black Americans was not civil rights or even racism, but rather the exploitation of labor by private capital. . . . They thought that the older, liberal methods of agitation for civil rights would not bring about such reform. The only viable method was for white and black workers to unite and force the necessary legislation because "the welfare of white and black labor is inseparable." The "problem" for these young radicals, unlike their elders, was essentially class, not race.[3]

Tolson identified with this wave of new thought. He probably also briefly tested it out in direct social action.

He frequently spoke of his experience organizing sharecroppers, both white and black. Two poems from *A Gallery of Harlem*

    2. Ibid., pp. 86–90.
    3. James O. Young, *Black Writers of the Thirties* (Baton Rouge, 1973), pp. 3–5.

Portraits, "Zip Lightner" and "Uncle Gropper," and "The Ballad of a Rattlesnake" from *Rendezvous with America,* one of Tolson's favorite poems for public reading, dramatize the experiences of sharecroppers. The Agricultural Adjustment Act of the New Deal administration triggered the organization of the Southern Tenant Farmers Union, the principal national effort to organize sharecroppers, in Poinsett County, Arkansas, in the summer of 1934. The movement spread to eastern Texas. Tolson's wife, Ruth, remembers only the sketchiest details of Tolson's involvement in this movement, but she does remember that it was agreed between them that it was safer for her and the children not to know of some of his activities. Arthur, Tolson's son, remembers his father, years later, telling him of being accompanied by armed guards as he helped organize a union in east Texas at secret meetings held late at night. Whatever action Tolson engaged in probably took place during the early stages of this movement in 1934 or 1935.

Meanwhile, Tolson was winning more and more recognition as a public speaker and as an extraordinarily successful debate coach. He also had begun to take an increasingly active interest in theater, as a director, actor, and playwright. By 1937, he had written at least one play, *Moses of Beale Street,* and probably also a second, *Southern Front,* but neither of the manuscripts has survived. Several of his "Caviar and Cabbage" columns refer to his experiences traveling with his debate team. Hobart Jarrett, a "pivot" man on the finest team Tolson coached, wrote an account, published in *Crisis,* August 5, 1935, of what it meant to be a Wiley College debater coached by Tolson. He refers to some of the experiences Tolson himself describes in "Caviar and Cabbage" and then summarizes:

> Down the years have come the tales of Wiley debaters. Legends have grown up on the campus. Traditions. They're in the atmosphere. When you join the debate squad you feel you're in for great adventures. Your colleagues tell you about the forensic giants of other days, and the strategy they used to beat distinguished opponents.

Jarrett was one of the debaters who defeated the national championship team of the University of Southern California at Bovard Auditorium on the USC campus in 1935. In "Caviar and Cabbage," March 26, 1935, Tolson mused on his experience as debate coach: "I used to boast of the number of Negro and Caucasian colleges and universities my 'system' defeated. . . . That wise old bird Emerson said there's a crack in everything God made, and I was able to find the crack in the debate systems of other coaches."

But "after the great debate with the University of Southern California," he "had become aware that there's more to life than winning personal victories. I was training my boys to go after the ugly truth and let the judges and respectable audiences go hang."

The skill and wit Tolson developed in his debaters for shaping and turning arguments, as well as his zeal for going after "the ugly truth," clearly helped train him for writing the short and pungent "Caviar and Cabbage" columns.

But Tolson was also gathering more and more acclaim as a platform performer in his own right, and while it is difficult to be certain at this late date what were the most important factors leading to the invitation to Tolson to write "Caviar and Cabbage" for the *Washington Tribune,* his reputation as an effective public speaker was almost certainly one. Tolson's first column was published October 9, 1937. His picture appeared in the *Tribune* on September 25, 1937, over a brief reference to the recent publication in the Omega Psi Phi monthly, Tolson's fraternity publication, of his article "denouncing colored leaders . . . which has caused much discussion." On November 6, the *Tribune* again carried Tolson's picture and an announcement that he would deliver " the main address at a mass meeting on 'Causes and Effects of Juvenile Delinquency Among Negroes' . . . at Rankin Memorial Chapel, Howard University. The meeting will climax the activities revolving around the National Achievement Week, a project sponsored annually by the Omega Psi Phi fraternity." These two announcements may also cause one to suspect that the editor of the *Tribune* was an Omega.

Meanwhile, Tolson's career as a published poet had begun, and it, too, may well have been a factor in the *Tribune*'s inviting him to write "Caviar and Cabbage." "Hamuel Gutterman" from *A Gallery of Harlem Portraits* was published in V. F. Calverton's *Modern Monthly* in April 1937. "Jacob Nollen" was published in the May issue, and "Dr. Harvey Whyte" was published in August. Calverton later published other poems from *A Gallery* as well. Calverton quickly became a close friend and vigorous supporter of Tolson. He introduced him to many influential friends in the publishing world, and in February 1938 he puffed Tolson's *A Gallery of Harlem Portraits* in his column, "The Cultural Barometer," which appeared regularly in *Current History:*

> One of the most interesting Negro poets of today is M. B. Tolson, who in his *Harlem Gallery* [*sic*] is trying to do for the Negro what Edgar Lee Masters did for the middlewest white folk over two decades ago. Mr. Tolson is a bright, vivid writer who attains

his best effects by understatement rather than overstatement, and who catches in a line or a stanza what most of his contemporaries have failed to capture in pages and volumes. The Negroes he describes in his poems come to life, candidly, unforgettably.

Calverton was known to black Americans particularly because of his *Modern Library Anthology of American Negro Poetry,* which Tolson referred to in his master's thesis. But Tolson apparently did not become personally acquainted with Calverton until 1937. A letter from Calverton dated November 23, 1937, begins, "It was damn swell meeting you the other day and I do hope your conference with Cerf was inspiring. I saw Max Perkins Friday, and he is very enthusiastic about your prospective novel— willing to give you an advance, etc. if you are really willing to get to work on it."

References to Calverton are frequent in "Caviar and Cabbage." In 1938 Calverton visited Wiley College for several days as a judge in a dramatic contest sponsored by the Southern Association of Dramatic and Speech Arts. Calverton's heroic drinking and aggressive sexual interest in comely coeds rocked the staid puritanism of Wiley College, but he was thoroughly professional as a dramatics judge. He also assisted the students he met at Wiley with their careers, just as he assisted Tolson with his. Calverton was generous, gregarious, and irreverent toward the racial and class prejudices of his time. His social radicalism reinforced Tolson's own. His friendship became one of the most deeply felt of Tolson's lifetime. His sudden death in 1940 stunned Tolson. Tolson missed Calverton's funeral because when the news reached him in Marshall he could not make it to the East in time by any means other than flying, but as a Negro he was jim crowed from flying. Instead, he wrote a tribute for the Calverton memorial issue of *Modern Quarterly*. He also wrote a poem, "The Man Inside," echoing the title of Calverton's own novel, as a memorial to his friend. In "Caviar and Cabbage," June 14, 1941, Tolson described Calverton as "The Squarest Man on the Negro Problem, I've Ever Known." Underlying all of Tolson's very sincere affection and admiration for Calverton must also have been a very deep gratitude for the man who first published his poems and who gave him such enthusiastic support among influential friends in the publishing world.

Another publishing venture may have been even more closely linked to Tolson's being invited to write "Caviar and Cabbage." Beatrice M. Murphy included three Tolson poems that were not a part of *A Gallery of Harlem Portraits,* "Roland Hayes," "The Auction," and "The Wine of Ecstacy," in *Negro Voices: An*

Anthology of Contemporary Verse in 1938. Murphy had been a columnist for the *Washington Tribune,* and, considering the time it usually takes to collect and prepare material for anthology publication, she almost certainly knew of Tolson's writing talents by late 1937. It is possible that she, too, played a role in the invitation to Tolson.

In any case, Tolson began writing "Caviar and Cabbage" just as his publishing career was getting off the ground. He was thirty-nine years old, but he would retain the intellectual zest and curiosity of a much younger man throughout his life. Nevertheless, for an English professor of Wiley College in Marshal, Texas, to be writing a weekly column for a Washington, D.C., newspaper calls for comment.

Lee Finkle in his study of the black press during World War II points out, "Unlike the white dailies, the black press featured columnists who were quite often not professional journalists by occupation. . . . If a black man had achieved any degree of success he was able to express his point of view in the pages of the black press." Finkle observes that these columnists represented a great variety of political perspectives and educational and geographical backgrounds. The great variety and freedom of perspective caused the black press to be "the black man's major forum for every ideological viewpoint, from conservatives such as F. D. Patterson, to the liberal Walter White, to socialist Layle Lane, and to Max Yergan, a member of the Communist party.[4]

The *Washington Tribune* principally served the black community in the D.C. area. It was not a national publication like the *Pittsburgh Courier* or the *Baltimore Afro-American.* Its principal competition in the D.C. area was the *Washington Afro-American,* a member of the Afro-American publishing family. In 1937, when Tolson began publishing his column, the *Tribune* had a Friday distribution of 22,411[5] but from 1937 to 1947 the circulation of black newspapers across the nation nearly doubled, a consequence of improving economic conditions and of public concern for the events of World War II.[6]

The D.C. area was special. As the seat of the federal government during a period when the whole nation looked to that government to lead the nation out of economic depression and to guide it

4. *Forum for Protest: The Black Press During World War II* (Rutherford, Madison, and Teaneck, 1975), pp. 55–58.
5. "Negro Statistical Bulletin No. 1" (Washington, D.C.: Bureau of the Census, 1937).
6. Vishnu V. Oak, *The Negro Newspaper* (Westport, Conn., 1948), p. 68.

through the increasingly threatening international conflict, and also as an area including one of the oldest and most aristocratically inclined black communities in the nation along with one of the proudest black universities, Washington, D.C., was a very challenging community for an English professor of Wiley College, living in Marshall, Texas, to address. It is at least credible, however, that Tolson's distance from Washington was one of his attractions for the editor of the *Tribune*. Dean Kelly Miller of Howard University, an eminent historian of conservative agrarian philosophy, was already publishing a regular column in the *Tribune*. Miller was one of the older leaders Tolson singled out for attack in the article that the *Tribune* referred to as causing "much discussion." Tolson probably was chosen to represent an alternative perspective, a younger generation, more aggressive, even radical, less hampered by his social and professional position, geographically and socially distant, hence freer to speak his mind, a literary man with a talent for the colorful phrase and situation, rather than the restrained, responsible historian. Whether that was the *Tribune*'s intention or not, that is the way it turned out.

The *Tribune*'s published policy was a curious mixture of sweeping generalities and very specific demands. It left plenty of room for editorial opinion, but it signaled concern for the social interests of the paper's clients:

Our Policy
Newspapers, like people, should have an excuse for living. Our excuse, which is also our purpose for living, forms our policy, expressed as follows:
To ever uphold, contend for and defend Human Rights, which should dominate over property rights.
Therefore, our policy is formulated into a nine-point program
1. Unemployment and Relief.
2. A Positive Purpose on Economic Security.
3. Law Enforcement and Law Observance.
4. Recreation and Citizenship.
5. Good Housing.
6. Good Health.
7. Suffrage for the District.
8. Comfort Station at Triangle at Tenth and U Streets, Northwest.
9. A Representative on the District Commission Board.

The *Tribune*'s insistence on the priority of human rights over property rights may have been a philosophical verity, but it also reflected the specific concern of a people whose racial history made them well aware of how often the assertion of the property rights of others had resulted in the violation or abrogation of their own human rights.

The *Tribune*'s coverage of events reflects a mix broadly representative of the black press at this time, but with an editorial posture receptive to Tolson's challenging outspokenness. The trials of some of the Scottsboro boys were still in the courts. On 1 May 1937, Angelo Herndon won a Supreme Court victory that saved him from twenty years in the Georgia chain gang and that favorably answered the question posed at the end of his autobiography, *Let Me Live,* published the same year. Dean Kelly Miller did a series of columns on the history of the Black Cabinet, those black Americans with access to the White House, finally speculating with wry pathos that Mary McLeod Bethune now held a role that was the closest contemporary counterpart to the powerful role Booker T. Washington had once assumed in a previous Roosevelt's administration. E. Franklin Frazier, chairman of the sociology department at Howard University and author of *Black Bourgeoisie,* a study Tolson often referred to enthusiastically in his later writing, was reported to have given a May Day talk to an audience of five hundred, "most of whom were members of the Communist Party." He was quoted as saying, "The white men are beginning to realize that they can't live on white supremacy alone. They are learning that they can no longer bring Negroes from the South to break strikes. They also realize that they can't organize white labor and leave black labor out. They aren't so dumb as they pretend to be." The *Tribune* editorially criticized Rep. Arthur W. Mitchell, the only black congressman, for introducing antilynching legislation that was weaker that Rep. Joseph Gavagan's antilynching bill then under consideration in Congress.

On November 13, 1937, on the same page as Tolson's third surviving "Caviar and Cabbage" column, a couple of literary items appeared that deserve noting. The first issue of *New Challenge* was announced listing the following contributors: Dr. Alain Locke, Sterling Brown, Henry Lee Moon, Eugene Holmes, Richard Wright, Margaret Walker, Verna Arvey, Owen Dodson, Charles Henry Ford, Frank Marshall Davis, Robert Davis, Benjamin Appel, Langston Hughes, and others. Richard Wright was also listed as an associate editor. Next to Tolson's column appeared a Continental News Agency article by Langston Hughes filed from Valencia where he was covering the Spanish Civil War.

There were as well, of course, the usual range of topics of more sensational, popular interest. Joe Louis knocked out James Braddock in the eighth round and thereby assumed the heavyweight championship of the world in June 1937. Meanwhile, rumors of the champion's marital troubles with his first wife, Marva Trotter, were diligently reported. Father Divine was becoming more and more hopelessly enmeshed in legal difficulties. Elder Lightfoot Solomon Micheaux declared religious war on his troubled rival, and Faithful Mary, "spirited wife and No. 1 angel" of Father Divine, recently ousted from her domestic niche, publicly accused him of being more than a spiritual father to hundreds of women who came under his spell. The absurd, the trivial, and the momentous issues of the day were all in the news and all fair game for the comments of the earnestly aggressive, nimble-witted professor from the Southwest.

The sporadic appearance of the early columns suggests that "Caviar and Cabbage" was begun on a trial basis, but it quickly became a regular feature and ran for almost seven years. Much was to happen, both to Tolson and to the world he lived in, during those seven years. At Wiley College, a new Ph.D. from the University of Chicago joined the faculty in 1938, and Tolson took him under his wing giving him effective encouragement and support to begin his writing career. Oliver Cromwell Cox thus became a stimulating friend and colleague of Tolson's for years to come. Like Tolson, he engendered extraordinary praise from professionally well-qualified peers but never gained broad public recognition. Cox taught at Wiley from 1938 to 1944, almost precisely the years Tolson wrote "Caviar and Cabbage," but he and Tolson continued to correspond for years afterward as well. Cox's major study, *Caste, Class & Race,* was published in 1948. In his preface he thanked four of his Wiley colleagues, along with others, for "face-to-face discussion and criticism of the substance of the book." From Wiley he named Melvin B. Tolson, Andrew P. Watson, V. E. Daniel, and Alonzo J. Davis.

In the preface to his book, Cox comments on the historic significance of World War II, which had only recently concluded and was a major concern of Tolson's writing in "Caviar and Cabbage."

> World War II initiates a new era in international sensitiveness, because the primary irritants had never existed in the world before. Feudal wars may be thought of as involving typically the personal power and prestige of great landed rulers, capitalist wars as mainly nationalistic conflicts over markets and exploitable resources: but the era centering about World War II began the fateful period of political-class wars, or the struggle for dominance of the capitalist world by the democratic masses.[7]

7. *Caste, Class & Race* (Garden City, N.Y., 1948), p. xxix.

In his book Cox attacks the assumptions of many contemporary sociologists, including his own teacher at the University of Chicago, Dr. Robert E. Park, that racial distinctions are significantly comparable to caste distinctions. Cox insists that they are radically different and argues that race as it is known in the modern world grows out of the capitalistic need for designating a large group of people as a cheap supply of labor and hence is of relatively modern origin. While the events of World War II do not figure prominently in his study, his prefatory comments and occasional observations make it clear that he sees "the capitalist alliance" as "interested in destroying the fascists as competitors for world markets and natural resources but in saving them as bulwarks against the proletariat."[8] Modern democracy, "still in its fetal stage," struggles to be born amidst the conflagration.

At one point a statement of intensely felt personal faith emerges rather startlingly from the ponderous sociological detail:

> Sometimes it is estimated that capitalism is basically interested in "the fundamental value and dignity" of the individual. This conclusion is seldom, if ever, demonstrated, but it is ordinarily associated with individualism. As a matter of fact, however, democracy is the supreme champion of individual worth and personal value because it reaches down irresistibly and facilitates the political upthrust of that major group of persons known as the masses; it concerns itself with the personalization of the least privileged individuals. Democracy tends to confer upon every individual a priceless sense of wantedness in the society—a sense of being a recognized part of a supremely vital organization. By this means alone the individual is able to form a positive conception of himself as a responsible social object. On the other hand, individualism champions the cause of the successful few and of the ablest, it despises the weak and jealously withholds its privileges and recognition from the common people.[9]

Despite his fervent belief in belonging to a collective, inclusive, democratic society, Cox jealously protected his individual integrity, both professionally and personally. His book was a direct challenge to Gunnar Myrdal's *An American Dilemma,* and he sharply criticized many of his most distinguished black colleagues for participating in Myrdal's study. Yet he also refused to identify with radical sociological groups and denied that he was a Marxist, although others frequently identified him as such, usually as a

8. Ibid., p. 198.
9. Ibid., pp. 238–39.

means of discrediting his arguments. Hughes, Calverton, and Cox all shared with Tolson a passionate egalitarian dream. All were harshly critical of capitalism. They saw it as the historical cause of international conflicts resulting in devastating wars, as the prime cause of racial slavery and colonial exploitation, and as engendering dangerous human traits of competitiveness and selfishness. The progress of the world, the realization of the full potential of the human race, depended upon developing a collective sense of cooperation and common human concern. They all came to these broad conclusions from varying experiences and perspectives. None of them ever joined the Communist party, although all of them were sympathetic with the professed aims of Communism, and all of them viewed the revolutionary events in Russia, at least in the early years, with hope and fascination. All of them, however, guarded the freedom of their individual judgments diligently and, on occasion, fiercely. All of them also were deeply suspicious of the manner in which charges of Communism and radicalism were used by American reactionary forces to discredit warranted and needed social change. Some of their views on the Russian experiment with Communism later shifted with historic events. Their indictment of capitalism as antithetical to the emergence of a fully realized democracy, however, never changed.

Of the four, Tolson's democratic dream and his indictment of capitalism seemed most rooted in Christian tradition. Calverton and Cox were secular skeptics. Hughes seemed closer to Tolson's position. Both Hughes and Tolson guarded their most personal religious feelings carefully, but the communities they identified with and consistently addressed were so pervasively Christian that each commonly shaped his dreams for the realization of a revolutionary democracy in terms of the concepts and parables of Christian faith. Tolson repeated many times the biblical charge that the love of money is the root of all evil. He used it as an indictment of capitalism and the values it engendered. It is for this reason that this collection of Tolson's "Caviar and Cabbage" columns begins with a section labeled "Christ and Radicalism."

Tolson's view of the world commonly seemed a blend of the visionary and the apocalyptic. The Great Depression and World War II were catastrophic in the pain and suffering they caused. Yet in the midst of each, Tolson insisted on seeing the seeds of a brighter future. In "Caviar and Cabbage," September 30 and October 7, 1939, he described how the depression brought white and black workers together in common interest. This shedding of racial barriers promised to reveal the cost and destructiveness of the racial bias that Tolson saw rippling through the culture with radically transforming effect. In "Caviar and Cabbage," July 25, 1942, a radio broadcast of Dimitri Shostakovich's newly created Seventh Symphony became for Tolson the occasion for the proclamation of a faith in a radically new international awareness that promised a new world order.

Tolson was never short on dreams. It is all too easy to look back on these occasions and mock his naive optimism with the disillusioning awareness that his dream of a classless international brotherhood of man seems as far from realization today as it was in 1942. But Tolson's dreams were only one part of an imaginative dialectical process. He also was a skeptic. In "Caviar and Cabbage" he wrote:

> I've lived in the Ozarks. Those folks are incredulous, skeptical, inquisitive, disbelieving.
> Plato says a wise mind is an interrogating mind. It wants to know why. It doesn't accept a thing because the Big Boys say it's right. It doesn't get on the bandwagon. A wise man thinks for himself. He questions everything. That's the only way to find the truth.

Apocalypse and prophetic vision, dream and skepticism, the artist both discovers and infuses the truth in history. The prophets of the Bible as well as such prophetic poets as Whitman and Tennyson may well often seem belied by the later events of history, but their visions also become a force in history, reminding mankind of a sense of purpose commensurate with its moral imagination.

The artist's role is the lonely role of the truthseeker. Tolson early and consistently assumed that genius often went unrecognized in its time. In "Caviar and Cabbage" he was surprised and gratified by the popular acclaim given Richard Wright's *Native Son,* but he was skeptical that Wright's message was being truly read. Eric Walrond's tragic death in World War II regrettably seemed according to script. The artists in Tolson's poems are seldom recognized for their true talents. Vergil Ragsdale in *A Gallery of Harlem Portraits* dies an early death and his manuscript is callously burned by his landlady. In Tolson's final masterpiece, *Harlem Gallery,* John Laugart and Mister Starks, both artists, die young. Hideho Heights keeps up a bravura public persona, but the Curator discovers a more disillusioned private poet when he reads Hideho's "E.&O.E." "E.&O.E." is also the title of a seldom read poem of Tolson's, and the lines attributed to Heights in *Harlem Gallery* are in fact lines from Tolson's own previously published poem.

The truthseeker lives in a world resistant to change. "In a world of change, people want to hold on to something. They hate to admit to themselves that they are like a ship without a rudder or a compass. The volcanic changes in finance and politics and religion fill them with helplessness and fear. They become panicky. They are terrified by the modern Noahs talking about the flood. They don't want to listen to the modern Daniels translating the handwriting on the walls of their ancient beliefs. In other words, they want none of the truthseekers" ("Caviar and Cabbage," April 1, 1939).

The early stages of World War II and the question of America's participation posed many Gordian knots for a truthseeker to untie. The black community, because of racial sympathy, registered the ominous message of Italy's invasion of Ethiopia much more sensitively than did the larger American community. As the conflict shifted to the European theater and the Roosevelt administration showed more and more evidence of actively supporting Britain and France against the fascist nations, the black press found itself in a particularly acute dilemma. One of the most important reasons for the existence of the press was to protest the racial injustices suffered by the people the press served. While the black press had no sympathy with the fascist cause abroad, particularly since Italy's invasion of Ethiopia so blatantly violated the rights of a black nation, it nevertheless found it difficult to join in what was increasingly being characterized as a struggle of free and democratic nations against totalitarian fascist nations. Fascism in America was all too vividly and oppressively present to the black community in its experience of racism. How could the press, or the black community for that matter, patriotically support a war against fascism abroad without seeming to be negligently closing its eyes to fascism at home. Lee Finkle in *Forum for Protest* documents the spread of the "Double V" campaign, initiated by the *Pittsburgh Courier,* with variations through much of the black press, as an answer to this dilemma. The essential element of this campaign was the recognition that two victories were needed: one against fascism abroad and another against fascism at home. Tolson opposed American entry into the war until Pearl Harbor made that position moot. Then he embraced the "Double V" enthusiastically.

There are significant gaps in the microfilmed records of the *Washington Tribune* in the Moorland-Spingarn Research Center at Howard University, the only source for copies of the *Tribune* I have been able to discover. Unfortunately, one of the most significant gaps is from January 3 to April 11, 1942, the period immediately following Pearl Harbor. This probably is the reason I found no "Caviar and Cabbage" column dealing centrally with that event, and hence have included none. Tolson's response to both the personal and the historical significance of this event is indicated by these lines from "Rendezvous with America" published first in *Common Ground* during the summer of 1942 and later as part of the title poem of his first published book of poems:

> I have a rendezvous with America
> This Seventh of December.
> The maiden freshness of Pearl Harbor's dawn,
> The peace of seas that thieve the breath,
> I shall remember.
>   Then
> Out of yonder Sunrise Land of Death
> The fascist spawn
> Strikes like the talons of the mad harpoon,
> Strikes like the moccasin in the black lagoon,
> Strikes like the fury of the raw typhoon.
>   The traitor's ruse
>   And the traitor's lie,
>   Pearl Harbor's ruins
>   Of sea and sky,
>   Shall live with me
>   Till the day I die.
>   *Here,*
>   *Now,*
> At Pearl Harbor, I remember
> I have a rendezvous at Plymouth Rock and Valley Forge
> This Seventh of December.

The loyalty and patriotism of the black press were sensitive issues in both World War I and World War II. Tolson confronted the issue directly in "Caviar and Cabbage," May 1, 1943. Warren Brown, employed by the Council for Democracy, published an attack on the black press in December 1942 in the *Saturday Review of Literature,* which aroused great indignation throughout the black community. Brown implied that most blacks were satisfied with the progress being made in race relations and alleged that the incendiary black press was capable of embittering the black masses. According to Brown, these newspapers were "Negro first and American second," and they created racial hostility by focusing on particular incidents. He predicted future racial clashes and described some already happening that were not "wholly due to white prejudice. They are also due to an irresponsible Negro leadership."[10]

Tolson scathingly described Brown's criticism as a hit below the belt "delivered by a black Uncle Tom." He pointed out that Brown's employer, the Council (Tolson refers to the "League") for Democracy, was inviting Negro editors to learn how to gain more advertisers. Since the principal economic support of the black press had traditionally been its subscribers and not its advertisers, thus allowing the press freedom from pressure to conform to the views of its advertising clients, the Council's efforts to increase advertising in the black press were, according to Tolson, the Judas kiss of betrayal. "Every dumbbell knows that he who pays the fiddler calls the tune." It was the white newspapers' dependence on advertisers that caused George Seldes, the editor of *In Fact*, to refer to the big white papers as "the Harlot Press." If the reader valued the columnist's freedom to speak his mind—and Tolson proclaimed with pride, "Never has the Negro had more manly journalism"—then buying a black newspaper was like buying a Declaration of Independence for only ten cents.

Tolson never conceded the ground of patriotism to his ideological adversaries. In 1939, Tolson's "Dark Symphony" won first place in the National Poetry Contest sponsored by the American Negro Exposition in Chicago. The poem was later published in *Atlantic Monthly*, September 1941, and it was through the interest of Mary Lou Chamberlain, then an editor at *Atlantic*, who later moved to Dodd, Mead and Company, that Tolson's *Rendezvous with America* was published in 1944.

"Dark Symphony" stakes out a strong claim for the New Negro as the product of a long history of American rebels and workers. Crispus Attucks, Nat Turner, Joseph Cinquez, Frederick Douglass, Sojourner Truth, and Hariett Tubman, as well as those "history-moulding ancestors" who

> Planted the first crops of wheat on these shores,
> Built ships to conquer the seven seas,
> Erected the Cotton Empire,
> Flung railroads across a hemisphere,
> Disemboweled the earth's iron and coal,

---

10. Warren H. Brown, "A Negro Looks at the Negro Press," *Saturday Review of Literature*, 19 December 1942, pp. 5–6.

Funneled the mountains and bridged rivers,
Harvested the grain and hewed forests,
Sentineled the Thirteen Colonies,
Unfurled Old Glory at the North Pole,
Fought a hundred battles for the Republic,

were all American progenitors of the "Hard-muscled, Fascist-hating, Democracy ensouled" New Negro.

The true American, like the true Christian, was for Tolson a rebel struggling to realize the democratic dream in the fullest human sense possible. World War II expanded but did not alter Tolson's democratic dream. In "Caviar and Cabbage," April 22, 1939, he wrote, "Every intelligent Negro has his eye on Europe and his ear against the United States. Every intelligent Negro is reading some fearless Negro newspaper in order to keep up with the drift of current events. The Atlantic Ocean of Teddy Roosevelt's day no longer exists. Figure it out for yourself. In order for a Negro to interpret the race problem in America, he must know the history of the world, yesterday and today. The race problem in the United States is a pimple on the diseased elephant of civilization." The economic depression of the thirties caused Tolson and other socially conscious blacks to submerge race into class. World War II caused Tolson to think no longer simply in terms of the "Big Boys" of American business, but also in terms of the European colonial nations who were the big boys of international power and who consequently shaped much of the world's vision of world history.

On Christmas Eve 1943, Tolson heard from Dodd, Mead that *Rendezvous with America* was accepted for publication. Meanwhile, Tolson's poetry was appearing frequently in *Common Ground* as well as in *The Modern Quarterly*. He was writing a novel, *All Aboard,* the story of Duke Hands, a Pullman porter and the people's hero, which he hoped would be a blockbuster. On May 1, 1944, P. L. Prattis, executive editor of the *Pittsburgh Courier,* proposed to Tolson the formation of a "thought" club to share views in writing on issues of the day. Prattis said he had discussed the proposal with Richard Wright, that their views were similar, and that he hoped to fill out the club with invitations to Manet Fowler, Horace Cayton, and Tolson. He proposed as the first "thought" piece an already published difference of opinion between Rose Wilder Lane (white) and Manet Fowler (Negro), both *Courier* columnists, on the importance of race-consciousness for Negro writers. Apparently the proposal never became more than a proposal. "Caviar and Cabbage" concluded June 24, 1944, the same year that *Rendezvous with America* was published.

Tolson's career as a poet underwent a transformation of style and increasingly impressive critical appreciation until the triumphant last year of his life, but broad popular recognition always eluded him. In 1947 he was named Poet Laureate of Liberia. He moved from Wiley College to Langston University, Langston, Oklahoma, that same year. He responded to the honor Liberia conferred upon him by writing *Libretto for the Republic of Liberia*. In the esoteric demands *Libretto* made upon its readers, it was a markedly more ambitious poem than anything Tolson had previously written, although there had already been some minor critical reservations about the learned quality of some of the poems in *Rendezvous*. In an interview of Tolson published in *Anger and Beyond*, for which Tolson probably wrote both questions and answers, the following exchange occurs about *Libretto:*

> Interviewer: Let us return to the idea of the seer. In the last section of the *Libretto*, you predicted the rise of African republics. You foresaw, as Tennyson before you, a Parliament of Man.
> Tolson: That has been by-passed by many a critic. In 1947, when I was elected Poet Laureate of Liberia, there were only two independent black countries in Africa. Today there are thirty-three. It is a vision, right out of the Apocalypse.

In "Caviar and Cabbage," October 19, 1940, Tolson explained the Ferris Wheel and Merry-Go-Round theories of history. The Ferris Wheel theory of history is based on the rise and fall of nations attributed to competition for power and dependent upon theories of class and race superiority. The Merry-Go-Round theory of history is based on economic and social brotherhood. The continuity of Tolson's ideas and the transformation in the style of his poetry can be measured in his heavily ironic use of these same metaphorical theories of history in *Libretto:*

> Between Yesterday's wars
> now hot now cold
> the grief-in-grain of Man
> dripping dripping dripping
> from the Cross of Iron
> dripping
> drew jet vampires
> of the Skull;

Between Yesterday's wills of Tanaka, between
golden goblet and truckling trull
and the ires
of rivers red with the reflexes of fires,
the ferris wheel
of race, of caste, of class
dumped and alped cadavers till the ground
fogged the Pleiades with Gila rot: Today the mass,
the Beast with a Maginot Line in its Brain,
the staircase Avengers of base alloy,
the *vile canaille*-Gorii-the *Bastard-rasse,*
the *uomo qualyque,* the *hoi barbaroi,*
the *Raya* in the *Oeil de Boeuf,*
the *vsechelovek,* the *descamisados,* the *hoi polloi,*
the Raw from the Coliseum of the Cooked,
Il Duce's Whore, Vardaman's Hound—
unparadised nobodies with maps of Nowhere
ride the merry-go-round!
Selah!

Libretto was Tolson's opening salvo in an effort to lead black writers into the modernist literary movement. He felt that a modernist aesthetic revolution had taken place across the arts and that black writers had to scramble to stake out their cultural claims for the attention of the future audiences that this modernist revolution was developing. *Libretto* won Tolson impressive critical appreciation from such critics as Allen Tate, Stanly Edgar Hyman, and Donald Spector.

After *Libretto,* Tolson projected an even more ambitious five-volume epic of the historical experience of black America from its origins in Africa up to the present. *Harlem Gallery: Book I, the Curator,* set in present time, was to be the first of the five volumes. *Harlem Gallery* was published in 1965, and Tolson died a year later. Knowing that he was terminally ill with cancer, he was still gratifyingly proud of the critical praise and recognition his final volume of poetry won for him. Karl Shapiro opened his introduction to *Harlem Gallery* with this challenging statement: "A great poet has been living in our midst for decades and is almost totally unknown, even by the literati, even by poets." Tolson was granted a second honorary degree from Lincoln University, his alma mater. He was elected to the book-review board of the *New York Herald Tribune.* The District of Columbia gave him a citation and

award for cultural achievement. He was asked to read at the
Library of Congress under the auspices of the Gertrude Clarke
Whittall Poetry and Literature Fund. He became the first professor
to assume the Avalon Chair in Humanities at Tuskegee Institute.
The American Academy of Arts and Letters awarded him a $2,500
grant. He was also awarded a Rockefeller grant, which only his
intervening death kept him from receiving.

Harlem Gallery, too, contains many echoes of "Caviar and
Cabbage." Tolson never changed certain basic convictions. On
July 29, 1939, he began his column: "I like truth better than
fiction—milk better than *skimmed* milk." He followed that opening with a discussion of the communal life of the ants compared to
man's self-centered mores:

> ants don't build fences. They are too intelligent, charitable and
> self-respecting. Man and the hog, whom Man resembles very
> much, need fences. Ants hold property for the common good,
> just as Man, in a bright moment, developed the postal service for
> the common good. How much would you pay for a stamp if Mr.
> Rockefeller owned the mail service?
>
> Ants care for the sick and disabled. Savages do the same thing.
> Civilized man thinks a poor fellow should make hay while the sun
> shines; that he should prepare for a rainy day. How many heart-
> less people do you meet who oppose old age pensions?

The Curator and Doctor Nkomo in *Harlem Gallery* also argue
the virtues of separating the cream from the milk or mixing it into
whole milk. Doctor Nkomo, who often voices Tolson's convictions, is given the final word against the Curator's elitist prefer-
ences:

> *"Mens sibi conscia recti,"*[11]
>   said Dr. Nkomo
>   —definitely—
> "is not a hollow man who dares not peddle
>   the homogenized milk of multiculture,
>   in dead ends and in boulevards,
>   in green pastures and across valleys of dry lanes."

Melvin Tolson continued to assume a prophetic role for the artist.
The artist's preoccupation with the multicultural nature of the new
world of man that was evolving might cause him to risk losing
contact with an audience bound by its provincial consciousness of

---

11. *Aeneid,* book V, line 604. "A mind conscious of the right."

its present world and unwilling to reach imaginatively beyond its immediate needs, but Tolson, along with Dr. Nkomo, believed that a true multicultural democracy was evolving and that the artist must announce it and prepare the people for its coming.

"Caviar and Cabbage" indicated clearly how the events of the Great Depression and World War II formed a matrix for Tolson's imagination. But Tolson was not simply malleable clay for the potter's wheel. He spoke with a voice and personality that affected others as well, and hence became an active ingredient in the history he recorded. Something of the power that others recognized in this man during the period that he wrote "Caviar and Cabbage" is attested to by a tribute written by Langston Hughes. The occasion was the publication of *Rendezvous with America,* which coincided with the end of "Caviar and Cabbage." Hughes's tribute thus forms an appropriate concluding comment to this introduction:

> That Texas is some state! I was down there once or twice myself. And I have found some very amazing things—including Melvin Tolson.
>
> Melvin Tolson is the most famous Negro professor in the Southwest. Students all over that part of the world speak of him, revere him, remember him, and love him. He is a character. He once turned out a debate team that beat Oxford, England. He is a great talker himself. He teaches English at Wiley College, Marshall, Texas, but he is known far and wide. He is a poet of no mean ability, and his book of poems, "Rendezvous with America," is a recent fine contribution of American literature. The title poem appeared in that most literate of literary publications, the *Atlantic Monthly.*
>
> But Melvin Tolson is no highbrow. Kids from the cottonfields like him. Cowpunchers understand him. He is a great teacher of the kind which any college might be proud. It is not just English he teaches, but character, and manhood, and womanhood, and love, and courage, and pride. And the likes of him is found nowhere else but in the great State of Texas—because there is only one Tolson![12]

12. Langston Hughes, "Here to Yonder," *Chicago Defender,* 15 December 1945.

I
Christis and Radicalism

The Death of an Infidel
April 2, 1938

It seems that I am always in the objective case. But the records show that Aristotle, Columbus, Pasteur, Socrates, and Jesus were in the same classification. So I'm in good company. I am not a yes-man nor an amen-brother. In fact, the only reason I can endure this worst of all possible worlds is this: I have a supply of brickbats and there are plenty of glass houses to throw at. The Big Boys have tried to buy me off and some of them have tried to cut off my meal ticket in this Christian country, but I go on my way hurling my rocks at superstitions and prejudices and cruelties. If I think a thing is right, I'm ready to debate any man, anywhere, and at any time. I let Joe Louis fight all my physical battles, but I myself meet all comers in the arena of argumentation. A.B.s, A.M.s, and Ph.D.s are not barred. I admit I do have some fear of D.D.s, for they may call upon me the wrath of an angry God. I am the son of a preacher, who was the son of a preacher, who was the son of a preacher. One time I spent four months eating and sleeping with about 500 white preachers. I shall tell you about that.

Mouth Christians

I want to say a few words about an infidel, the late Clarence Darrow. He did not live the way an infidel is supposed to live; he did not die the way an infidel is supposed to die. He was a thorn in the side of the good Christians. His life of unselfishness was an everlasting challenge to the Christianity-talking followers of Jesus. All they could do was condemn old Clarence Darrow for the things he said. You see, the Christians talked about the Golden Rule and the brotherhood of man, while this old infidel practiced the Golden Rule and the Ten Commandments. The question is: Who will get to heaven first—the man who talks or the man who acts?

By their fruits shall ye know them! Anybody who is scared to die can cry, "Lord! Lord!" It's easy to love God. It's easy to love

26

Jesus. It's easy to pray for the heathen African ten thousand miles from the house where you live. It's hard to call a lousy tramp your brother and set him down at your table. It's hard to keep from feeling superior to Aunt Dinah and Uncle Tom in the one-room shack on Misery Alley. The only test of a Christian is this: How does he treat the poor? How does he treat the lame, the halt, and the blind?

People who believe in a black aristocracy, in capitalism, in jim-crow churches, in exclusive fraternities and sororities, in the perpetual ignorance of the masses, in the I-thank-God-that-I-am-not-like-other-men theory—these persons are no more followers of the poverty-stricken Jesus than a cannibal in the equatorial jungles. Such a person is a mouth-Christian. If Jesus were here today, he'd be calling the lowly Nazarene a Red; and Jesus would be calling him a viper and hypocrite. It's easy to love a man who lived in Jerusalem 2,000 years ago. It's respectable to be a mouth-Christian.

An Infidel Champions the Underdog

With death closing in on him—and if a man is ever serious, it is when he must meet the grim reaper alone—old Clarence Darrow said that the greatest satisfaction of his life had been spurred from his efforts in behalf of the underdog, and that his hardest task had been trying his hardest to overcome the cruelties of the world. That's greatness talking.

Once I censured a student for making an error in grammar. The student told me that Shakespeare made mistakes. I told him that when he was able to write a masterpiece like Shakespeare's *Hamlet,* I would say nothing about the errors he made in his themes.

Darrow doubtless made mistakes, like you and me. But his virtues towered above his weaknesses like the Rocky Mountains above a molehill. The evil that men do lives after them, but the good is not interred with their bones.

Darrow defended Eugene V. Debs, the Socialist leader who had been accused of conspiracy in the railway strike of 1894. I wish I could have been there when old Darrow and Debs met beyond the grave, two defenders of orphans and broken-down workers shaking hands and talking things over. If you have a spark of humanity in you, read the life of Debs; then see if you are worthy to unlace the shoes of a Debs. A daily newspaper informs me that the last recorded act of this infidel was to go to Joliet state penitentiary to

secure the parole of Jesse Binga, 71-year-old Negro ex-banker
serving a term of ten years for embezzlement. Race meant nothing
to Clarence Darrow—only human suffering.

An Infidel and the Song "America"

Clarence Darrow believed in practical democracy. He believed
that society is responsible for most of our crimes. He studied hard
and got the facts. Nobody answered the facts. Instead of attacking
the facts, ignoramuses, as usual, attacked the man. You can't
destroy an idea by attacking a man. It took Americans, intelligent
Americans, fifty years to discover that the old lawyer was right.

Once Darrow said publicly that if a Negro sang "My Country
'Tis of Thee," he was either a fool or a crook. Some of the big
Negroes were shocked. Big Negroes are always being shocked by
the truth. It's a wonder that more of them don't die of heart
failure—so the race can move ahead. Death solves more problems
than logicians. God knew what He was doing when He let death
roam up and down creation.

How can a black man honestly sing "My Country 'Tis of Thee'
when he doesn't own enough of his country in which to bury a
cockroach? How can a black man honestly sing "Sweet Land of
Liberty" when, if a white man heard him whisper that he wanted to
vote in thousands of Southern towns, it would cost him his life?
Black men were afraid to say that; so old Darrow told the truth for
them. No wonder the good white folk and the "yessah" Negroes
thought him a dangerous man!

Darrow is gone. I'm sorry. He was a fighter. He loved the lame,
the halt, and the blind. He loved the lousy underdog. I'm sorry that
every Negro newspaper and preacher and teacher didn't say something to black America and white America about this great man's
life. I'm sorry they didn't mention his death. But I'm always in the
objective case.

A Warning to Black Men

The case of Clarence Darrow points a lesson. Black folk are too
easily deluded by superficial facts. Call a man an infidel or a radical
and you can hoodwink us to death. Why should a black man fear a
radical? The abolitionists were radicals in their day. At one time it
was radical in America to say "I believe the black man has a soul; I
believe a black man can be educated." If it had not been for the
radicals, every black man would be in a cotton patch with a white
man standing over him with a forty-four and a horsewhip three
yards long.

And whenever you hear anybody denounce radicals, remember

this: persecuted races get their rights only through the agitation of radicals. The man who denies the truth of this is as dumb as Balaam's jackass. Amen!

Portrait of Jesus, the Young Radical
June 4, 1938

I have read a lot, heard a lot, and thought a lot about Jesus. I am the son of a preacher who was the son of a preacher who was the son of a preacher.

A sermon is a word-picture painted by an artist-preacher to be hung in the gallery of memories. A good sermon thrills me as I am thrilled by Peter Paul Rubens's *Landscape with the Rainbow* or Leonardo da Vinci's *Mona Lisa*.

But so many third-rate painters have attempted to do the word-picture of Jesus that it's hard to tell just what He looked like. You've seen those cheap snapshots that rookie cameramen make of you for ten cents at the circus. Well, in thousands of cases, bad photographers have messed up the likeness of Jesus.

On Mother's Day I attended the chapel services at Wiley College and got a marvelous portrait of Jesus the young radical. The word-picture was done with that imaginative quality that possesses the amazing accuracy of truth, just as Shakespeare's Julius Caesar in *Julius Caesar* is more real, more lifelike than the historical Julius Caesar who walked the streets of ancient Rome.

I was thrilled by this vivid picture of Jesus the young rebel. My soul was uplifted all day. I found myself in Nazareth. I was standing in the presence of the young man Jesus—Jesus the only radical in a village that time and progress had forgot.

Dr. James L. Farmer, the Artist-Preacher

A great preacher is a great artist. Words are his tubes of paint. Verse, his brush. The souls of men the canvas on which he portrays the truths caught in moments of inspiration. The God-man is a man of imagination.

No two painters see an object through the same eyes. No two artists give the same interpretation of a scene. Jan Van Goyen's pictures of the sea are not like those of S. van Ruisdael. Frans Hals's portraits of women reveal moods and nuances in the subtler sex not found in the pictures of Van Dyck. But both are fine artists.

Likewise, no two preachers derive the same thoughts from the same text; no two pulpit orators give identical pictures of the world-character that came out of the village-rut that was Nazareth. Why is this? Well, a man sees Jesus through the eyes of his experiences, through his native imagination, through his moral and intellectual training; and the picture that he gives us of Jesus is determined by his ability to use words.

Dr. James Leonard Farmer's personality is the product of an interesting career. When you enter his study and look around at the massive rows of books reaching to the ceiling, you realize that the gates of scholarship didn't close in his face when he received his Ph.D. degree from Boston University in 1918. As a liberal scholar, his researches have carried him into many fields, giving his intellect a catholicity of taste and interest.

As dean of Rust College, registrar of Samuel Houston College, professor of the Old Testament at Gammon Seminary, dean of the Gulfside summer school and professor of philosophy at Wiley College, he has made noteworthy contributions to the field of education. His sociological and philosophical articles in some of the leading magazines of the country have created a favorable reaction among outstanding scholars in these spheres. He emphatically represents modern scholarship in the church, as typified by Dr. Harry Emerson Fosdick and Rabbi Jonah Bondi Wise and Professor William David Schermerhorn.

Jesus, the Friend of the Masses

In a few striking sentences on the subject "The Young Man Jesus and His Parents," Dr. Farmer etched in the social background of Nazareth and placed against it Jesus.

Said Dr. Farmer: "Jesus was teaching contrary to the social and religious traditions of his people. . . . They thought one thing, but practiced another. As a consequence, wherever He went He made many enemies for himself among the social and religious leaders."

Yes, the Big Boys were against Jesus, and if He should return today the Big Boys would be against Him. They would call Him an infidel, an atheist, a radical, a red.

In one clean sentence, Dr. Farmer pointed out the dilemma of a man like Jesus—a man who wants to help the people: "The more popular He became with the masses, the more hostile these leaders became toward Him, and the more determined to destroy Him."

Martin Luther would sanction that and John Wesley, and Frederick Douglass, and Abe Lincoln, and Oliver Cromwell, and Franklin Roosevelt!

If you become a defender of labor, you become an enemy of capital. If you are a lover of the masses of people, you may expect the Big Boys and their flunkies to get on your trail like a pack of hungry wolves. Jesus found that out.

Jesus' Mother Tried to Save Him!

Dr. Farmer painted one of the finest pictures of a loving mother and her son that I have ever seen. When Jesus broke away from the moss-back teachings of His parents and community, He gave himself a very bad reputation. The gossipers in Nazareth said He was crazy, criminal, wayward. The priests and respectables denounced Him. His mother was grieved as any other mother would have been. Youth has vision! Old age, dreams.

It's easy to be a Christian today. It puts you in the best society. But I wonder how many of us would have had the guts to follow Jesus when the mob was on His trail! It's easy to love Him now since He's been dead some 2,000 years.

Jesus was a radical, as Dr. Farmer pointed out in his striking analysis. He didn't knuckle to the old folk. He wasn't considered a model boy, by any means. He loved His parents but He loved His duty more. Truth was His pole-star. He was a God-man. The greatest God-man working for the ages.

Christian Youth and Parents

I don't have space to reproduce this sermon masterpiece. It's like trying to put Samuel Taylor Coleridge's unforgettable "Kubla Khan" in stammering prose.

But, I suppose the core of the sermon was the conflict between the hypocrisy of parents and the frankness of youth, the mouth-Christianity of parents and the demands of youth for the everyday practice of the teachings of Jesus.

It's refreshing to find a preacher who faces the challenge of youth with intelligence and poise. It's wonderful to find a parent who does not call a questioning youngster a smart guy. Parents say that "under our present competitive system we cannot successfully practice the ideals of Jesus," and youth replies, "Why not change the system?"

Dr. Farmer sees clearly the dilemma in which an honest man finds himself in a dishonest world. "You must neither practice what you preach nor preach what you practice." I've never seen that put better. Again: "You must say that you believe the right, but you must not do it. And you must do what you believe not to be right; but you must not say it!"

And then the eminent doctor of philosophy takes his stand with old Martin Luther and John Wesley when he says, "If ever there

was an occasion for radicalism, I declare it is amply provided here.
Not an axe to fell the tree, but a spade to undermine its roots, is the
urgent need of the times."

Parents say, "Take the world as it comes, and make the best of
it." Christian youth says, according to Dr. Farmer, "Change the
world and make it what it ought to be."

I'll take my stand with American youth and Dr. Farmer and
Jesus, the young radical.

Paul Robeson Rebels against
Hollywood's Dollars
March 25, 1939

It was years and years ago on the gridiron at Lincoln University.
A magnificent bronze god was helping Fritz Pollard get the Lions
ready for their attack on the Bisons. The brown god was scrimmag-
ing against the varsity. I saw him pick up bodily our All-American
tackle, hurl him into the advancing backfield, and break up an
off-tackle play. The bronze god was Paul Robeson, the All-
American of all time. Yes, if old Walt Whitman, America's greatest
poet, had seen that, he would have included Paul Robeson in
America's greatest epic, *Leaves of Grass*.

Football and boxing are my favorite sports. They require guts.
Great white players who encountered Robeson in his days as a
collegiate and professional athlete admired the youth's intestinal
fortitude. But a man can be physically courageous and morally
craven. You see that in politics, religion, and education. Paul
Robeson's moral courage equals the physical fortitude of his magnificent body. He is a MAN.

And it takes a man to turn down Hollywood's dollars. In fact,
you can tell a man by his attitude toward the dollar. Listen to a man
when he gushes about his love of humanity and Jesus and God. But
you'll learn more about him when you see how he acts toward a
dollar!

I say that to say this—Mr. J. Danvers Williams, the international
columnist, writes from London, home of monkey-faced Chamberlain's sell-out gang, that "Paul Robeson has broken with the big
commercial film industry."

That's news for dark America. But it hasn't been discovered by
the copies I've seen of the Negro press. Robeson refuses to be
what my friend, Langston Hughes, calls "the international Uncle
Tom." Black boy, I feel like jumping up and cracking my African

heels together! But I have to get out this article before the deadline.

Robeson has met the big shots of the white world. You know what Woolcott, the big-time critic, said about Paul in that bestseller, *Where Rome Burns.* You know what Gertrude Stein, the famous American patron of the arts and literature, said about Paul in her celebrated *Autobiography of Alice B. Toklas.* Yet Paul Robeson said: "I never felt that I was a man until I visited Russia."

Now, Robeson wants to return to Moscow to make a picture under Eisenstein, the world's greatest producer. Like Marian Anderson, he received a tremendous ovation in Russia. There is no American DAR there to jim-crow black artists and windjam about democracy—the mockery.

Robeson wants to make a picture of that heroic Chicago Negro, Oliver Law, who died leading white soldiers in the International Brigade of Spain against the Ratzis.

Listen to what Robeson says about Hollywood: "I shall not attempt to make my picture about Oliver Law for any of the big companies, for I know only too well that the directors of the industry wouldn't consider it 'policy' to depict a Negro leading white men into battle."

And yet didn't I hear, over the radio, the President and the Chief Justice of the Supreme Court, commemorating our 150 years of liberty under the Constitution? Didn't I hear an opera singer hymning in the House of Representatives:

> "My country 'tis of thee,
> Sweet land of liberty"?

Black boy, maybe I'm wrong. Maybe Paul Robeson is wrong, but that makes me think of a bad-smelling Diogenes, who hasn't had a bath for many years, trying to sell you and me a bottle of exquisite perfume.

Robeson takes a slam at the atrocious lies of the Hollywood industry. These films picture rich young men who fall in love with girls in the five-and-ten-cent stores, or heiresses who marry the family chauffeur—once in a million years. The musical comedies play up half-naked girls wriggling like Minnie the Moocher, to arouse the desires of adolescents and bald-headed husbands yearning for a last fling before seeking oblivion.

Robeson is the New Negro in action. He is not a rugged individualist. He is not a snob. He does not scorn the masses. He is not concerned in rising from the ranks, but in rising with the ranks. Negroes have to learn that. He wants life in the arts; not sentimental romanticism. Robeson believes in ours for us; not mine for me. Robeson wants the films to show actual people; factory workers, farmers, shipbuilders, longshoremen, cottonpickers. We've had enough of the top hats, evening gowns, and limousines. Robeson wants the films to show real people with real problems, with the masses aspiring and militant as masses. Robeson wants Mr. Average Man and Miss Average Woman put on the screen!

Marian Anderson, a Southern Paper, and a Negro Drunk
April 15, 1939

It is Easter, goodwill to men. A study in contrasts. The famous contralto, barred from singing in the concert hall of the un-American Daughters of the American Revolution, makes her debut in a free, open recital on the steps of Lincoln Memorial before a crowd of 75,000.

At the feet of the Great Emancipator whose likeness is preserved in marble within the classic memorial, the magnificent voice of the Negro singer rings across a continent.

"My country 'tis of thee,
Sweet land of liberty . . ."

One thousand and five hundred miles away, sitting pressed against my radio, I try to visualize the Negro singer. I try to imagine what she is thinking as she utters the ironical words, "Sweet land of liberty." I try to figure out what is running through the minds of the white listeners. What does Secretary Ickes think? In his fine address did he say all that was in his heart?

Beyond Constitution Hall, from which women have banned her—women who would be honored by her genius and character— the dark angel's voice sweeps the profound theme of "Ave Maria" into millions of homes.

A thousand years from now, when the 1939 un-American Daughters of the American Revolution shall have been forgotten in scattered dust, the name and voice of Marian Anderson shall be known at the fireside of American womanhood.

An item for future historians: Easter, 1939. The *Shreveport Times* gives Marian Anderson's recital 4 words; the editor gives Abraham Bell, a Negro Drunk, 49 words in the same paper.

Easter at Medicine Park, Okla.
April 15, 1939

Medicine Park, Okla., is a small mountain village. This morning

175,000 people are gathered to see the spectacle of the crucified
and risen Christ. Men and women and children sit on the sloping
mountain. They have come afoot, on horseback, in cars to witness
this thirteenth production.

As Jesus dies between the two thieves, some of the people burst
into tears. As the sun comes up over Fort Scott and Jesus rises
from the dead, thousands cry hallelujahs.

The only road from the scene, according to E. C. Wallis, who
reports the dramatic happening, is a graveled road just wide
enough for two cars. And there are 50,000 cars that must wind
around mountains and cross streams to get back home with their
pilgrims.

But all the scores of thousands of good white citizens are happy
this Easter morning. They have been deeply moved by the crucifixion and resurrection of Christ.

A few Indians look on at the mighty biblical drama. Also a few
Negroes. But the white spectators, while sitting on the Indians'
mountain, do not think about how their paleface ancestors stole the
Indians' rich oil lands in Oklahoma and killed off the Indians. And
the pious white spectators, of course, do not see the crucifixion of
the Negro race in the crucifixion of Jesus.

So this Easter morning the white citizens leave Medicine Park
with their souls uplifted, and go back to their jim-crow schools and
jim-crow churches and jim-crow politics. The Indians go back to
their gloomy reservations. The Negroes go back to their daily
crosses. Next Easter, Medicine Park will give its fourteenth pre-
sentation of the crucified and risen Christ.

Easter in Europe!
April 15, 1939

A mighty array of Italian infantry, motorized units, tanks, and
bombing planes roll into Albania, and again that freedom-loving
country finds itself the slave of a foreign power.

Four Italian warships blast the town of Durazzo. King Zog and
his wife, with a baby three days old, flee before the onrushing
hordes of fascists. Four hundred planes thunder over the little
country, every whir of four hundred motors proclaiming death on
earth, ill will to men.

Italian heavy guns face each other across the narrow neck of the
Adriatic, and the famous six-foot Grenadiers push on across the
mountains to the borders of Yugoslavia.

Today is Easter. Peace on earth! Yet in London, old Chamberlain cuts short his holiday and hurries to call a meeting of the

cabinet, "fearful of a lightning attack by Germany without a declaration of war."

In Paris it is Easter. Good will to men. Yet Premier Daladier calls
hastily his military, naval, and air chiefs to map out plans to
counter the vast army movements on the other side of the Rhine.

And now Pope Pius XII raises his voice in his first Easter
message from the throne of St. Peters in an eloquent appeal for
peace and charity. His scholarly address is delivered in Latin.

That is just as well. Hitler and Mussolini don't know anything
about Latin: so they won't know what the Pope is talking about.
Hitler and Mussolini understand only the language of bombing
planes and machine guns. Hitler and Mussolini don't fear the Pope
as long as he talks in Latin.

1,900 Years after the
Resurrection of Jesus!
April 15, 1939

It is Easter. Centuries and centuries ago the Lowly Nazarene
walked and talked among men. Never a man spoke like Jesus, the
friend of the lame, the halt, and the blind. He came into a world
torn with political strife, domestic disharmony, racial animosities,
and the greed for gold.

He preached a straight doctrine. He didn't beat around the bush.
He was an agitator. His enemies said: "He stirreth up the people."

Here on my wall hangs a picture of Him talking to the rich young
man. I look at that picture a great deal. I showed it to a big white
merchant who came to talk to me about Jesus. The sweat popped
out on his forehead as he read the words of Jesus:

"Take what thou hast and give it to the poor."

It is Easter. Spring is here. Life is flowing into bud and leaf and
flower. In the grand cathedrals of the earth mighty organs thunder
the message of the Christ. In a hundred lands millions of mouth-
Christians sing hosannas. The Risen Master! What does He see?
What does He hear? What does He feel?

He did not build a church of brick and mortar. He built His
church in the hearts of men. He was not interested in isms. He
wanted to make a better world. He lived to rid men of envy,
jealousy, the lust of power, and the lust for gold.

He said to His followers: "Take nothing for your journey, neither staves, nor scrip, neither bread, neither money: neither two
coats apiece."

Jesus looks down upon His followers this Easter. What are they
taking on their Christian journey? Some of them are taking Cadil-

lacs, ten-room houses, trunks of fine clothes, delicious foods, and all the money they can get out of other folks' pockets.

What does Jesus think about these people as He looks at them this morning? Jesus was humble; these mouth-Christians are proud. Jesus was poor; these mouth-Christians are rich, or breaking their necks trying to get rich. Jesus stood for His principles, died for His principles; these mouth-Christians are "practical" and "diplomatic" and "expedient." Jesus loved the poor; these mouth-Christians scorn the lousy and ignorant. Jesus said that only the pure in heart shall see God; these mouth-Christians have explained things so that anybody can see God. Jesus denounced the hypocrisies and exploitation of the Big Boys; these mouth-Christians worship high positions and material success. Jesus whipped the money-lenders out of the temple; these mouth-Christians take in anybody who has a dollar.

Jesus said some straight things. The man who says he loves God and hates his brother is a liar and the truth isn't in him. You can't serve God and Mammon. By their fruit you shall know them. He who is without sin, let him cast the first stone. Judge not that ye be not judged.

One thousand and nine hundred years after His resurrection, Jesus is still holding up His principles. Jesus doesn't want words; Jesus wants deeds. Jesus wants Christians; Jesus doesn't want mouth-Christians. Fears and supersititions and traditions make mouth-Christians. Everybody who is scared to die or lose his job will make a good mouth-Christian.

Jesus didn't believe in jim-crow churches, jim-crow cars, child labor, snobbery, exploitation, slums, Uncle Tomism, big society. If you believe in these things you are not a Christian. You can't hold on to these things and hold on to Jesus. Let that sink in! Jesus is all wrong. Why are things in such a mess after 1,900 years of talking about Jesus? Perhaps there's been too much talk!

The Negro and Radicalism
August 12, 1939

Radicalism is spread in the United States. Every Negro who knows anything about Negro history is glad of this. Radicalism is the Great Emancipator of Negroes. When I see a Negro kicking off radicals, I know he is either dumb or crooked.

Conservatism is the Negro's worst enemy. The South is the most conservative part of the country, and therefore it is the graveyard of Negro rights. In our most radical cities, Negroes enjoy the widest freedom. Your biggest Negro haters are the most conservative people. That is true in Boston, Dallas, Tucson, Washington, and Waycross, Ga. Conservatism breeds every kind of prejudice. I've heard educated Negroes in the South say that they like to live in "a wide-open town"; that is, a town where anything goes. Of course, such a town is not conservative. It is a place for a good time. These Negroes I refer to are respectable citizens. But they have observed that in "a wide-open town" the cops don't beat up Negroes for pastime. Then, too, the white citizens don't spend the day and night keeping Negroes in their place.

A conservative is a man who is opposed to change. Since he is all right, he imagines that everything is all right. God deliver me from a conservative Negro!

I realize that there are some places in the Land of the Free where there is no freedom of speech. But even in such hellholes a Negro can give the radicals a silent Amen. The Devil himself cannot keep a man from thinking. Then, too, if you are scared to be radical, you can cheer the man who has the guts to speak out for human rights. You can write him a letter of appreciation and tell him to burn it up.

Escaped from Chattel Slavery

The Negro would not have escaped from chattel slavery if it had not been for radicals of all classes, isms, ologies, and sects. Don't forget that. For 150 years before the Civil War, radicals kept up a continuous fight for Negro freedom. Many of them were lynched.

Conservatives have stood for prostitution, blood-letting, polygamy, illiteracy, ignorance, witch-burning, voodooism, piracy, plagues, child labor, social diseases, and cannibalism. Why? Conservatives have always opposed change at all times and in all places.

Conservatives have always believed: "Whatever is, is right."

Conservatives have always laid the blame for everything on either God or human nature. When the filth in London produced the Black Plague that killed unnumbered thousands, conservatives called the Black Plague "an act of God." When a man dies because he is ignorant of the laws of health, the conservative says: "Too bad. But his time had come."

The conservative is a peculiar bird. He always has a hundred good reasons for doing nothing. If you pull on the oars, he declares you're trying to upset the boat. If you want to organize the Negroes, he sees a massacre of the Negro race. If Negroes picket a white man's store, he sees 12,000,000 Negroes losing their jobs.

Anytime you want to make a change, the conservative sees the collapse of the universe.

The conservative is always talking about the eternal truths he has discovered. This is whistling in the dark near a graveyard. A new idea gives a conservative a spasm of fear. Thus all conservatives die of heart failure.

Yes, if the Negro had waited for the conservatives to free him, he would still be in chattel slavery. It took radicals like Douglass, Garrison, Lovejoy, Greeley, and John Brown to arouse the conscience of a nation to the brutalities of slavery. Economic materialism plus radical propaganda turned the trick.

A favorite excuse of the conservative is this: "The time is not ripe."

This statement is a feather bed in which the conservative sleeps from the cradle to the grave unless he is rudely awakened by a strike, a revolution, or war.

Radicalism Comes to the Defense

When I was in college, the Negro was the victim of vicious propaganda in all the sciences. He was described as unintellectual, unintelligent, immoral, irresponsible, childish, brutal, lustful, undependable, and criminal.

Conservative sociologists, historians, educators, statesmen, anthropologists, and novelists filled thousands of pages with Uncle Toms, Aunt Dinahs, Sambos, black rapists, black Al Capones, and grinning crapshooters.

After the World War, white radicals came to the defense of the Negro in larger and larger numbers. Negro art, music, and literature flourished. The Harlem Renaissance seems now a long way off. But it took place in the 20's. It is quite recently that the Negro has been considered a human being in American life and literature with the virtues and vices of human beings.

Can you remember when Dr. Du Bois and the late Dr. James Weldon Johnson were making their valiant pleas for the Talented Tenth? It seems like a far-off dream. What professor would dare write a book now on contemporary American literature without including Negro poets and novelists?

I may say here that no race is civilized until it produces a literature. A great work of literature is a race's ticket to immortality. Races do not live in history because they have produced Henry Fords. Some so-called educated Negroes haven't discovered that well-known fact yet!

Rome owned a great material civilization, but Rome will be but a name to antiquarians when future generations will still be studying and admiring the great thinkers and writers of Greece.

Science, literature, and art have been the tireless defenders of Negroes. These three fields are renowned for their production of radicals.

The Most Powerful Thing

Propaganda is the most powerful thing in the world. It controls the destinies of men and nations. Every dictator knows that.

"Seize the press," says the dictator when he gives his first command to his flunkies.

The Negro didn't have a chance to be a man as long as conservative writers were depicting him either as a clown or a rapist. The seeds of racial prejudice were sown in the minds of millions of innocent schoolchildren and college students. This had gone on for generations.

Then came the radicals. With them came a proletarian literature and art dealing with the masses. These radicals said that a man was the product of social and economic forces. These radicals proved that a man is not the master of his fate and the captain of his soul.

This social philosophy marked the second emancipation of the Negro. No longer could the enemies of the Negro condemn him for being ignorant, illiterate, immoral, and criminal. The radicals said if you want to change the Negro, change his environment. Nurture changes nature.

In intellectual circles, you don't hear intellectuals arguing now about heredity and environment. Of course, we still have a few Negro snobs boasting about their heredity. But they are not geniuses like Richard Wright, Langston Hughes, and Paul Robeson.

I am glad to see radicals raising hell. The more hell they raise, the better it is for my people. Minority groups escape into the Promised Land only when radicals are raising hell.

Radio News Flash:
"Jesus Lynched in America, 1939!"
December 16, 1939

This is the Age of Hypocrisy. As Dr. Leonard Farmer has said, "You must neither practice what you preach nor preach what you practice." As long as you talk and write about Heaven, the Garden of Allah, the Promised Land, Sodom and Gomorrah, the Hebrew Children in the Fiery Furnace, Abe Lincoln, the Constitution,

Hitler, Stalin, Mussolini, the Reds, David and Goliath, Beauty, Patriotism, Jesus, Virtue, the Book of the Seven Seals—as long as you write and talk about somebody or something away off, the 2x4 respectables will give you the big hand.

A preacher may preach about David's stealing Uriah's wife: but he'd better not breathe a word about Deacon John Doe who stole Deacon Littlejohn's wife.

It's okay to describe Jesus driving the moneylenders out of the Temple 1,900 years ago; but you'd better not talk about the 1939 racketeers in the Temple.

Quacks Rake in the Money

No wonder that great scholar, Samuel D. Schmalhausen, in the *Modern Quarterly,* dubbed this period "The Age of Lies."

Everybody knows we are rotten with hypocrisy. Everybody knows we tell lies by direction and indirection—black lies and white lies. Everybody knows that while we mouth Christian platitudes we practice devilish vices. Everybody knows that while we talk about heaven we're on our way to hell with a one-way ticket. Yet most of us are scared to face the truth. We're like a guy with the syphilis who is scared to see the doctor; therefore, he visits a quack.

Our society and its institutions are diseased. So we call in quacks of all sorts. Dale Carnegie comes along with *How to Win Friends and Influence People.* So we buy a million copies containing his bunk. A dusky mulatto with showbutton eyes and straight hair puts on an Oriental costume; and we pay four bits when he tells us how to win success and love. Somebody starts a chain letter that ends in the outhouse.

In spite of the iron fact that Big Business has ruined the white man, simpleminded Negroes and college professors shout: "Business is the salvation of the Negro." Now and then some big Negro, with his belly stuffed with roast chicken, comes along and tells the little Negroes "to think on higher things."

Dr. Flunky of the famous Pow-wow University shoots craps with some statistics and writes: "Business is on the upgrade. Prosperity is just around the corner. All you need is faith. All you need is hope. Fellow citizens, the dirty radicals tell you the Old Ship of State has hit a rock. Beware. Beware of such hasty generalizations! The Old Ship of State has just sprung a leak. That's all."

Condemnation of the Rich; Exaltation of the Poor

Nothing is more beautiful than genuine service. The early

Christians had it. Taking neither two coats nor scrip, neither gold nor silver, they went about doing good. They were the first Communists: that is, they held everything in common. They were not social climbers. They did not cater to the selfishness of the Big Boys. If Luke had a loaf of bread, he shared it with Mark. They had Christianity: they didn't know anything about modern Churchianity.

The early Christians rendered a great service. I think V. F. Calverton has summed it up best in his recent best-seller, *The Awakening of America:* "It elevated the concept of man as man, regardless of his position in society, his wealth, his office in the state. It made all men equal in the eyes of the Lord. It condemned the rich and exalted the poor."

Why did Christianity grow? Well, the early Christians practiced what they preached. Its revolutionary democratic ideal in a world of human slavery and poverty appealed to the masses. That's the reason Christianity made a vigorous appeal to the black slaves.

How Jesus Differed from Other Christs of His Day

Why was Jesus lynched? Why were the ancient Christians burned at the stake? Mr. Calverton gives us the answer: "The Roman emperor did not attempt to suppress Christianity because of its religious content, but because of its political and economic threat. Roman civilization was full of too many Christs, too many messiahs of all kinds—Mithraic, Zoroastrian, Manichean—to be alarmed about another Savior born of the Jews."

Then why did the Big Boys in Rome get scared of Jesus? Why did they single out Jesus? Why did the Unholy Three of ancient times—the Pharisees, the Sadducees, and the Sanhedrin—plot the downfall of Jesus?

Mr. Calverton tells us: "It was the revolutionary doctrine of this particular Christ, who associated with fishermen, carpenters, tradesmen, whores, that terrified the Romans and made them drive his followers to the hills and the catacombs and finally to the lions when they were captured."

This stern fact is overlooked by 9,999 persons out of every 10,000 who go to church every Sunday.

If Jesus Came to America in 1939?

The essence of the teachings of Jesus is democracy, as contained in the Golden Rule. He who says he loves God and hates his brother is a liar and the truth isn't in him.

The disciples of Jesus were poor. His followers were the riffraff, the down-and-outers, the scum of society. The fox has a hole, the bird has a nest; but the lowly Jesus didn't have a place to lay his head.

You recall the high tragedy of the rich young man who came to Jesus. He had kept all the commandments from his youth up. But that was not enough. Needless to say, that rich young man could have joined any church in America. By our low standards, he would have been okay. But not by Jesus'.

Jesus said: "Take what thou hast and give it to the poor."

The rich young man did just what most of us would do today. He told Jesus good-bye.

Let us quote one of those ole-time Christians of the seventeenth century, Winstanley, by name: "At this day the poor people are forced to work for 4d. and corn is dear. And the tithing-priest stops their mouth and tells them what 'inward satisfaction of mind' was meant by the declaration, 'the poor shall inherit the earth.' I tell you the scripture is to be really and materially fulfilled."

Doesn't that priest sound just like some of these mouth-Christians who say: "You'll eat pie, in the sky, bye and bye"?

And when grand old Winstanley told the Big Boys about piling up goods on earth and building up classes, doesn't he sound just like a soapbox radical? Jesus came to level things. Great men were to be servants; not exploiters. Jesus didn't believe in economic, racial, and social distinctions.

We look upon servants—the scrubwoman and the street sweeper—with contempt. Am I telling the truth? Amen! You talk about Karl Marx, the Communist! Why, don't you know Jesus was preaching about leveling society 1,800 years before the Jewish Red was born?

Listen to old Winstanley: "You jeer at the name of the Leveller. I tell you Jesus Christ is the Head Leveller. The day of Judgment is begun . . . the poor people you oppress shall be the saviours of the land . . . and break to pieces the bands of property." Then come the English Revolution, the American Revolution, the French Revolution, the Russian Revolution!

Jesus Is Lynched in America in 1939!

That's what you would see in your newspaper if Jesus returned to America in 1939. Why? What did Jesus do to get lynched?

Well, Jesus did some radical things. Because of his un-Americanism, the Dies Committee called him in. Jesus had white Christians and black Christians meeting together at Okay, Arkansas, thereby violating the State Jim Crow Law in that Christian

State. Jesus said He wasn't going to have any jim-crow churches. So the whites and blacks got together for the first time and ran Jesus across the state line.

Then Jesus wanted the rich Christians to take what they had and give it to the poor. Henry Ford and the Supreme Court and the Big Negroes asked Jesus: "What you trying to put over, you Red?"

Then Jesus said He wasn't going to have any more preachers knifing other preachers in the back to get bigger churches and positions. Jesus started abolishing fraternities and sororities; that caused the Alphas and Omegas and Kappas to gang Jesus. Then Jesus ran around with bums: He didn't know how to pick the right company. Jesus went into the colleges and universities and started the students thinking. Then Jesus walked into Wall Street and started breaking up the rackets He found there. That's the reason they lynched Jesus!

An Easter Sermon—Without a Preacher
March 30, 1940

It is Easter. Before me lies the greatest Easter sermon. It is not the work of a preacher. Thousands of sermons will be delivered today, but not one will equal this. It is a sermon without a preacher. I'm not joking, either.

Before me lies a huge metropolitan newspaper. I wish every man in the world could read it, as I shall read it. Now, the owner and editor of this newspaper didn't intend to put out a sermon this morning. This Easter edition was simply a business proposition.

At the top of the page is the word *Easter* in large, Old English type. In the center is a fine-looking church. To the right and to the left, handsome boys are singing in a choir. Then, there are beautiful doves flying above serene meadows.

Christians and the Battlefield!

I read an article from the Associated Press. It says: "Christians turn from battlefield to church for day of rejoicing. Holy City is a Mecca for thousands."

Do you see the contradiction, my friend? Do Christians, battlefield, and church go together harmoniously? You would think that the devil himself wrote that sentence. Yet it is the truth. We are a race of hypocrites. We hate and shoot each other down like dogs; then go to church!

The article continues: "The eyes of the Roman Catholic world turned to Vatican City, where Pope Pius XII personally arranged to celebrate mass in historic St. Peters.''

Read that quotation again. We are told that the message of the Pope will be a vigorous appeal for peace. And yet the Pope is having a bomb-proof room built in the Vatican! I take these facts from the magazine *News-Week*.

Easter Parade in a Thousand Cities

This morning, in a thousand cities, ladies of refinement and culture are on parade in their Easter dresses. Before me lies a full-page picture of four ladies smiling among beautiful flowers. When I was a young man in Atlantic City, I used to see ladies in $10,000 fur coats taking a stroll along the famous Boardwalk. Our civilization is very kind to—some ladies.

This morning, in a thousand cities, overworked, poverty-stricken mothers and daughters got out of filthy beds in man-made tenements. Millions of poor women didn't have the new dress to wear to church.

This morning, in Waco, Texas, Bob Crowder, 50, killed his sister-in-law and wounded his wife and killed himself. He used a 12-gauge pump shotgun. The husband of his sister-in-law lost his job and the murdered woman came to live with her sister.

Then Bob Crowder lost his job. Despondent for weeks, Crowder decided to fix things so that they wouldn't have to worry any more about jobs. Ten million men in America woke up this Easter morning—without jobs. Jobs for husbands and fathers would help a great deal in bringing "peace on earth; good will to men.''

A Picture of the Risen Lord

Here before me lies a beautiful picture of the Resurrection. It was painted by that genius, Fra Angelica, about the middle of the fifteenth century.

To the left of this masterpiece is an article on the political and economic situation in Old Mexico. The Mexicans are having trouble, with Big American Business, over oil properties. Mexico is about to hold a presidential election. The issues revolve around these oil properties. Dollars are making a mess out of things—as usual. The greatest enemy of Jesus is the dollar.

The article says a revolution is expected, because guns and ammunition are being smuggled into Mexico from the United States. American Business started the trouble by blackjacking the Mexicans out of their oil wells; now American Business sells guns to the Mexicans so they can murder each other over the oil wells.

Many "Christians" won't see anything wrong with this on Easter morning.

Across from the picture of the risen Lord is a picture of children called "The Junior Red Cross." The children have a truck loaded with provisions. I wonder if the Junior Red Cross is getting ready to send aid to the Mexicans who will kill each other with the guns produced in our "Christian" country. And I bet those Big Businessmen are sitting in church this morning with their wives and children! Are the gunmakers also in church, singing: "Peace on earth; good will to men"?

What Is the Title of This Sermon?

Now, the title of this newspaper sermon is "Hypocrisy." For 1,900 years we have preached one thing and practiced another. We are so hypocritical that we don't know we are hypocritical. A white American can denounce Hitler for persecuting 500,000 Jews, and at the same time see nothing wrong in persecuting 12,000,000 Negroes.

We are so downright dirty that we can take sacrament and plot the destruction of another human being. We can say we love God—whom we have not seen—and hate our neighbor next door. We can give to the Red Cross, and sell guns to murder other men. We can say God hates a liar, and lie faster than the Broadway Limited can run. We can say the truth will make you free, and then do our best to destroy any man who has guts enough to tell the truth.

We are a race of vipers and hypocrites! If Jesus returned, we'd lynch Him before a cat could sneeze. We put on our fine clothes and talk about Jesus. Jesus wouldn't have a thing to do with us. Jesus was interested in bums. The lame, the halt, and the blind followed Jesus. If the dirty mobs that walked after Jesus came into one of our fine churches, the good "Christians" would turn up their noses and call the police!

All that Jesus said can be summed up in the Golden Rule. When I hear anybody talking about God or Jesus, I simply look to see if he's practicing the Golden Rule. If he isn't practicing the Golden Rule, he's as far from Jesus as the earth is from Jupiter.

Only radicals can be Christians.

What Shall the Negro do to Be Saved?—
U.S. Department of Labor Auditorium
on April 26, 27, 28, 1940.
April 27, 1940

When it comes to private affairs, I never like to butt in. When you butt in, somebody may butt you out. Every man's house is his castle—until the Big Boys come along with a mortgage or eviction papers.

If they don't get you that way, there is the Law of Eminent Domain. Let us get down to brass tacks.

Today I'm butting in for the good of the race. I'm asking the little Negroes, the big Negroes, and the little Negroes who think they're big to attend the Third National Negro Congress. I say this with malice aforethought. For I realize that if you attend this all-important congress, this will interfere with some of the backbiting, gin-drinking, bridge-playing, hip-shaking, joy-riding, and fornicating in the nation's capital.

Cynics say Negroes won't get together. That's a lie. Negroes are together when pleasure comes before business.

I heard a dirty Cracker wisecrack: "If you want to put Sambo to sleep, start reasoning with him. Then, if you want to wake Sambo up, tell a joke."

What Shall the Negro Do to Be Saved?

That's the big question before the Negro National Congress. The Negro, for fifty years, has depended on somebody else to save him. With his eye fixed on a piece of pie in the sky, bye and bye, he has let his enemies degrade his women and rob his children. He has bowed down to the white man, and received a kick where he sits down like the Fool in the King's court,—he has tickled the vanity of the Big White Man to get a few crumbs.

He has shunned KNOWLEDGE as if it were an army of Devils. Yet men perish for the lack of KNOWLEDGE. He has opposed every radical idea that would save him, and depended on the broken crutches of charity.

But there is a New Negro in America today. He knows that a man who would be free himself must strike the blow. He knows that KNOWLEDGE is power. He realizes that one man cannot stand alone. He knows that the united Negro masses can change America. He knows that one Negro, sneaking up to the back door of the White House for a handout, is an enemy to the race and to himself.

Frederick Douglass Knew the Way to Salvation!

When I stop admiring old Frederick Douglass, I want some Al Capone to rub me out. White folk don't say much about old man Douglass. Their silence is a tribute to his greatness. Douglass was a New Negro. He knew how to save the race.

If I had the power, I'd glue this quotation inside the head of every Negro in America.

Read and reread and reread these words of old man Douglass:

> The whole history of the progress of liberty shows that all concessions have been born of earnest struggle. If there is no struggle, there is no progress. Those who profess to favor freedom yet deprecate agitation are men who want crops without plowing ground. Power concedes nothing without a demand. It never did and it never will.

Yes, I've read hundreds of books on the History of Man—on Civilization and Culture, Liberty and Democracy. But I'll be doggone if old man Douglass didn't sum up everything in one paragraph! If Abe Lincoln said anything deeper than that, I've never seen it in Carl Sandburg's great biography of the Great Emancipator.

Douglass was a slave. He agitated from tombstones for his people, when he was hungry and homeless. Some Negro leaders can't agitate at an interracial dinner where the tables groan with baked chickens. Perhaps the chickens keep them from agitating!

The National Negro Congress agrees with Frederick Douglass. It knows that agitation is as necessary as the plowing of ground to plant beans. That truth ought to be clear to a dumbbell!

A Cross of Gold

William Jennings Bryan did one good act in his life—and died. At that, he beat Methuselah, who, like some dead Negro leaders, did nothing.

William Jennings Bryan said to the Big Boys: "You shall not place this crown of thorns upon the brow of labor. You shall not crucify Labor on a Cross of Gold."

The Negro is a laborer, when he has a chance to labor. The National Negro Congress is determined that the Negro laborer shall not be crucified on a Cross of Gold.

This is a Land of the Free—where everybody is free to starve.

Especially Negroes. If the Negro masses can't find jobs, then the Negro doctors, teachers, businessmen, and civil-service employees can't bring home the bacon to their high-yellah mamas. That means the high-yellah mamas will raise hell with their hungry papas. When the Wolf comes in the door, Love flies out the window. Hunger is the most dangerous rival a man has.

When hunger comes in, mama says to papa: "Papa don't love mama no more."

Facts that Speak for Themselves

Millions of Negro people in America are hungry and jobless. Yes, the Negro is the last to be hired, and the first to be fired. The Negro is the last to get on the WPA, and the first to get off. Negro snobs are always saying that the race suffers because Negroes have no self-respect. If those same self-righteous Negroes were dirty and hungry and homeless, how much self-respect would they have? If a man is reduced to begging, he loses his soul. Jesus fed the people before He preached to them. How can a man think about his soul when he is thinking about his belly? Two thoughts cannot occupy the same place at the same time!

I often hear dumbbells kicking off Negro youth. A captain whose ship is safe in the harbor can always kick off the captain whose ship is on the stormy seas. Do these cross-eyed elders have any jobs to give Negro youths?

Negro youth lives in a world that it never made. Youth wants love, education, recreation, a home, and a steady job. If you think I'm lying, ask black boys and girls what they want. Don't act like Crackers and tell them what they want.

Already the dark forces of oppression are plotting to reduce the Negro to his place—the place of galley slaves. The dark forces of un-Americanism are advancing behind a smoke screen of Americanism. Attend the Third National Negro Congress and help save the race!

Should Negroes Join NAACP?
The Mystery of Doctor Frank
March 8, 1941

I wish some of you wise birds would solve for me the mystery of Doctor Frank. Of course, the Doubting Thomases want to know what this has to do with the NAACP. I would say: As much as one of the Siamese twins has to do with the other.

Should Negroes join the NAACP? Whenever you ask me about an organization, I start looking into its record. I am a fiend for facts. Let the record speak. Let the china fall in President Roosevelt's lap or Senator Bilbo's hair. It makes no difference to me.

When you mention the NAACP, my mind does a Lindy Hop. I hear the voice of James Weldon Johnson in Convention Hall, Kansas City, Mo., when I was a boy, denouncing fascist mobs before 15,000 people.

I see on July 28, 1917, 10,000 New York Negroes silently marching down Fifth Avenue to the sound of muffled drums. The procession is headed by little children dressed in white, followed by women in white. Their banners speak to America: "Mother, Do Lynchers Go to Heaven?" "Mr. President, Why Not Make America Safe for Democracy?" "Your Hands Are Full of Blood." "Patriotism and Loyalty Presuppose Protection and Liberty."

I see a mob in Chicago bombing a Negro church. I see American white-savages attacking the home of Dr. O. H. Sweet, a colored physician in Detroit. A mobster is killed. I hear the voice of Clarence Darrow pleading for Justice and Democracy for black men. These are the things I see and hear when you mention the name of the NAACP. The Negro is in an awful condition. But only God knows how much worse his condition would be if the NAACP had not battled for the Negro all these years! Put this statement above the door of every anti-NAACP-er.

The Mystery of Doctor Frank

Should Negroes join the NAACP? Remember after the last World War Negroes were lynched wholesale. In East St. Louis I saw thousands of Negroes burned out of their homes. What will happen after this war? Already 90,000 Ku Kluxers are organized in Pennsylvania!

Bear these facts in mind as I write about Doctor Frank. I do not know what his real name is: But he published a book in 1924 called *Negrolana*. He had to use a false name. This is all I know about him: he was "a business man of high standing in the state of Texas and a superintendent of public schools for twenty-five years."

Should Negroes join the NAACP? I shall let the record of Doctor Frank speak for itself. Then, you may make your own decision. Sit tight. I warn you. If you have a weak heart, you'd better put down this paper right now.

This is a white Southerner writing. His facts should carry weight. He believed in the NAACP. He even risked his life to write down the facts. I wonder if, as Negroes, we appreciate those noble Southerners who've fought for us. When I think of them, I feel like damning to everlasting hell those hat-in-hand, me-too-boss, parasitic Uncle Toms.

The Stories of Eyewitnesses from *Negrolana*

From the *Vicksburg Herald:* "In an exchange of shots between Holbert and James Eastland, between whom trouble had risen, Eastland was killed. Holbert, with his wife, fled but was captured by a mob. They were tied to trees, and while the funeral pyres were being prepared they were forced to suffer the most fiendish tortures. The victims were forced to hold out their hands while one finger after another was chopped off. The fingers were distributed as souvenirs. The ears were cut off. One of Holbert's eyes was knocked out. The eye hung by a shred from the socket. A corkscrew was bored into the flesh of the arms, the legs and body, and pulled out, the spiral tearing out big pieces of raw, quivering flesh. . . .

"Had this man outraged a woman? Oh no; he had merely killed a man who was shooting at him. His wife had committed no crime, but simply fled with her husband. Yet she was made to share his fate. . . ."

This account is taken from a Southern paper. I started to tell several of these eyewitness stories. I shall tell more. Here you have Judge Lynch in action. Now, the NAACP, through its heroic propaganda, has stirred the conscience of the nation and the world. Over 4,000 men and women have been lynched. That is the official report. Of course, no man knows how many thousands of unknown lynchings have occurred.

Will Judge Lynch March Again?

Have you read *Kneel to the Rising Sun* by Erskine Caldwell, the author of *Tobacco Road?* Or *Court House Square* by Hamilton Basso? Or *The Cathedral* by T. S. Stribling? Be sure to read these books. They are white Southerners. They picture lynchings. These white novelists give Negroes the best reason for joining the NAACP.

At 3 A.M. in a fog, I passed through a mob raising hell for five miles along the White River. We got down in the car, and our white Negro driver saved us. I'll tell you about it sometime. It was a thriller. I'll never forget those bloodhounds baying in the swamps. The two Negro tramps were innocent—it was discovered later! That has happened many times.

I don't have to theorize about mobs. The NAACP has fought for Negro rights on many fronts. But its greatest service has been its heroic work to blot out lynchings. That's enough to justify its existence.

I am looking at a play by Ann Seymour, who received the prize award given by the Society of Southern Women for the Prevention of Lynching. These white women of the New South have earned my gratitude. I only wish every Negro had done as much for my people.

Now, we may go to war. If we do, God only knows what the terrible aftermath will be. A depression is sure to come. And with it a new wave of lynchings. The Negro must be prepared to meet anything and everything. To do this, he must be organized. With the world turned upside down, this is no time for petty bickerings. If Negroes can't bury the hatchet and get together, the hatchet will be buried in their skulls. He who would be free himself must strike the first blow! So get out your rusty bucks and join the NAACP!

Fighting Preachers in the District of Columbia
April 12, 1941

I like a fighting preacher. My father is one. His Gospel has the TNT of Joe Louis's fists. You've read James Weldon Johnson's *God's Trombones*. It takes imagination and knowledge to read those old Negro sermons. You've seen a trombone in an orchestra. It's proud and self-assured. Well, those old Negro preachers were the trombones of God, the whole show. When they let out their blasts at the altar, they scared both the Devil and Man.

At revival time, when I was a boy, my Mother used to put me to bed. But I'd get up and listen outside the church. Yes, I had to hear those trombones of God.

Those old Negro preachers had showmanship, drama, color. They were mighty men, born to leadership. I used to watch my Dad in the pulpit and feel proud. I was like the Athenians listening to Demosthenes thundering from the bema. The trombones of God were fearless. During slavery times, they were always doing subversive things. Yes, most of those slave revolutions were planned in the church. There was the Rev. Nat Turner, with his gun in one hand and his Bible in the other. No wonder the Governor of Virginia hid under his bed!

Fire and Cloud

Before Dick Wright became famous I told you to read that great story, "Fire and Cloud." If you haven't done it yet now is a good time to meet Reverend Taylor, one of God's trombones. Reverend Taylor led his half-starved congregation in a hunger march. Yes, against the Big Boys. You'll find all about Reverend Taylor in *Uncle Tom's Children*. This paper displayed the story when others slept on the job in 1938. Of course, now, all the papers, black and white, are discussing Dick Wright. Enough of that. Time changes things.

The antebellum Negro preacher was a greater diplomat than Mr. Roosevelt and Mr. Churchill. Paul Laurence Dunbar pointed that out. Some of the loudest blasts against slavery came from God's trombones in the Deep South. Dunbar tells it in his "Ante Bellum Sermon." Why not look it up?

There is majesty in old John Milton's *Paradise Lost*. But no greater majesty than that you'll find in one of God's old trombones. At his best, the old preacher had the poetry of word and motion—if you get what I mean.

When I was a boy, I heard Dr. Walker recite "Thanatopsis." And I shall never forget it. Just as I'll never forget Richard B. Harrison as "De Lawd." I heard Professor Teeters say, in a lecture, at Milwaukee: "When I saw Richard B. Harrison in *Green Pastures,* I knew the meaning of sublimity."

A Great Preacher Deals with Practical Problems

So true. The biggest problem in the world is poverty. Jesus knew his economics. He fed the people—and then preached to them. It's hard for a man to think about his soul when his empty belly is debating his backbone. No lie. That's the reason you find so many intelligent clergymen who're Socialists. Jesus was always kicking off the Big Boys. It's significant that not one of His followers was a rich man. He was interested in the widows and orphans. He created hope in the lame, the halt, and the blind.

He told His followers to take on the journey neither gold nor silver—neither scrip nor two coats. These mouth-Christians try to follow Jesus with bankrolls and Cadillacs. No lie, Sambo. Our good white friends try to drag along their race hatred. That's the reason Hitler has so much fun denouncing democrats and mouth-Christians in England and America. They ought to have enough sense not to throw stones if they live in a glass house!

Yes, a great preacher is militant against the Big Evils. Jesus was tolerant with the woman caught in adultery. But He gave the Big Boys who condemned her a moral blitzkrieg. I wish I'd been there to see it.

After all, prostitution has an economic basis. A study made by the University of Chicago proves that. Thus, most problems come down to the question of bread and meat. If young people are no account, it's the result of our tooth-and-claw civilization. Most scholars haven't sense enough to see that. Economic instability produces moral instability. Lose your job, and you lose a lot of things worthwhile. A jobless man is homeless even when he's in a house. A depression twists the character of the haves and have-nots. We're all members of ONE body.

Ministers Campaign for Jobs

I'm glad that the thinking clergymen in the District of Columbia have joined the Negro National Congress in its campaign for jobs. The shortest route to a man's soul is through his job. A man without a job is a ship on the ocean of society.

The Interdenominational Ministers Alliance is right in saying: "Happiness is based on work." These gentlemen of the cloth are philosophical in declaring that this policy of Jobs for the Jobless "will be carrying out the program of Jesus Christ." Negroes need to prepare to live. "Feed my sheep" is still a dynamic program for the Church. Men will support any institution that supports men. Good jobs make better men. Work helps the soul.

Gentlemen of the cloth, like F. W. Alstork, Julius S. Carroll, I. E. Elliot, Robert R. Brooks, and William H. Jernagin, are to be praised for their initiative, foresight, and humanitarianism. They have captured the militant spirit of those old Fathers of the Church.

I'm glad to see these gentlemen taking up such everyday problems as the rising cost of living, high rents, poor housing conditions, high food prices, insufficient health protection, job insecurity, jim crowism in Uncle Sam's industries. Such ministers will have behind them the united support of the Negro masses. Let the Church take care of the earth. God will take care of heaven.

The Glenn L. Martin Company will employ shortly 40,000 workers, and yet it refuses to hire a single Negro. Still these Big Boys received $322,000,000 in Government contracts. The Negro National Congress and these clergymen are demanding 7,000 jobs for Negroes. That's a big idea. But it takes big men to conceive a big idea. Some Uncle Toms will say it can't be done. But the Uncle Toms have never done anything—but sell out the Race!

II
Race and Class

Is the White Man Worse than the Negro?
January 29, 1938

I tried this question out on several of my friends, and they thought I was a little crazier than usual. Now, since it soothes your vanity to think that another man is crazier than you, I pass the inquiry on to you. Some people are never comfortable unless they are feeling superior to somebody else. That's specially true of little men in big places and little men who are trying to get in big places. But enough of that.

I put it to you, Reader, straight from the shoulder: Is the white man worse than the Negro? There is just one place in the world where you will find the answer to that question. That is in the books that white people have written about themselves. If you want the lowdown on a race, read its books. By that I mean, read what the poets and the storytellers have to say. Let the histories go. Historians are the biggest liars in the world. They may get the facts, but when they get through interpreting the facts and perverting the facts, it would take God's X-ray to find the grain of truth. When the exceptional historian comes along, you have a poet. The first really big liar was Herodotus, the father of history. He was followed by Tacitus, Bede, an army of college professors, and H. G. Wells.

If you want to get the lowdown on the ancient Greeks, read Sappho, the Minnie-the-Moocher of her day. If you want the behind-the-scene doings of the Italians, read Boccaccio. If you want the lowdown on the French, then go to Zola, Balzac, Hugo, Proust, and the Negro, Maran. The whole Bible—you've doubtless seen only part of it—will let you know all about the ancient Hebrews. Those men were poets who wrote the Bible.

Our Good White Folk

I hear Negroes grumbling because Negro writers portray the vulgar side of Negro life. They make me think of the woman who sweeps the dirt under the bed and says "There ain't no dirt!" It's a

55

storyteller's duty to his art and his God to tell what he sees. Since some of the boys like Shakespeare and Horace and Old Walt Whitman did this, future generations have honored them. Negro writers don't tell enough.

Just as you have narrow-minded Negroes who are afraid to face the facts of life, you have Frenchmen, and Englishmen, and Americans who are the same way. But the true poets and storytellers say with Walter Duranty in his justly famous book, "I write as I please!"

I've said all of the things I've said by way of preface to the important question: Is the white man worse than the Negro?

If you read the big writers of today, your answer will certainly be a thunderous yes. These big white poets and novelists certainly give us the lowdown on white folk. They follow them into Congress, as T. S. Stribling did in his famous *The Sound Wagon*, and you discover that Senators and Congressmen are quite different from what they teach you in the colleges.

Then Sinclair Lewis comes along with his *Elmer Gantry* and you get the lowdown on the white preachers. You talk about Father Divine. Well, he's a saint! No lie. Then there is old Theodore Dreiser. When he gets through revealing the crookedness and immoralities of the big businessman in his immortal *The Financier*, you won't want to hold the white man's civilization up as a model to black children.

But I haven't given you any examples to talk about. Some of you turn up your delicate noses at the poor Negroes of Mississippi. Don't do that until you read William Faulkner's *Sanctuary*. What that white man did to that girl from the University of Mississippi will make your eyes pop out.

Then I must not overlook Caldwell of Georgia, who wrote *Tobacco Road*. Good white folk kicked off the play. Well, the play is a Sunday-school book beside *God's Little Acre*. No lie! Novelist Caldwell from Georgia said to his white friends that no Negro could become as degraded as a white man. Then he proved it. White Georgia is shaking yet!

Then there is the novelist from the town where I was born, accidentally. I'm thinking of Jack Conroy, who wrote that remarkable book, *A World to Win*, which, by the way, contains the most heroic picture of a Negro I've seen in a novel.

That Negro showed the trembling whites how to live and die in this worst of all possible worlds. Fatfolks represents the Crispus Attucks of 1938. I want to meet Jack Conroy and shake his toil-worn hand. I don't see how he stays in Moberly, Mo., where I was born. I had to leave when I was three months old. No lie!

Is the White Man Worse Than the Negro

Yes, undoubtedly, he is in our modern fiction, but not in life itself. Why? Well, the big white writers, the poets, and storytellers who are writing for immortality are pulling the lid off things and writing the truth.

Jessie Fauset, our Negro lady novelist, said that she wanted to write a best-seller. Well, she'll have to put some chitterlings in her mouth and write like Dostoevsky and Dos Passos and Dreiser. She'll have to be in harmony with the big writers of 1938. She'll have to forget that she's a colored woman and write God's truth.

I know it is hard. But if Negro writers don't get busy, the white man will monopolize the field. Radicalism is making it possible for the Negro to write like a man. Race is nothing. Genius is universal. Our day is a day of debunking. A writer does not have to prove that his race is great. A great book proves that. I forgot. Race is a myth, anyway. Why not read Paul Radin's *Myth of Race*? Oh, God, I hope I live long enough to see just one Theodore Dreiser with a black skin. Then I'll die happy!

My People
May 7, 1938

My people are still singing "You may have all this world; give me Jesus." And the big white man has taken the world. My people are still hip-shaking to the swing music of Gabby-Gay and his Red Hot Rhythm Boys, while a second depression follows in the footsteps of the Wall Street crash of 1929. My people still grope in the midnight of Professor Kelly Miller's antiquated philosophy, while the words of the new Negro fall upon ears stuffed with the cotton of unreason. My people still believe that the miracle of a phantom Negro business will solve their problems in America, while fascism begins its murderous march across these benighted states.

I fear for the safety of my people; not because they are black, but because they are poor like the 1,500,000,000 poverty-stricken masses of the world. I have no dope of hope and faith to give my people. I have no exciting, racial plan to collect the pennies of washerwomen and cooks.

Black Shadow over a Black World

A black shadow hangs over the black world of America. Our Big Negroes and Great Big Negroes have not seen it yet, and the Little Negroes are in a wilderness of ignorance without that pillar of fire that Professor Kelly Miller sees when his stomach is heavy with roast chicken.

That black shadow is fascism. Hitler and Mussolini are the greatest dangers that confront dark America today, but the Negro press tells the Negro masses nothing about it. Here and there a Negro scholar raises his voice in protest, but that voice is lost in the ballyhoo of self-styled leaders picking up the scattered pieces of silver.

The Jew Fell Asleep

The Jew fell asleep on the job. He tried, in most cases, to keep apart from the rest of the world. He tried to save himself by building up Jewish business for 2,000 years. He did not see, as a race, that race pride and race unity would not save him in a world bloody with interracial strife. From time to time, Jews have risen with a vision that reached beyond the Jewish barriers, but the Jews did not accept them. You remember Jesus and His "Go ye into all the world and preach my Gospel." But the orthodox Jews wanted none of this. They had a program for the salvation of the Jew. Isolation! Isolation! Isolation means destruction of any people. You remember China and her mighty walls. They kept civilization out. But they could not keep out the guns of the Japanese. No people can live alone.

Fascism and the Jew

Fascism or Nazism—they're both Siamese twins—took advantage of the Jewish philosophy of racial identity and unity. Thus the Jew became Hitler's goat. If the Negro should follow the racial isolationist policy of Professor Kelly Miller and the more learned but equally deluded Dr. W. E. B. Du Bois, the result will be racial suicide. The philosophy of racialism is obsolete, for this is an era of interracialism and internationalism. The industrialization of the world has brought these things about. Whoever pursues another course needs a course in the economics of 1938. The feeling of race pride may lull the unthinking into a coma of false security, but they will be awakened by the crash of relentless facts in the marketplace.

A blinded Jewish leadership did not see this. I have just finished reading several copies of a magazine called *The American Jew,* published by Joseph H. Biben and Saul Eichen. The Hebrew gentlemen have not learned the difficult lesson that Hitler has written on the map of Europe. They have not studied the Jewish history of 2,000 years.

Isolation means racial suicide. The Jewish race is a poverty-stricken race, like all other races. They are not Shylocks, for as a boy I lived in a Jewish neighborhood in Iowa and played and ate and slept with Jewish boys. In fact, I knew more about them at that period than I did Negro boys. Their parents worked hard at a variety of tasks, like the parents in other races. They were no more grasping than others. I had Jewish pals in the university. Jews resent the stigma of moneylender as much as black men resent a synonym for black man with a small "n."

The Jew in Germany

The Jew in Germany was better off than the Jews in any other part of the world. Yet look at the facts. I take them from the February issue of *Current History*. The Jew owned but one-half of one percent of the national wealth of Germany. Out of 4,958 university professors, only 200 were Jews—a meager 4 percent. There were 21,700 big officials, but only 270 were Jews. Hitler came along and told the ignorant Germans that the Jews were hogging everything, and on that Jewish goat he rode into power.

If there are Negroes who still believe that the salvation of the Negro lies in a policy of economic isolation, then the case of the Jew has proved to the world that Negro success will create jealousy and lead to the Negro's annihilation.

If you grant that the Jew was a successful businessman—as most Negroes like to believe, statistics to the contrary and the millions of poor Jews to the contrary—then Hitler has smashed that argument with Nazism.

What better argument could an American Hitler have than this: "Here you poor whites are in the bread lines, and there goes a n——— in a Cadillac! Are you white Americans going to stand for that?"

In Germany mobs pursue Jewish pedestrians. Hundreds of Jews have had their skulls caved in. Jewish businesses have been smashed. Jewish women have been raped. The great Rothschild had to flee like a common thief for his life. Thomas Mann, perhaps the greatest novelist in Europe, had to leave. So did Einstein. So did René Remarque. Jewish intellectuals have been scattered over the face of the earth like dead leaves in a wintry gale. This is not the first time it's occurred in history. It has happened repeatedly. Yet ignorant Negro leaders tell the Negro to ape the Jew. For what? Isolation has never worked and it never will. That's Exhibit A in history.

I could write eloquently about racial unity and economic solidar-

ity and make you feel good. But the price of beans would be the
same at the corner grocery store. The only thing that will help now
are the cooperatives. But we don't have sense enough to take these
up—even in our "A" class colleges.

Senator Bilbo

Don't try to laugh off Senator Bilbo and his back-to-Africa
movement. Marcus Garvey initiated that before him. Prejudice is
prejudice. Ignorance is ignorance. So don't be surprised that Garvey and Bilbo had things in common.

The gentleman from Mississippi is a dangerous man in these
times. He and Hitler are Siamese twins in mentality. Listen to
Senator Bilbo: "There are twelve million unemployed in the United States. There are twelve million blacks in the United States.
Move the blacks to Africa . . . and your problem of unemployment
is solved by the simple process of elimination!"

That will appeal to hungry, jobless white men who have been
taught by the propaganda of big business and politics that the
Negro is nothing. Do you remember the Ku Klux Klan? Think on
some of these things. I am afraid that fascism is coming to the
United States and that the Negro will be the goat. Secretary Ickes
also fears this. Mr. Roosevelt is deeply concerned. Fascism is the
biggest enemy facing black men at this moment. Why doesn't the
Negro press wake up and warn the people? Why? Why?

Why Negro Leaders
Are Charlie McCarthys
January 7, 1939

At the Race Pride Barber Shop in Okay, Arkansas. At the Eat
More Hotel in Frog Town, Nebraska. At the Ladies' Progressive
Club in Tombstone, Arizona. At the Big I Fraternity in Washing-
ton, D.C. At the Art for Poverty's Sake Pow Wow in Harlem. It
matters not where you go in the Land of the Spree and the Home of
Burma Shave, you will hear the Sambos and Aunt Hagars grumb-
ling about the way black leaders sell out black folk to the Big White
Man.

The best Charlie McCarthy in the world is the average Negro
leader. And there is a good reason for this. Leaders are made . . .
not born. The soil in which a plant finds itself determines whether
the plant will be a giant of its kind or a pigmy.

Napoleon Bonaparte, minus his egotism in one of his sanest moments, declared: "I am the creature of circumstances."

Circumstances mold the leadership of all nations and races and classes. A study of Franklin D. Roosevelt as President of the United Snakes gives incontestable evidence of this.

The Hand That Feeds the Negro Leader

If you want to get the lowdown on a leader in Harlem or Los Angeles or Rome, Texas, study the hand that feeds him. For generations and generations it has been beaten into our skulls that we must not "bite the hand that feeds us." Now, in the case of Negro leaders, it doesn't matter whether that hand is the hand of Mr. Rockefeller or Mr. Randolph Hearst or the Superintendent of Schools at Chittling Switch, Alabama.

Mr. Edward Warner Brice tells us that on the walls of the registration building of a university hangs this motto, placed there by its founder: "Whose bread I eat, his song I sing."

We talk foolishly about freedom of speech and action, when freedom of speech and action exists only in the dictionary. How many of my readers say what they think and act the way they want to act? If freedom of speech and action were water, we would not have enough to take a bird bath. And many of us have been enslaved so long in body and mind and soul that we don't know we are wearing a ball-and-chain.

We talk about the dictatorships in Germany and Italy and Russia unaware of the brutal fact that we are shackled by a Dictatorship of the Almighty Dollar.

The Guy Who Pulls the Purse Strings Pulls the Leaders

So the Negro leader says to himself: "Whose bread I eat, his song I sing."

So the Negro leader says to his dumbbell admirers: "Follow me, and I'll lead you into the Promised Land."

So the Negro leader lives in his fine house, eats his roast chicken, rides in his high-powered car, thanks God for His many blessings, and tells his black followers: "Troubles don't last always. Prosperity is just around the corner. If you live right, you can eat turkey for Christmas like me. I started out in a log cabin, and now look where I am! Work hard, be efficient—and before you know it, you'll be sitting on top of the world with your toes hanging down. Look what they did for me. Things ain't so bad. Money don't make people happy. You think you're hungry, but it's just in the mind.

As a man thinketh, so is he. I was just in D.C. the other day talking
to Dr. Doolittle, and he said "everything's okay."

But if you want to get the lowdown, watch the guy who pulls the
purse strings. For the guy who pulls the purse strings pulls the
leader. No lie.

It's the same in the Delta Stomp Night Club, where the little
Sambos and Mary Janes strut their stuff, as it is in the High Brow
$$$$$ Club, where the 400 steal each other's wives and husbands.
What do I mean? I mean this: the guy that tips the orchestra leader
calls the tune.

Now, Black Boy, if your eyes are open and your ears are unplug-
ged, you can understand WHY your Negro leaders, when they get
in these interracial good will meetings, sing these Uncle Tom tunes
that make you sick below the belt.

You Can't Offend the Boss and Hold Your Job

I went to hear a Big Negro Educator at Columbia University and
his Uncle Tom tune was so rotten that many Negroes got up and
walked out. When the lecture was finished, I couldn't hold up my
head among the white friends I had invited to hear this great leader
of my people. If you have any manhood or womanhood, I suspect
you have had similar experiences. Now I know what to expect.

Few men have the guts to challenge the word of the boss. That's
true in factories, in hotels, in colleges, and in governments. For a
man to do that, he must be bigger than his job. A job is the most
enslaving thing in the world. Now, remember that I'm talking
about men who think independently for the People, not men who
think about getting ahead and feathering their own nests.

A man that the Big Boys like is a man who doesn't rock the boat.
You can measure the size of a man by the size of his enemies. Look
at history. Jesus was about as peaceable as any man that ever lived,
but the Big Boys in Jerusalem accused Him thus: "He stirreth up
the People." As long as a Negro stays in his place in Waycross,
Georgia, or in Washington, D.C., the white folk will call him: "A
good Negro. A safe and sane leader." By the way, that's the worst
thing the white folk can say about one of your leaders.

What would happen if the CIO permitted Mr. Henry Ford to
appoint the leaders of the CIO? I believe the Negro race in America
is the only race in history that has permitted another race to
appoint its leaders. Even the African tribes appoint their own
chiefs. The Indians, a barbarian people, had sense enough to do the
same thing. Would whites let Negroes appoint their leaders? Even
in Germany the Jews don't let the Germans do that!

Watch Your Leader's Hands Instead of His Mouth!

During slavery times the white planters found it profitable to appoint Negro leaders, and the custom is still in vogue. Elect your own leaders. And fire them when they double-cross you. Mary White Ovington, who has sacrificed her life for the Negro people, says that most Negro institutions tend toward a monarchy. That is, Negroes tend to follow leaders rather than principles. That's bad. Put your trust in principles rather than in men. There are Judases in every group. He who is greatest among you should be the servant of all. See that your leader serves you instead of himself.

What good does it do you to have a leader living in a fine big house when you are living in a shack?

What good does it do you, Black Boy, to have a leader rolling by in a Rolls Royce while you are footing it in the road?

What good does it do you to have a leader eating roast chicken while you are eating black peas?

Wake up. Elect your own leaders. Put them in the chair of leadership and jerk them out when they don't go right. Then the race will go places during 1939. God bless you. And make your leaders help you. Remember, Black Boy, you are the Big Boss; your leader is your servant. No leader can be any bigger than the People let him be. The measure of a leader's greatness is not in the size of the leader's pocketbook but the size of the pocketbooks of the People whom he leads!

For 1939, you don't want leaders who will make you feel good. You want leaders that will make you eat well.

For 1939, let your leaders enjoy the good feeling. You enjoy the good eating. Whenever you see your leader picking up the money box, you say to him: "Where thou goest, I will go."

For 1939, when your leader starts talking about service, you see that he serves you instead of himself.

For 1939, when your leader tells you to support him, you see that he supports you. Watch your leader's hands instead of his mouth.

Then you won't have any regrets in 1940!

The Oldest Problem in the World!
April 8, 1939

A few years ago I was sitting in a vast auditorium at Columbia University. World-famous educators of many races had spoken from that platform on many occasions. The scholarly Dr. W. E. B.

Du Bois had just taken his seat. For an hour we had listened to his powerful speech on the Negro question. Now his hand was pressed to his head, as a group of Negro singers sang a haunting Negro song. I studied the silent, upturned faces of the whites present. I thought many conflicting thoughts. I concluded, then, that Dr. Du Bois was the most tragic figure in dark America. He was an artist groping in the black prison of race, baffled by the icy walls of color.

I thought of his many tragic books—*The Souls of Black Folk, The Suppression of the Slave Trade, John Brown, Darkwater, The Gift of Black Folk,* and *The Dark Princess.*

Dr. Du Bois is essentially an artist turned into a scholar by the awful alchemy of racial prejudice. He is a black John the Baptist crying in the white man's wilderness.

Mary White Ovington, the white friend of black folk, tells a powerful anecdote about this dark Hamlet. Once a young white man read a short story by Dr. Du Bois, threw the book across the room, and cried: "No man should dare to write like that!"

And while Dr. Du Bois sat there with his head bowed, I imagined I heard him repeating the lines from his poem, in free verse, written after the Atlanta race riot in 1906:

> "From lust of body and lust of blood,
>   Great God, deliver us!
> "From lust of power and lust of gold,
>   Great God deliver us!
> "From the leagued lying of despot and of brute,
>   Great God, deliver us!

The Negro problem in America is something over three hundred years old. The race problem in India is five thousand years old. In 1917 Russia, occupying one-sixth of the earth's surface, had one hundred and eighty-eight race problems. Today there is not a single race problem in Russia. Call the Communists everything that men called the early Christians. But, as I heard a bitter enemy of Russia say: "Those ——— Reds have solved the race problem! I saw it with my own eyes."

The Black Man Should Study the Race Problems of India

What causes a race problem? Do races instinctively hate each other? Lord Francis Bacon, the father of the modern scientific method, called racial prejudices "the idols of the tribe." Common sense tells us that every idol is man-made and man-exalted. No man is born to worship an idol. A man picks up an idol as he picks up the flu or a cootie. A man gets rid of an idol as he gets rid of a bedbug. Racial prejudice is an idol. Bacon was right on that, even if he did steal some money from the Big Boys in London.

When I was a collegian, I heard a learned scholar say that the terrible caste system in India was built on racial prejudices. Ten years later I discovered that the great scholar was either a liar or a dumbbell. The caste system and racial discrimination in all countries are built on economics.

Look at the world's oldest race problem. Away back in 3,000 B.C. a host of Aryans rushed through the Khyber Pass in Northern India and conquered the native Dravidians. The white masters made the dark-skinned tribes do all the dirty work, just as white masters at Jamestown, Virginia, made their white slaves and black slaves do all the dirty work. Today the Italians are doing the same thing in Ethiopia. The Japanese are doing the same thing to the Chinese in China. The Germans are doing the same thing to the Jews in Germany. And black Liberians are doing the same thing to black natives in Liberia.

To keep the Dravidians in their place, the Aryans "created an artificial structure." Now all conquering white races talk about racial purity. But at the same time they beget a horde of illegitimate mulattoes, quadroons, and octoroons. The whites did that in India. They've done the same thing in Africa, America, South America, Australia, Asia, and a thousand islands of the sea. They preach racial purity and practice racial impurity.

Five thousand years ago the Aryans in India set the example for future Aryans. Having taken the women and lands and riches of the dark-skinned Dravidians, the gentlemanly Aryans proceeded to set up "an artificial structure" — the infamous caste system. This kept the mulatto sons and daughters from cashing in on Daddy Aryan!

This happened so long ago that shortsighted scholars can not see the economic basis underlying the caste system of India. Then the Big Boys in India called in the priests and scholars to write some histories and "holy" books. What did they write? You know, money talks in all lands. Well, the flunkies wrote that Brahma said he had created from the beginning of the world four castes—priests, warriors, merchants, and slaves. Brahma said (according to the flunkies of the Big Boys) that from his head sprang the priests, from his arms the warriors, from his thighs the merchants, and from his feet the slaves. The "feet" of India are the millions and millions of Untouchables. Thus the conquerors have been able to set up about 2,400 castes in that benighted country. Each caste has a catechism.

Therefore a cleaner of outhouses will say: "I was born a cleaner. I am a cleaner. I must die a cleaner."

In the same manner a black peon at Chittling Switch might say: "I was born a peon. I am a peon. I must die a peon."

Thus the cleaner of outhouses in India stays in his place. Thus the black peon in the Bible Belt stays in his place. Mortal man cannot rise above the level of his thinking.

You remember the story of the eagle that was raised among chickens. The eagle ate like a chicken, walked like a chicken, and thought like a chicken. You see, that eagle didn't know anything about eagles. One day a hunter came by. He picked up the eagle and climbed to the top of a mountain. He pointed the eagle toward the sun.

The hunter said to the bird: "You are an eagle. You don't belong down there."

The hunter then cast the eagle into space. The eagle started falling rapidly. To save himself, he began flapping his wings. And then turning toward the sun, with a triumphant cry, he mounted upward, upward, upward. Thus it is with a race of men who have been degraded by a so-called superior race. Somebody comes along and says: "You are a man. You don't belong down there."

Great Britain and Gunga Din

If you reap what you sow, then the white man has a monopoly on hell. His greed has written the pages of humanity in words of blood. How he can talk about God all the time puzzles my peanut brain.

Look at India. Vasco da Gama sailed around the Cape of Good Hope in 1498 and reached India. His Portuguese countrymen followed him and began stealing from the natives. The Dutch came running after the Portuguese and grabbed up all they could. Later the French gave the Dutch a rush act. And after the other mouth-Christians had started loading their ships with the riches of the poor natives, in stepped pious old England and booted them all into the sea. Caesar was bad. Napoleon was bad. Hitler is a John Dillinger. But England is an international Al Capone.

England says to the other nations: "Thou shalt not steal. Just leave that to me."

Who Is the Most Dangerous Man in India?

Is he little skinny Gandhi? No. Not by any means. You hear a great deal about Gandhi. His story is dramatized all over the world. He gives the English some trouble with his passive resistance. Last month Gandhi tried to starve himself to death because the Big Boys didn't act right. But passive resistance never did free a people. Toussaint L'Ouverture knew that. John Brown knew that. Abe Lincoln knew that. Ex-President Beneš of Czechoslovakia knows that in exile. Haile Selassie knows that today in exile. George Washington didn't rely on passive resistance to win American independence. Neither did the ancient Hebrews.

Great Britain has a standing army of 500,000 men. Seventy-five percent of that army is now stationed in India. Why? There is a dangerous man in India. Do you know him? The English know every move he makes. English spies and detectives watch him night and day—watch his every move every second of the day. That man's name is Subha Bose. Subha Bose! The name of Subha Bose sends icy chills up and down an Englishman's spine. Why? Because Subha Bose is "a razor-minded radical who believes in active resistance." Subha Bose has studied history. He believes like the white man: "He who would be free, himself must strike the blow."

The English want Gandhi to live. The English do all they can to keep old man Gandhi alive. If old man Gandhi should die, Subha Bose would become the leader of the Indians. And Subha Bose believes what the English believe—that is, that force rules government. The English consider Subha Bose the most dangerous man in India!

Big Fish Eat Little Fish— and the Color of the Fish Doesn't Count
May 13, 1939

Above are the words of a black sailor who was born in Shanghai, the son of a Harlem cabaret singer and a Chinese merchant. He had mixed with all races and classes of men in faraway ports of the world. He had sailed the Indian Ocean, the Aegean Sea, the Atlantic, the Pacific, and the Mediterranean Sea. He knew life from the inside. He had a Ph.D. from the University of Hard Knocks. I encountered him on a dirty wharf in New Orleans—the same wharf I had visited one day with the famous Negro artist, Aaron Douglass. If I were the president of a college, I would have that black sailor with the Chinese eyes on my faculty. I would have him deliver to my students a series of lectures of "Life." Then I would resign before the Board of Trustees kicked me out.

The sailor had studied fish in the deep seas. He had discovered that the size of a fish counts and the color of a fish doesn't matter. Big white fish eat little white fish. Big yellow fish eat little yellow fish. Big black fish eat little black fish.

Men Are Like Fish

So said the black sailor with the Mongolian eyes. Big Englishmen will work little Englishmen for nothing in the mines of Wales. Big Japanese fleece the workers of Japan in the rice fields and factories. Race doesn't count. Color doesn't count. Only size counts! Men are like fish, all over the world.

That sailor was saying the same thing that Paul Radin, the great anthropologist, was saying in the University of California: Race is a myth which the Big Boys use to exploit the little boys.

If I could get that one fact through the skulls of the white masses and the black masses and the yellow masses, I could change the history of mankind in twenty-four hours!

When the Big Boys have some dirty work that they want to put across to get a dollar, a franc, a yen, a ruble, or a mark, then the Big Boys will appeal to race and religion. They have done that for 5,000 years. Dr. Charles A. Beard, the historian, has come to the same conclusion. I tell you that black sailor with the Chinese eyes had everything on the ball. He'd been places and seen things. You couldn't fool him!

Get the Facts for Yourself

Any man who has enough common sense to fill the brain of a bedbug knows that thinking is the best guide a man has. Thinking solves problems. Thinking has brought man from cannibalism to modern civilization. Yet, a rascal can come along with the most crooked scheme wrapped up in the paper of racial or religious prejudice and hoodwink tens of thousands. Why? Because they stop thinking.

Hitler—the "incapacitated" bachelor who can never be a husband—unites with the Big German Boys and appeals to race prejudice to put over his nasty policies, while the little Germans eat sawdust sandwiches. Mussolini whoops it up against the Ethiopians, while the little Italians starve on 25 cents a day for twelve hours' work. Ed Cotton comes to the United States Senate on a platform of racial hate, while the poor Crackers eat sow's belly and corn pone. The poor Crackers sing "My Country 'Tis of Thee," and they don't own enough of their country in which to bury a cockroach! The Big Negro tells the little Negro to be proud of his

race and that God will take care of him, while the little Negro's
belly is so empty it rubs against his backbone. Yes, big fish eat little
fish and the color of the fish doesn't count.

I Have Only One Life to Give to My Country!

That's true. And the Big Boys will see to it that you give that one
life. American boys in Flanders were killed with guns made in
America. The *Lusitania* was sunk by a submarine the patent of
which was made in the United States. The United States, a lover of
peace, tried to stop the Bolivians and Paraguayans from killing
each other with guns manufactured in the peace-loving United
States! Vickers, an English company, sold guns to the Germans to
kill English soldiers.

Answer this question, you wise guys: Did you ever hear of
bombing planes dropping bombs on an enemy's munitions works?
No. No. No! You never will. They bomb cities, cathedrals, the
houses of innocent children; but you have never heard of an enemy
plane bombing factories that produce arms and ammunitions.
Seemingly, that's the first thing they would do. Destroy a nation's
arms and it can't fight. Well, these great arms-producing companies, like Krupp and Vickers, and Du Pont, have international
agreements. They are protected. They make billions of dollars
selling arms and munitions to enemy rake-off. So what? Read the
congressional investigations on this subject and find out for yourself.

Big Fish Swim Together!   Little Fish Swim Together!

That's a law of the sea. It's also a law among men. You little boys
have to discover that stubborn fact for yourselves. For six months
I made a study of the Supreme Court of the United States. Before
Mr. Roosevelt came into power, people thought the judges were
scholarly and impartial men. Now, we know that's a lie. Putting a
black robe on a man doesn't make him give just decisions, any
more than putting a suit on a monkey makes him a man. A prejudiced scholar is more dangerous than a prejudiced ignoramus.
He knows how to sugarcoat his unjust decisions with legal tech-
nicalities and it is harder to trap him. The radicals told us that truth
before Mr. Roosevelt announced it over the radio. They told us
that fifty years ago. Didn't the Supreme Court decide time after
time in favor of human slavery? Didn't old Abe Lincoln kick it off a
dozen times? Your memory is short, maybe.

Big fish swim together. Who are the friends of judges? With
whom do they smoke fifty-cent cigars after they take off their black

robes? Think of that. Their friends are Big Boys. The same was true of the Sanhedrin Court that sent Jesus to be lynched. It was controlled by the Big Boys of Jerusalem. Jesus didn't have a chance. What deals are pulled off behind closed doors? Why were so many bills beneficial to poor men like you and me declared unconstitutional?

Big Boys eat together, play together, sleep together. Birds of a feather flock together. Then you little boys are always wondering why you get the dirty end of the stick. What else do you expect to get, you dumbbells? When the Big White Boys and the Big Black Boys sit together behind closed doors around a table of roast chicken, what do you expect to get? Read *The Treason of the Senate*. Read *The Shame of the Cities*.

The poor, white and black and yellow, will have to learn to swim together. Therein lies their salvation. The CIO is teaching the little white man that, thank God! The masses of blacks and whites must come up together. Race is a myth. Big fish eat little fish and the color of the fish doesn't count! It took me twenty-five years to learn that.

The King and Queen: Behind the Headlines
June 17, 1939

These are the times that try men's souls—and, also, their pocketbooks. Wake up, Black Boy! I know you're tired of looking at the monkey-tricks of white folks. But wake up. Their Majesties, King George VI and Queen Elizabeth, are here!

Black Boy opens his eyes and says: "So what?"

A big question. No lie! Robert Burns, the immortal poet of Scotland, gave us the lowdown on kings away back yonder when British kings were building castles out of the sweat and blood and agony of African slaves.

Read thoughtfully Burns's poem, "Is There for Honest Poverty?" Burns dined with the nobility—entertained, not wisely but well, the bored wives of aristocrats. Burns saw through the shams and hypocrisies of kings. Then Burns wrote: "The rank is but the guinea's stamp."

Kings and Pounds

Black Boy, that Scotchman knew his stuff! The almighty dollar is the measure of a king. Take the dollars or pounds away from George VI, and he's no more than Sambo Doolittle.

What am I stammering to say? This: George VI and Queen Elizabeth represent the billions of dollars gobbled up by the aristocrats of Great Britain. Thousands of men and women are better off physically, morally, culturally, intellectually, and spiritually than the king and queen. Do you get me? You don't eh?

George VI and Joe Louis; Elizabeth and Mrs. Bethune

Then let me get personal, Black Boy. Joe Louis has a better physique than George VI. Dr. W. E. B. Du Bois has a greater intellect than George VI. Dr. Alain Locke has more culture than George VI. Professor Sterling Brown has more genius than George VI. Father Divine has more spirituality than George VI. Duke Ellington is better looking than George VI. Lord, Lord, Robert Burns was right: "The rank is but the guinea's stamp."

On merits, pure and simple, Queen Elizabeth could not hold a light for Mrs. Mary McLeod Bethune or Miss Marian Anderson. For personality and good looks, I know a thousand colored women who would put her in the shade, in spite of her wealth, training, and high-powered publicity.

Their Majesties, George VI and Queen Elizabeth, are what they are because they are the symbols of the wealth of the British ruling class—and that wealth was accumulated, through the centuries, by the exploitation of the masses of poor Englishmen and the brutal subjugation of colonies all over the world.

Sun Sets on Hungry Britons

The average Englishman is plainly a dumbbell. If he were intelligent, he wouldn't let owl-faced Chamberlain and the Big Boys of London impose on the poverty-stricken masses of Englishmen a figurehead king with a dozen palaces.

Historians say the sun never sets on the British Empire. This, however, is the truth: the sun sets on hungry Englishmen. The masses of Englishmen are ignorant, illiterate, exploited, and bad-smelling. Read the scholarly books of Dr. Robert Briffault, Sir John Strachey, and Dr. Harold Laski, famous economist of the University of London.

English literature has produced a William Shakespeare; English science, a Charles Darwin. The masses of Englishmen have reduced themselves to abject poverty in order to produce a George VI.

Tea with J. P. Morgan

The newspaper report on the king sipping tea with J. P. Morgan occupied but one sentence in the Associated Press. Thousands of words were written about the royal activities. This incident was buried beneath a mountain of trivialities.

Yet this little tea was the most important thing that happened. This little tea was a private tea. Who was there? Black Boy, you were not invited. Poor White Man, you were not there either. Poor White Man was not there because he was poor. Black Boy was not invited because he was poor and black. Selah!

Around the table at this little tea sat King George VI and Queen Elizabeth, representing the billions of the British nobility; Mr. and Mrs. Garner, representing the robber barons of Wall Street, and J. P. Morgan, representing the world's greatest international bankers.

A Waiter Was There

Oh, yes. I almost forgot. A Negro waiter was present. But since the time of the Pharaohs, away down in Egyptland, Negro waiters have served kings and queens. The bejeweled Medicis of Italy used to import black slaves to handle the gold platters.

Why did the king and queen have that little tea with Mr. Morgan and Mr. Garner? Well, Mr. Morgan has made and bossed Presidents. President Coolidge used to call up Mr. Morgan every morning to learn what he (Coolidge) should do and how he (Coolidge) should do it, as President of the little old USA.

Mr. Morgan does not have a deep affection for President Roosevelt. Mr. Morgan cannot boss Mr. Roosevelt. Franklin D. kicks off the sixty families too much. This interferes with Mr. Morgan's financial octopus too much. So Mr. Morgan would like to see Texas Garner in the White House. Mr. Garner believes in the divine right of Big Business, which is the modern interpretation for the divine right of kings.

If Mr. Morgan can make Mr. Garner President, then the Big Boys of Wall Street can get together with the Big Boys of the British Empire. For that sinister purpose the king and queen left Buckingham Palace to visit the Land of the Spree and the Home of Burma Shave.

Garner Makes a Hit

Mr. Garner made a big hit with the king and queen. Mr. Garner clapped the king familiarly on the back and gave him a big hug at the embassy blowout. Mr. Garner and the king did some backscratching, like the big whites and big Negroes at an interracial banquet. Mr. Garner said the king was okay; and the king said Mr. Garner was a jolly good fellow. J. P. Morgan smiled.

While the Big Boys of Great Britain and the USA were having their little powwow, millions of people were wearing themselves out waiting to get a glimpse of royalty. Who was the cynic who said: "Where ignorance is bliss, 'tis folly to be wise?"

King and Queen Listen to Native American Music

Be not deceived. Kings and queens have always listened to the music of the masses. I cannot explain this. The songs of the masses strike many a tragic note. Tragedy is a hound that dogs the footsteps of the common folk. One of the old czars of Russia used to weep when the peasants sang their sorrow songs in his palace; but this did not cause the old czar to stop fleecing and flogging peasants.

Southern lynchers like to hear Negroes sing spirituals. Kings of England have liked Irish folk songs, but that did not keep them from sending soldiers to shoot down freedom-loving Irishmen.

So the king and queen heard Negro spirituals. But no report has come that the king and queen said anything about the 5,000 Negroes who have been lynched in the Land of the Free. The queen heard our beloved Marian Anderson sing. But the queen said nothing about the barbarous jim-crow action of the DAR.

No sensible person expects a king and queen to say anything that is something. The English beheaded one king who talked too much. The English king is supposed to be seen and not heard.

Royalty at Hyde Park

Having been cheered by millions of unthinking Americans, the king and queen entered the broad reception room of the Roosevelts at Hyde Park. On the walls were rare old prints depicting the courage of the American navy in the war of 1812. I wonder if any black sailors are in the pictures. They fought, all right. What would Commodore Perry have done without his black sailors?

Philip Freneau, poet of the American revolution, hated English kings and what they represented. He advocated sending American frigates to capture George III. His poems inspired Washington and the patriots.

Did the king and queen think about the words of Freneau as they gazed at the pictures in Hyde Park? Were those pictures embarrassing? Why didn't Roosevelt take down those pictures? Ask me another. Freneau wrote:

As Samuel hew'd the tyrant Agag down,
So hew the wearer of the British crown;

> Unpitying, next his offspring slay,
> Or into foreign lands the fiends convey:
> Give them their turn to pine and die in chains,
> Till not one monster of the race remains.

That's what Freneau and Washington and Patrick Henry and Thomas Jefferson thought about English kings. You will remember that when Franklin D. Roosevelt was pointing out the Lincoln Memorial, King George VI was looking thoughtfully at the monument of the rebel, George Washington! What was the king thinking about? You will never know. The English king is to be seen—not heard.

A Discussion of Hogs, Dogs, Fish, and the Declaration of Independence
July 22, 1939

Have you observed how people are flocking to the country? Have you ever wondered why? Nature made the country. Man made the town. Man messed up his job. People run away from a messed-up job. All these Back-to-Nature movements prove that. Advertisements picture woodland scenes and invite us to steal away from the city and forget our troubles in rural bliss. When things got too hot for Mohammed, he retired into the desert. When Jesus became tired of the monkey business of the ancient Hebrews, He went up into the mountains.

Back in September, 1817, William Cullen Bryant wrote a poem called "Inscription for the Entrance to a Wood." By that time the Big Boys had messed up New York City, where Dr. Bryant was editing the *Evening Post*.

The editor said: "that the world is full of guilt and misery" and that he had seen "enough of all its sorrows, crimes, and cares." I don't know what Bryant would have written if he had seen the New York of Tammany Hall, Jack Legs Diamond, and the Prohibition Era. So Bryant told his readers to go into the woods. The poet said:

> Thou wilt find nothing here
> Of all that pained thee
> In the haunts of men
> And made thee loathe thy life.

Isn't this an awful denunciation of man-made cities even in the good old days of 1817, before 14,000 unemployed embarrassed this land that God has blessed! Taking the advice of William Bryant and a dozen of the Black 400, I made a pilgrimage to Caddo Lake on the Fourth of July.

I Am Denounced as a Bad Driver!

We left the main highway and plunged into the back country. The road twisted as the matted underbrush of the lowlands closed in on our car. We ran into ruts, treacherous bridges, and rocky bumps. The laughter and jokes died an unnatural death.

The backseat drivers yelled at me: "You bum! Who doped you and told you that you could drive? I'd rather walk. Oh, God, deliver us from such a chauffeur!"

I sought consolation in philosophy. I thought of Mr. Franklin D. Roosevelt. But as the denunciations increased, I said: "Don't blame me. Blame the road."

We struck a deep rut, and one lady struck the top of the car. This opened the door to the lady's subconscious mind; and an oath rushed out.

You know how they curse Mr. Roosevelt when the New Deal strikes a bump. I reminded the lady that it was the roughness of the road and not the inefficiency of my driving. Mr. Roosevelt is also driving in a car called the New Deal. The road of capitalism is full of ruts and bumps. Why damn Mr. Roosevelt for the road? He didn't make it. Neither did I make that road to Caddo Lake.

I said aloud: "If Mr. Roosevelt and I had a different road our driving would be different."

"Oh, yeah," said the lady, scornfully.

While the members of the Colored 400 were playing bridge and Chinese checkers, I was listening to a Negro fisherman who was talking to some poor whites. He was explaining his fish-trap.

It was made of wire, in the form of a huge funnel. He would place the trap in the water and leave it there for two days. The leader of the fish would swim into the ever-narrowing trap and the others would follow. After they got inside, they didn't know how to get out. The Negro laughed and the whites looked amazed.

I said to the Negro: "That makes me feel bad."

The Negro fisherman looked up at me, as he knelt by the crude illustration he had drawn upon the ground.

"How's that?!" he asked, with a puzzled expression.

"You see," I said, "that trap and that leader of the fish make me think of the poor folk in this country."

The black face and the white faces showed utter perplexity and wonder and doubt.

"How's that?" the old Negro repeated.

"You see," I continued, "the Big Boys lay a trap for the poor folks; and a bogus leader leads the poor folk into the trap of racial hate and economic slavery. Then the poor fish, white and black, don't know how to get out of the trap."

There was silence. The Negro drew a circle on the ground. The poor white men looked at each other; then at me. As I left, I heard one of them drawl: "——— ———, he's right about that."

A White Boy and His Black Companion

I went down to the lake, near two or three empty skiffs. A white boy and a Negro lad got in one of the boats. The young Negro was teaching the white boy to row. They almost upset the skiff. Then the white boy, encouraged by his companion, caught on to the trick. Rowing in unison, they moved away, their bodies and paddles rhythmical in the sunshine. My heart beat excitedly.

Here was a lesson for America on Independence Day. For centuries, the dollar men had played black and white against each other. Today, black and white did not know how to row together. Sometimes this ignorance almost upset the Old Ship of State, in what people called race riots.

I said to myself: "Today's New Negro must teach the young white man how to row this boat called the race problem. This will be difficult, for there are so many misleaders, white and black, who shout the wrong instructions from the bank. If these disillusioned and prejudiced old heads would keep their mouths shut, the young Negro and the young white man would learn the trick of moving their bodies and paddles in union. Old men dream dreams; young men see visions."

The Raid of the Hogs and Dogs!

The members of the Colored 400 spread a big dinner and enjoyed the fat of the land. But this was Independence Day. The hogs and dogs near Caddo Lake were hungry—like so many poor folk without the rights of life and the pursuit of happiness. But the hogs and dogs had more sense than some of the poor folk. Therefore, the hogs and dogs made a raid on the 400.

They got in a fine box of cakes. They were led by a huge, red-looking hog. The fine ladies yelled at the ugly, dirty, bad-smelling beasts. That's what the British nobility did when the American rabble got in the cake box of liberty 163 years ago and got out the Stars and Stripes.

One lady wanted to know why I was howling with laughter.

I replied: "Madame, I was just thinking about the Declaration of Independence and the CIO."

She was too much of a lady to say it aloud, but I knew she was thinking: "I always thought you were a fool."

Our little camp was in an uproar. The Colored 400 got sticks and tried to drive off the hogs and dogs. But the red-looking hog continually returned his gang to the attack. Hunger had made him wise and courageous.

"What's wrong with those filthy hogs?" inquired one of the ladies, innocently.

"It's that red agitator!" I cried. "Those hogs wouldn't know they're hungry if it wasn't for that red agitator."

A learned professor then took me to task. He said: "Don't you know the hog is the most individualistic animal in the world."

Hog in Cake Box

"True," I admitted. "But hunger can make even hogs and dogs get together. Look at that ravaged cake box."

And hunger is going to make the whites and blacks in America declare a new Declaration of Independence. An empty stomach is the greatest defender of liberty. "Taxation without representation" is the cry of exploited men. "All men are created equal" is the cry of jim-crowed men. "Give me liberty or give me death" is the cry of underprivileged men. "A government of the people, by the people, and for the people" came from the lips of a poor white man who was the son and grandson of poor white men.

"We shall not work while others reap" is the cry of wage-slaves. "A man is a man for a' that" is the cry of a peasant who has seen his fellow peasants degraded by the drudgery of the aristocracy.

These words mean nothing on Independence Day, to the 400, whether the 400 are black or white, yellow or brown.

Masses of Negroes Are Ahead of the Whites!
August 19, 1939

I am not joking. I never was more serious than I am now. I have studied the white man's civilization from every angle. I am familiar with his achievements in the arts and sciences. I have stood before the mighty edifice of his Industrial Revolution and marveled. For many years the white man's culture gave me an inferiority complex. That was inevitable. I was born an animal. I became a human being molded by the standards and customs of America.

My African ancestors worshiped many gods. The white man

gave me one God. My African ancestors, living close to nature, developed many high virtues. The white man wiped these out and substituted vices that have plagued my people.

Dr. Boas's and Dr. Briffault's works in anthropology have revealed the many good things in the lives of "savages." White civilization has been the scourge of Africa. Even a casual reading of George Schuyler's *Slaves Today* and Rene Maran's *Batouala* proves this point.

White Was Perfection

By a vicious system of propaganda the white man drummed into my mind the idea of his superiority. White became the symbol of perfection. Everything that was good was declared to be white. God was white. Angels were white. All great scientists, artists, and leaders were white. The devil and his imps were black. Sin was black; virtue, white. A black cat was evil. Thus everything connected with the white man became superior. "Good hair" was straight hair. "A good complexion" was fair or light.

Racketeers made millions of dollars, therefore, on hair straighteners and skin whiteners. Mulattoes thought themselves superior. Professional men went into the market for high yellow women. Black persons were anxious to marry mulattoes so as to improve the race!

Certain sororities and fraternities emphasized taking in mulattoes. It was not an accident that yellow coeds won the beauty contests staged in Negro academies miscalled colleges. The white man's propaganda worked well until the Great Depression. Hunger knows no color line.

A Changing World and the Negro Masses

Concepts change. Right becomes wrong. Virtue becomes vice. The rejected stone becomes the cornerstone. That is the story that history tells. The last shall be first and the first, last. What I think or what you think cannot stop change.

Tremendous economic and social forces push men about. You cannot stop the tide by standing on the seashore and shouting: "Stop!" Some people don't know this until they are engulfed.

Yesterday people laughed at Negroes because they liked loud colors. Today loud colors are popular. Yesterday people scorned the philosophy of the Negro masses. Today science justifies that philosophy.

The white man's civilization is based on money-getting. He has ravaged the world to make profits. He has contaminated the arts and sciences and religions to make dollars and pounds and francs and marks. He made Big Business god. Did this produce happiness?

The negative answer is found in every newspaper. Ernest Hemingway has pictured it graphically in his powerful novel, *To Have and Have Not*. I shall never forget the scene that night in Havana Harbor aboard those elegant yachts. There one discovered the futility of the white man's quest for dollars and his boredom, vices, and unhappiness.

Whites and some Big Negroes intellectually enslaved by whites have taunted and denounced the masses of Negroes for not swallowing the white man's philosophy of rugged materialism. But my people have lived in a world of dollar madness without becoming a part of it—without succumbing to the dreadful disease that has made white men the most unhappy of men.

Eyes Are Opening

A change has set in among the good white folk. No lie. Their eyes are beginning to open. Economic competition has not brought happiness—the thing that every man is looking for. Economic competition has made three classes of people unhappy: (1) those who have money; (2) those who are trying to get money; (3) and those who don't have money. It would require a book of five hundred pages for me to explain this. Just look about you and see this truth on every side.

Economic competition appeals to the basest instincts in men. Did you ever see two dogs fighting over a bone? Well, that's the way men fight over dollars. A dollar is a piece of meat. A dollar is a loaf of bread. A dollar is a home. A dollar is a car. You see what I mean. Now, since in our great civilization, we can produce enough meat, bread, cars, houses for everybody, why should men fight over these things? That's what American thinkers want to know.

Live and Let Live

The slogan of the bright new world of tomorrow is this: "Live and let live!"

This has been for centuries the philosophy of the masses of Negroes. This has not been the philosophy of our white civilization. Therefore, the Negro masses are ahead of the whites. The Negro, when he has not been contaminated by white professors, believes in having a good time himself and in letting everybody else have a good time. The masses of Negroes are not hoggish.

Negroes don't believe in piling up riches on earth. Negroes

believe in living today and in letting tomorrow take care of itself. White people like to invest in bonds, stock, and real estate. Negroes like to invest in good times.

When Angelo Herndon said, "Let me live," he expressed the sentiment of black folks.

Millions of whites are saying that now. The New Deal and Labor are getting on the Negro's bandwagon. In this new world ahead of us the Negro will be the world's most famous teacher. The Negro is going to show the white folk how to enjoy themselves. He is already pointing the way. He is teaching them how to dance and sing and play. The white man forgot how to do those things while chasing the lousy dollars.

The whites crowd into Harlem cabarets because they want to enjoy themselves. Look what a big kick they get out of Negro spirituals and jazz! When you see Negroes doing the Lindy Hop and the Big Apple, who gives a tinker's dam about investing in stocks and bonds?

Rejuvenation through Joy!

The white man's civilization with its inhuman economic competition and rugged individualism has produced millions of physical and mental wrecks. It has produced enough vices to fill Dante's hell. Nine-tenths of the people who reach forty are suffering from shattered nerves. Husbands and wives fuss continually from maladjustments growing out of our national mess-up.

What we need is rejuvenation through joy. The Negro has had enough of that to give every dollar-crazed American. The world was made for Man to enjoy himself. He isn't here long. And he will be dead a long, long time.

Live and let live! Is there a better philosophy anywhere for anybody? With each able-bodied man working only four hours a day, we could produce more than enough for every sensible man. The rest of the time could be spent enjoying oneself. Books, pictures, travel, opera, shows, games, parties, outings—a hundred and one things could be done in our leisure time.

Some will say this is all bunk. They are Dumbbells who haven't read history. Once a man wasn't considered a man unless he worked fourteen hours a day. Before 1929 if a man had suggested that the government spend billions to give men jobs, he would have been called a fool.

It's a silly snake that won't shed its skin. It's a short-sighted man who can't see the day coming when men will live to enjoy themselves. There's no need of slaving eight hours a day if a job can be done in four.

A man is not a mule. Culture makes man a human being. A minimum of physical labor is good for the soul. The day is coming when men will work intellectually. That tomorrow will mean rejuvenation through joy. It will mean the maximum of happiness for everybody.

I Am Thankful for the Great Depression
September 30, 1939

As a black citizen in a white democracy, I consider the Great Depression the brightest blessing that my race has experienced since Mr. Lincoln issued the militarily brilliant and economically profitable Emancipation Proclamation. This is a measured and dispassionate judgment that contains nothing of irony or rationalization, sophistry or defeatism.

If public pronouncements indicate the private beliefs of public servants, I am quite sure that this optimistic generalization will not receive the pontifical sanction of such eminent Negro leaders as Dr. W. E. Burghardt Du Bois, Dean Kelly Miller, and Dr. Walter White.

Afro-American radicals and ultraconservatives, polemarchs and intellectuals, Hitlers and Gandhis have castigated the Negro masses as the most disunited racial group under the Caucasian sun—ethnically heterogeneous, economically centrifugal, politically unorganizable.

Dark messiahs, national and provincial, taking a cue from the demagogs of the great white world, have used every known instrument of exploitation, economic and political and ecclesiastical, to secure blood money through chauvinistic appeals.

The Afro-American scene reveals the wrecks of Back-to-Africa movements, Pan-Negro conclaves, Forty-ninth State programs, interracial good-will palavers, Hamitic congresses, Jesus-was-black powwows and salvation-through-the-dollar leagues.

Middle Class Emerges

A Negro middle class emerged, nurtured by the Dale Carnegie philosophy of Dr. Booker T. Washington and the aristocratic titbits of Dr. W. E. Burghardt Du Bois. Negro weeklies flourished, displaying the buxom charms of high-yellow society matrons basking on the jim-crow beach at Atlantic City.

The black masses were kept religiously informed concerning the closed worlds of the dark 400 in Boston, Philadelphia, Los Angeles, and Atlanta. Negro novelists and cabarets catered to white sophisticates. Negro singers of blues and spirituals bought elegant apartments on Harlem's Sugar Hill.

Negro columnists and tuxedoed orators extolled the "progress" of the Negro and in the next breath lamented the fact that the race was judged by the ignorant, illiterate, poverty-stricken masses, who caused the whites to ostracize Negro respectables.

In No-Man's-Land

In that heyday of the Afro-American middle class, the black masses wandered in a No-Man's-Land, subjected to the crossfire of calumny from the batteries of prejudiced whites and the Negro respectables, whom Dr. Herskovits, of Northwestern University, has called "the most bourgeois of the bourgeoisie."

When the bottom fell out of the stock market, the dark 400 took an ignominious tumble and the Negro masses sank lower in the bog of poverty. Under the NRA, racial discrimination spread like a virulent disease.

Vulgar tasks that the Negro had considered his own were usurped by underprivileged whites. The economic topsyturvydom threw white-collar workers into the ranks of the black-collar workers.

Negroes were the last to be hired and the first to be fired, the last to get on relief and the first to get off. The sufferings of whites were terrible; the miseries of the blacks intolerable, indescribable. Out of an agonizing spirit the Negro cried:

"Nobody knows the trouble I've seen, Nobody knows but Jesus."

In spite of all this, I am thankful for the Great Depression, as a black citizen in a white democracy.

A sunken-faced Negro woman, sixty-five years old, said to me the other day: "Son, I was borned in a depression."

To America's largest minority group, color is a birthmark and poverty a birthright; the Bill of Rights is a book sealed with seven seals; and the quest for a job, in prosperous times, takes on the hazard and ingenuity and sensation of a Homeric episode. The simple prerogatives and opportunities which white citizens take for granted are luscious fruit beyond the reach and grasp of black men. The Negro suffers all the disadvantages of being poor, plus the proscriptions of being black.

Light in a Dark World

Men and women of good will among the Caucasian group have realized this. Without the moral, and in many instances the financial, support of those humanitarians on the other side of the wall, the world of dark folk would have been darker. To call the honor roll of the Negro's friends would be to name some of our finest spirits: Jane Addams, Clarence Darrow, H. L. Mencken, Zona Gale, Pearl Buck, Arthur Spingarn, V. F. Calverton, Sinclair Lewis, Oswald G. Villard, Norman Thomas, Theodore Roosevelt, Will Rogers, Julius Rosenwald, Eugene O'Neill, Eleanor Roosevelt, John D. Rockefeller, Jr., Albert Einstein.

But the patronage of white intellectuals could not solve the race problem. Perhaps racial bias and religious prejudice are two of the most stubborn things to combat. Becoming fixed in the mind of the child during its tenderest years, these tough predilections sink their roots deep in the dark recesses of the unconscious. I am wondering if an argument ever convinced a Negrophobe!

Now, the Great Depression accomplished something for the Negro that no phalanx of facts by scholars was able to do. It convinced white labor organizations that the bar of color is an impediment to the cause of labor.

For decades liberal economists had observed that wherever existed the worst exploitation of black workers, there also existed the most infamous degradation of white workers. The South was the classic example. The Negro middle class grumbles that racial prejudice is strongest among the ignorant and illiterate whites and that these compose largely the lynching mobs. This is true.

Deep-seated Reason

There is a deep-seated reason. The masses of poor whites and blacks are in the deadliest competition for jobs. The basis of racial prejudice in the United States is economic. It has always been. The 4,000,000 Negro slaves were owned by 350,000 families. This slave labor, together with 500,000 free Negroes, competed with white labor. The masters, for two centuries, played the poor whites against the poor blacks; and the masters gathered the fruits of racial enmity. Uncle Toms got the rinds.

Before the Great Depression, skilled labor was arrayed against unskilled labor and both drew the color line against the Negro. When 1,000,000 black workers entered Northern industry during the World War, racial antagonism took on a phenomenal growth. Job rivalry caused bloody riots in East St. Louis and Chicago. The Ku Klux Klan unfolded like a malignant flower. Negro slum areas were cancerous growths in our cities. Syphilis drew no color line.

Seven Lean Years

Then came the seven lean years. A miraculous change swept through the ranks of labor. Union after union cried: "Down with the color bar!'' White pickets and black pickets walked side by side in Washington and New Orleans, in Chicago and Birmingham. Down in Arkansas whites and blacks in the sharecroppers' union were saying: "Ours for us."

And in Houston, Texas, white and black unionists beat up white scabs! Nobody had ever heard of that before in the South. Some Negroes thought the Judgment Day had come.

I Am Thankful for the Great Depression
October 7, 1939

The never-failing enemy of the Negro, the poor white, shocked by the Great Debacle, like a modern Saul on the road to Damascus, entered the Negro church and appealed for labor solidarity. To the Negro middle class, this was a Houdini trick.

Scholars and reformers had told them that the solution of the race problem would come from the top. Education—epitomized in Booker T. Washington's "Atlanta Compromise" and Benjamin Franklin's "The Way to Wealth"—had been offered as the magical panacea. White religionists interested in black souls had tendered the balm of Gilead. And now the wall of racial bias was cracking up below!

White and black labor united on the American stage for the first time in history. *Turpentine,* a powerful drama of militant workers in the Florida swamps, held forth at the Lafeyette Theatre in Harlem. Langston Hughes's *Mulatto* and *Don't You Want To Be Free?* trekked across the continent. *Stevedore* became a Broadway hit. *A Southern Tragedy* dramatized the coming of the sharecroppers' union to an Arkansas town; and this produced a sensation at the annual meeting of the Southern Association of Drama and Speech Arts.

Porters, Redcaps Organize

The pullman porters have organized. The redcaps have formed a union. In the major industries white workers have consolidated with the blacks. In many large hotels the Negro waiters have closed ranks with the other employees. White and Negro members of the Newspaper Guild picketed a big Negro weekly and won the strike.

Negro employers, in many instances, have been compelled to raise wages and shorten the hours of the employees. And while I sat in a Negro church in Port Arthur, Texas, the preacher announced that there would be a meeting of the cooks and washer-women to form a union.

And the funny thing about the movement is this: there is as much opposition to the union among Negro businessmen, who have continually denounced the Negro masses for not uniting, as there is among the white economic royalists!

When tens of thousands of white and black workers picket together, discuss their mutual problems together, and strike together—then, we are no longer haunted by spectres like the riots in Chicago and East St. Louis. The Great Depression advanced the cause of Negro labor a hundred years.

History and Minorities

History shows that a minority group has an opportunity of raising its status only during a period of social awakening. As long as the vast majority of Americans believed in the theory and practice of rugged individualism, it was inevitable that the Negro should remain a John the Baptist crying in the white man's wilderness.

As long as the frontier spirit permeated American life, in spite of the passing of the frontier, the Negro was doomed to slums and peonage farms. The economic and social tragedies now revealed by Faulkner and Caldwell and Stribling, Negroes have known for years.

I heard a Negro professor say once: "Tobacco Road is a black road, and it stretches from Key West, Florida, to Harlem."

The Mencken Formula

H. L. Mencken said that imagination can solve any problem in the world. I suppose imagination is as scarce as radium. It is difficult to tell about a shoe until you put it on. The sudden impoverishment of hundreds of thousands produced a tidal wave of charity. Vast numbers of white Americans realized for the first time that perhaps the Negro's low social status was caused by something other than biological inferiority.

Concepts underwent terrific changes. Was it Shakespeare who first discovered the relation between hunger and thinking? Anyway, the man in the bread line started thinking. The Great Depression popularized the social sciences. A proletarian drama and literature developed. Hollywood was not left untouched. Inevitably this revolution in the thought-life of the American people benefited the Negro.

When novelists, poets, artists, and scholars concentrated their attention on the lower levels of life, the poor Negro, who had been there all the while, came in for his share of study and delineation. For the first time, since the Emancipation Proclamation, Uncle Sam noticed his black stepchild. With startling immediacy, a Black Cabinet was formed.

The learned experts shook their heads sadly and told the general public that the black patient was suffering from a terrible complication of diseases, physical, social, economic, cultural, educational, and political.

Southern governors and legislative bodies swung into action, under the momentum of the WPA, forgot momentarily the defense of states' rights, and went through the gesture of putting a Negro on the jury here and there and building Negro schools from the cast-off materials of white schools.

Lynching in Tailspin

The vigorous crusade of the NAACP sent lynching into a tail-spin. The American Youth Congress, representing over four and a half million youths of all races and creeds, declared themselves guardians of democracy. The Federal Theatre Project brought to the masses *Haiti, Macbeth,* and *The Swing Mikado.*

Famous orchestra leaders, like Benny Goodman, employed Negro players. Negro writers, like Langston Hughes and Richard Wright, placed the problems of the Negro author before the Fascist-fighting Writers' Congress. Philip Randolph, president of the Pullman Porters' Union, pleaded the cause of Negro labor before the AF of L.

Negro scholars were appointed to the faculties of several white universities. Booker T. Washington could not have imagined interracial cooperation on so many fronts!

Out of the Great Depression came our most powerful Negro writer, young Richard Wright, the orphan from Natchez, Miss. He defeated six hundred other writers in the WPA Novel Contest, sponsored by *Story Magazine* and *Harper's.* "Fire and Cloud" and "Bright and Morning Star," two of his drama-packed short stories, received prizes as distinguished fiction of the year. Edward J. O'Brien included the latter in his anthology, *50 Best American Short Stories—1914–1939.* Perhaps the work of no other storyteller has received more unstinted praise from eminent critics of contemporary fiction.

Negro Became Human

During the seven lean years the Negro became a human being in the theater, in literature, in the social sciences, in labor, in the everyday experiences of millions of Americans.

Therefore, as a black citizen, I consider the Great Depression the brightest blessing my race has experienced since Mr. Lincoln issued the immortal Emancipation Proclamation.

However, a larger view demonstrates the advantages of disadvantages, the logic of illogic, the religion of irreligion, the wordliness of otherwordliness, the finite of the infinite.

Dr. William Durant says: "Nothing educates us like a shock."

It requires the brutalities of fascism to make Americans appreciate democracy, the Declaration of Independence, the Bill of Rights, and the Constitution. Dreadful diseases summoned into existence the miracles of modern medicine and surgery. The exploitation of fallacies and untruths by the sophists ushered in the science of logic. Gangsterism and corrupt politics mobilized the forces of Law and Order.

The malpractices of the packinghouse industries brought in the Pure Food Laws. Tyranny gives birth to liberty; vice, to virtue; laissez faire, to government control; and rugged individualism, to social conscience.

Therefore, it required the Great Depression to open the eyes of the American people to the economic, cultural, social, political, and spiritual values inherent in a great democracy. For this I am thankful. As a distinctly finite being, man learns only through tragic experiences. Progress and Pain are Siamese twins.

Tigers and Lions and Men
July 27, 1940

Away back in the eighteenth century, when the robber aristocrats of England were carrying the Bible and syphilis to "uncivilized lands," there lived in London an un-English Englishman named William Blake. This artist and poet was unpatriotic. He was interested in "mankind and all other creatures." He was so crazy that he advocated and practiced charity and forgiveness, while the robber aristocrats were raping Africa and America.

Once William Blake saw a tiger, in a deep jungle. Of course, tigers roam the jungles of India. Of course, Blake never visited India or the Far East. Just the same, Blake saw a tiger in the tiger's native jungle. Only a poet can be Here and see something Over There, 5,000 miles away. Without going to India, Blake wrote the world's greatest "tiger" poem.

Seeing the tiger, thinking about the raw savagery of the tiger—Blake wondered how God could make both the tiger and the lamb. Of course, that puzzles both the learned theologians and the scholarly professors. If the theologians and professors are as wise as William Blake, they will not try to answer the question; they will say: "Ask me another?"

Did He smile his work to see?
Did He who made the lamb make thee?"

The Beast No Man Can Tame

In the Marsalis Park Zoo, at Dallas, Texas, there is a tiger named Tom. I am now looking at Tom's fierce picture in the *Dallas Morning News,* a newspaper that can teach liberalism to many of your pretentious Eastern and Northern dailies which give lip service to the Constitution.

The unknown reporter who writes about Tom gives me food for thought. With his facts, I shall begin my philosophy. Philosophy always begins where facts end.

Now, Tom is a black-striped 350-pounder with a body as yellow as the gold—nineteen billion dollars—buried by our learned New Dealers. Now, don't get smart, Sambo, and ask me why the white folk dig gold so that they can bury it? I simply give you the facts. Mr. Franklin D. Roosevelt and his experts can give you the philosophy.

But let us talk about Tom the tiger. After eighteen years of captivity, Tom still snarls and shows his railroad-spike claws. Yes, Tom hates Man as much as the Big Boys who exploit Man. Hour by hour, Tom paces up and down his cage. In 1921, Frank Buck, the Bring-'Em-Back-Alive trapper, captured Tom in the Sumatran jungle. Tom is still untamed and ferocious. Tom is a cat.

Man loves the dog because the dog is fool enough to trust Man. On the other hand, the cat obeys the Scriptures: "Put not thy trust in things." The cat is like the wise man: he trusts a principle; not a man of principle.

In some ways the tiger is superior to Man, who is always disgracing God by boasting that he's "made in the image of God." Tigers do not live on men unless tigers are old and toothless. There are parasitic, money-loving men who live on men all the days of their youth and old age.

The Tiger Is Capitalist and Rugged Individualist

Behold the tiger, ye admirers of rugged individualism! The tiger glories in his own strength. The tiger, even in captivity, believes he is the master of his fate and the captain of his soul. Clyde Beatty, the famous animal-trainer, says that a tiger can whip a lion. Well, why is the lion the king of beasts? If you put lions and tigers in a jungle, the lions will kill off the tigers. Why is that?

Mr. Beatty gives the logical reason: Lions fight in packs; a tiger fights by himself. The tiger is a rugged individualist. I shall never forget that remarkable picture, *Bring 'Em Back Alive*. The tiger always went through the jungle by himself. He attacked everything—the crocodile, the python, and whatnot. Whenever you see one lion in the jungle, beware of the pack!

The tiger hunts alone and eats alone. He believes in the survival of the fittest. He believes in Might. The race of tigers is being exterminated by other animals. The tiger has no sense of adaptability. Under all conditions, he remains the rugged individualist. Although Tom is caged in the Marsalis Park Zoo, he still tries, by himself, to kill his keeper. Don't be surprised if you hear of the death of Tom! Tom is like some deluded Americans: he doesn't know that the day of rugged individualism has passed forever.

Civilization Builds Cages for Men

There was a time when a man could stand in his back door and shoot in any direction. The Law has stopped that. The coming of cities put a stop to that. Ford and Rockefeller made their fortunes before the great era of monopoly finance. The Golden Period of the Robber Barons has vanished forever.

Old Horace Greeley could say seventy-five years ago: "Go West, young man."

Out there in the Golden West was gold for the digging. The miserable Oakies in *The Grapes of Wrath*—600,000 families—prove that the land of opportunity has vanished. No lie. Civilization, as we know it, builds cages for young people. Only the adult who is a fool will try to dope young people today. These economic cages have trapped our citizens by the millions. Ignorant of the causes of their misery, hundreds commit murder and suicide. Others waste themselves in vices. Tom, the tiger, is not the only caged animal.

The big, healthy tiger walks the jungle, killing other animals. He is the confident, rugged individualist. Sometimes, I think self-confidence is all that the rugged individualist has. The tiger, in his prime, does not know that he'll become old and toothless some day. Old age will dim his sight. Then, the animals that he preyed upon will prey upon him. Being a rugged individualist, the tiger travels by himself when he is too old to defend himself.

Weak and toothless, the old tiger whimpers like a baby when he is attacked by "inferior" animals. He cracks up. I never saw a rugged individualist who could take it when he got down and out. You hear rugged individualists say continually: "I don't want to get old and helpless." But suppose they do get old and helpless. In our gambler's civilization, anything can happen. Children desert parents. Wives desert husbands. Husbands desert wives. Healthy tigers don't worry about sick tigers. I'd rather be an ant than a tiger; healthy ants take care of ants that are old and sick. It's better to have a society where all of us have something than to have one in which a few of us have all.

The Merry-Go-Round and the Ferris Wheel of History
October 19, 1940

The history of man heretofore has been the history of the rise and fall of nations. I presume to call this the Ferris Wheel Theory of History. G. W. G. Ferris, hoping to amuse us while he plucked the nickels from our pockets, invented a giant power-driven steel wheel which carried cars around its rim. However, before the birth of Mr. Ferris, Man had invented his theory of racial superiority.

Have you ever looked philosophically at a Ferris wheel? The car-riders go up—and come down. No particular car stays at the top. Why? Because the giant power-driven wheel is always turning. Now, follow me. The Ferris Wheel of History turns on the axis of Time. Rome was at the top 2,000 years ago; today Germany occupies the top seat in Europe. Tomorrow—another conqueror, of course.

The Glory That Was Greece

Edgar Allan Poe thought about this Ferris Wheel of History and wrote two immortal lines that say more than a hundred volumes of history. The essential difference between poetry and prose is the terrific condensation of poetry. In the poem, "To Helen," the man who kept his dying wife warm with a cat wrote these lines:

> . . . the glory that was Greece
> And the grandeur that was Rome.

When a man writes two lines like that in succession, he ought to go on to heaven and get his wings. The word *glory* gives us the complete achievement of Greece in the fine arts and sciences:

Phidias, Sappho, Aristotle, Euripides, Plato, Herodotus, Aristophanes, and all the other shining intellects of Athens. The word *grandeur* is the only word in our language of 650,000 words that will describe Roman civilization, which was materialistic and pragmatic like ours, huge geographically and financially.

You know the old saying: "All roads lead to Rome." That means the Big Boys said to the little Sambos: "Bring us the dough."

Where Are Greece and Rome Today?

You will remember that Edgar Allan Poe knew his history of the Ferris wheel. So he put the "glory" of Greece and "grandeur" of Rome in the past tense. Those great civilizations are dead. Poets like to write about dead civilizations, which, at the height of their power, never thought about dying. It wouldn't hurt you to read Sterling Brown's "Memphis Blues" and Carl Sandburg's "Four Preludes on Harp Strings of the Wind." The old prophets of the Bible continually referred to the destruction of proud cities.

Now, here is something that's an eye-opener. Every nation at the top got there by force—and force caused its downfall. Every nation at the top invented a theory that proved to itself its own superiority. Each top-nation scorned all other nations. The ancient Greeks called all other peoples "barbarians." I shall never forget Sandburg's poem describing a "Dago," the descendant of Aristotle, laying a roadbed for the Anglo-Saxons of today! In Aristotle's time the Anglo-Saxon was a savage, and today we're all wondering what Hitler will do to the Anglo-Saxons in England. The Ferris Wheel of History!

Nations have had their hour of glory and grandeur, and then faded into oblivion. You remember the proud Spaniard who lived under Ferdinand and Isabella. France, under Napoleon, dominated Europe. The Ptolemies of Egypt, the Pharaohs of the Nile, the Czars of all the Russias, the Sultans of Turkey, the Kaisers of Germany—kings and potentates have had their day and disappeared in the lower depths. The slaves who served the kings of yesterday are the rulers of today.

The history of man heretofore has been the history of the rise and fall of nations. I presume to call this the Ferris Wheel Theory of History.

Advice—That Will Not Be Heeded!

The vanity that makes a people think itself superior to another people is the vanity that leads to its defeat. Pride goeth before a great fall! A ruling class never learns anything from the downfall of other ruling classes. Capitalists will learn nothing from the feudal lords whom the capitalists overthrew. There are Big Boys in this country who think you can solve economic problems by hunting down Reds.

A fascist is either a capitalist with capital or a capitalist without capital. A Communist is a man with an empty belly knocking at the door of a capitalist. Until the Big Boys see through these two definitions, they'll continue to put nails in their own coffins. In the meantime, the Ferris Wheel of History will continue to turn on the axis of Time. Nobody can stop that. But as I said in the beginning, rulers never learn anything from the downfall of other rulers. Power blinds all rulers.

The Merry-Go-Round of History

There can be no democracy without economic equality. Thomas Jefferson said that when he wrote the Declaration of Independence. There can be no brotherhood of man without a brotherhood of dollars. I have another theory. It is based on economic and racial brotherhood. I presume to call this the Merry-Go-Round of History. On the merry-go-round all the seats are on the same level. Nobody goes up; therefore, nobody has to come down. That is democracy, as I see it. In a brotherhood, all the members are equal.

Racial superiority and class superiority produced the hellish contraption called the Ferris Wheel of History. Democracy will produce the Merry-Go-Round of History.

We talk about democracy in the Senate, over the radio, in the classroom, and in the pulpit; but God knows we're liars. We don't want democracy. Those who cry out against class antagonisms are the chief producers of class and racial antagonisms.

If Jesus tried to bring a real democracy to America in the year of our Lord 1940, Jesus would not die on the Cross a second time. No, the capitalist with capital and the capitalist without capital would lynch Jesus before He could get to the Cross.

As long as there are upper classes and superior races, there will be wars and revolutions. The class or race that is up today will go down tomorrow. I shall stay on the merry-go-round of history 'till the day I die. I am a democrat in theory and in practice. I do not ask for myself what I shall not give to others.

Black Cats—Black Women
—and Black Spirits
March 29, 1941

Physically, the white man is closer to the ape than the Negro. The ape and the white man have these things in common: thin lips, straight hair, and hairy bodies. The unpolluted Negro has thick lips, kinky hair, and little hair on his body. Yet the Negro does his silliest to ape the white man who is the closest relative of the ape.

Madame Walker and Madame Malone made a million bucks straightening the kinks of Negroes with hair superior to the white man's. For years I've been trying to think up a formula to whiten black skins. Such a prescription would bring me in a billion bucks. Then I could make some big contributions to the NAACP, the Negro National Congress, the Urban League, and the Negro Alliance.

Whenever you hear Negroes singing "I Shall Be Like Him," they mean that some day they'll be white. There are Negroes who are dumb enough to believe that a white skin means the solution of all earthly problems. The white man through everlasting propaganda has made the blacks and browns and near-whites believe that achievement and salvation lie in whiteness.

God and the Devil

A wise man said: "Every man paints God in his own image."

There's something to that. Therefore, the white man paints God white. The Africans have black gods. Dr. Carter G. Woodson and Dr. Alain Locke can tell us about that. But when the Sambos and Aunt Hagars become "civilized," they get a white God. They also get a black Devil. When I was a boy, the black Devil scared me and I got "religion."

Now, the white man pictures all angels as white. On the other hand, all imps of the Devil are black. In fact, everything that's bad in the universe is black—according to the Bilbo whites and Uncle Tom blacks.

Hell is black, in spite of the flames that should light it up. Negro mothers tell innocent children that "the black, evil spirit" will get them. Some ghosts are white, but they put on white so that you can see them in the darkness! You know the ghosts are black, because only evil spirits come back—and all evil spirits are black!

Having made God white, the Caucasian proceeded to stigmatize blackness. He did it so well that whiteness became a badge of superiority. When the slave said Master, he saw a white man. When a native in India says Sahib, he means an Englishman. When I use the term American, people see a white face. Virtue is white. Sin and evil are black. When I say slave, everybody sees Sambo and his wooly head. Yet there were white slaves in America. On the stage, a villain is usually dark. In American fiction, a Red is generally a dark, foreign-looking person. The same is true in the movies. A dark deed is engineered by a dark villain. Gangsters must be dark persons. Genuinely white individuals don't commit dark crimes! I know a friend who couldn't act as a pallbearer because he didn't have a dark suit!

The Evil of Blackness

I had an aunt who was a good woman. But she believed that black persons are evil. Dirty Negroes are always worse than dirty white folk! And they always have worse odor. I've heard Negro aristocrats say that. They were duped and doped!

You mustn't let a black cat cross your path! It means seven years bad luck. A black "professor" ran off and left me one night when he saw a black cat. If a blackbird perches on your roof, it means death! Of course, death is also black. Anything bad is dark. Black is immoral, wicked, mournful, calamitous. So thought even Shakespeare, the white Englishman.

Let us turn back. It was on April 14, 1360. It was so cold that many men in the army of Edward III died from exposure while laying siege to Paris. So that day was called Black Monday. During the reign of George I some of the wise boys blacked their faces to hunt deer. The King passed the Black Act, and many of them landed in jail. In England, the cattle raised for slaughter are called black cattle; the white are dairy animals! Of course, pirates used the black flag. In the fourteenth century, a terrible plague spread over Asia and Europe; although it came from yellow China, it was called the Black Death!

If a member of a white family goes wrong, he is called a black sheep. It seems that, while a black sheep is still a sheep, he's different from a white sheep. That differentness means he's evil. The Black Belt is, like War—Hell! The whites at Greenville, Texas, put up a sign: THE BLACKEST LAND AND THE WHITEST PEOPLE. The only black thing that you don't have to apologize for is black gold—the oil the Big Boys need for their war machines.

Improving the Negro Race

How shall we save the Negro? We can do that by improving the Race. How shall we improve the Race? By having near-white children. The average Negro mother feels that a calamity has come upon the family if she brings a black daughter into the world! I saw a black girl pass the house, and a Negro woman assured me that she was ruined!

From the pictures of Negro women in Negro newspapers, I'm sure there are no black women in America. Society leaders are near-white. There are no black women in Negro colleges, for "Miss Chittling Switch College" and "Miss Freedom College" are queens who're near-white. No good-looking Negro women have kinky hair. Negro doctors, businessmen, and professors marry (accidentally) high-yellow women. Chorus girls are (accidentally) high yellows.

Even black women speak of improving Sambo's Race by marrying yellow men. Ain't it the truth? Brownskins are flattered when you tell them they look Spanish, Hindu, Italian, Japanese—anything but African. Society matrons invite me to "A Night in Africa"?

Yet the blacks and yellows and browns assure me that they're proud to be Negroes! They urge me in this column to speak for the Race. They tell me to butt my wooly head against the white man's barriers of racial prejudice. Yet, on every hand, I'm confronted with the Color Lines within the Color Line! Because my hair is wooly and kinky, as God made it, they tell me my hair is "bad." Who in the hell says straight hair is "good"? The white man, of course! And his Uncle Tom Negroes! I've got Caucasian blood in my veins, but I'm ashamed to tell you how it got there!

Every Negro in the United States
Is Important!
August 29, 1942

I am an optimist. I believe a better world is coming by and by. I believe that human nature can be converted, changed, reconditioned. I do not believe man is born to be selfish, poverty-stricken, ignorant, unthinking.

There are critics who say that I hit with the kick of a Missouri mule. If I fail to do this, it ain't no fault of mine. I don't hold malice.

I don't hate persons.

I hate ideas and customs that keep people from happiness. Personal vices don't shock me. I've seen about every "sin" in the little old USA. And what I haven't read about the "sins" of civilized Anglo-Saxons and so-called savages is minus zero. I'm not interested in the fact that people do wrong. I try to find out WHY they do it. So gossip, for the sake of gossip, bores me.

I believe in Democracy. I believe in the little people. I believe in equality. I practice as well as preach that. Democracy begins in a man's house.

All Races Are Important to Me

I love the white race as much as I do the black race. I hate the ideas of those white crooks and dumbbells who try to practice Hitlerism, fascism, jim crowism, mouth-Christianity, social injustice. I also hate the ideas of black snobs and jackasses.

A man lives with other men. He cannot escape this. What a man does to himself is his private business. What he does to his neighbor is the world's business. I believe every race should stay in its place. And its place is not on the heads of other races. All men up. No man down.

Civilization is a mountain. This mountain is large enough for every man to stand on its top, facing the sun of Democracy. In our period of the world's history, no man should live in poverty, slums, ignorance, fear. I hate the guts of Hitler and Governor Talmadge of Georgia, because they hate Democracy. They want to turn back the clock of civilization to the Dark Ages.

I believe the little people of all nations want the Four Freedoms. They are often duped and doped by two-bit politicians. The world is in a hell of a mess, because the Big Boys put it there.

Two-bit minds scorn the little people. I am not one of these. If we had real Freedom of Speech, Governor Talmadge would be hooted out of Georgia by the little white people of Georgia. The trouble is the press and schools and radios of Georgia are controlled by Big White Boys.

The Importance of the Little Negro

The little Negro (LN) is apt to think he's unimportant in the world's affairs. That's the reason he confines his talk and work to a little lodge, a little church, a little circle of friends.

A little Negro doesn't realize that every time he takes a step he shakes the universe. That's science. If all the little people in the world stepped at the same time, they would upset the Laws of Nature to a degree.

Nothing is lost in the universe. That's science. An invisible germ can change the course of history. A seed of coffee changed the history of Brazil. A leaf of tobacco changed the history of the United States and Europe.

If Shakespeare hadn't stolen a rabbit, the history of literature wouldn't be what it is. He was just a little boy then. I get this from Sir Sidney Lee's biography.

So the little people and little things count, good and bad. Often what looks good is bad, and the other way around. Time tells.

So I like to write for little Negroes. They are important. Of course, they don't know it. The little Negro is thinking today. Like the ants and the bees, the little Negroes are getting together. The salvation of America is in the hands of little Negroes. If the Race problem can't be solved, America cannot lead the world.

Tomorrow belongs to the little people. The Big Boys are through. He who is greatest among you, let him be the servant of all. We used to think a big house, a big car, a big salary, a big position—made a big man. Those days are gone forever. A big man now is a big servant of little people.

Our Good White Friends Get Cold Feet
January 23, 1943

Some of our good white friends are getting cold feet. Like a cat in the presence of a dog, their bellies of charity are turning over. The blood has left their hoofs, and they stand in great fear.

Now, don't get me wrong. Some of our white liberals and radicals are getting stronger. They have just begun to fight. Labor is working more and more closely with Negro workers. As Walter White said a short time ago, bigger and bigger gains are being made. These should spur us on to greater unity, greater courage, greater vision.

Of course, more violent attacks are being made upon us. We expect that. Freedom will not come to us on a gold platter. Nothing is worth a tinker's dam that you don't have to fight for. We have the best leadership we've ever had. We have fewer Uncle Toms in big places.

The Theory of Cold Feet

In times of peace it was profitable for certain educated white men and women to pose as friends of the Negro. It gave them a special niche in American life. They attracted attention to them-

selves. They were invited to attend big meetings, where the golden
brown chicken sagged the tables.

Then, too, they gained the spotlight by sponsoring Negro celebrities. They had a good excuse for crossing and recrossing the
Color Line. It was a big adventure. I could go back to ancient times
and show cases similar to this among the Greeks, Ethiopians, and
Persians.

Of course, the Bilbos denounced these good white friends. But
the Bilbos are uneducated, uncultivated, unsophisticated, un-this
and un-that. So the white liberals felt superior. They wrote sentimental articles and stories in the Southern and Northern magazines. They spoke about the Negro with authority. Yes, life was
pleasant in those peaceful days.

In this very *Saturday Review of Literature,* which carried
mushy-mouthed, pussyfooting, bootlicking Dr. Warren Brown's
denunciation of the Negro Press—in this very magazine, V. F.
Calverton, editor and novelist, carried an article, two years ago,
which said that no white man was anything who didn't have a
Negro writer as a friend in the Jazz Age.

Why They Get Cold Feet

Those good old days of Negro patronage have gone forever.
White people have always accepted the Marian Andersons and
Richard Wrights. These liberals admire Negro genius. Even in the
South, they will eat and drink with a Negro celebrity in the privacy
of their homes. But that doesn't mean they accept as citizens, the
Negro masses.

Today, the Negro masses are on the move. They are no longer
innocent, spiritual-singing, tap-dancing children. The battle is on
for human rights. All over the world the tide of freedom is rising.

As a result, the South is getting scared and brutal. The South
talks no longer about Negroes being inferior. The South says now,
with Northern Big Business, that the Negro must be kept in his
place for economic and political reasons.

The battle is on for the Four Freedoms, at Home and Abroad.
The interracial chicken dinners are things of the past.

Peter got scared and denied Jesus three times. Peter got cold feet
when the showdown came. Today, our good white friends are
doing the same thing. Rats desert a sinking ship. Would-be friends
do the same thing in a crisis. These days of battle are too hot for the
Virginus Dabneys!

Who Said: "This Is a White Man's Country"?
July 31, 1943

Out of the mouth of a liar comes the truth. Hitler, who now sees the handwriting on the wall, once declared in a moment of sanity: "If you tell a lie big enough and long enough, the world will call it a truth."

Nobody has suffered from lying more than the Negro. In Congress and in the Bible Belt of Dixie, the liars are busy on Sambo and Labor. Loud and long are the tongues of our enemies. But the tragic thing is this: We Negroes often swallow the lies of our foes.

The biggest lie ever told in America is the following: "This is a White Man's country."

I hear Negroes repeating this lie North, South, East, and West. When I spoke to Negro soldiers at Camp Wolters, I tried to refute this lie. Out of this lie came defeatism, jim crowism, churchianity, Bilboism.

No self-respecting Negro will tolerate this lie. It means the death of the Declaration of Independence, the Bill of Rights, the Emancipation Proclamation.

What Is a White Man's Country?

A Negro who thinks this country—the United States—is not his country is a damned fool. My native land! Where is it? It is where my mother gave me birth. My hometown is where I was born. Jesus was a Nazarene, because He was born in Nazareth. I am just as much an American as President Roosevelt. And for the same reason. We both were born in the United States.

I love Africa. But Africa isn't my country. Africa belongs to Africans. I know some foreigners raped Africa. But still Africa belongs to Africans. That is their vine and fig tree.

A man's country is his motherland. In the last war I entered the United States army. I wasn't drafted, either. It has never entered my belief that this is a White Man's country. That is a damnable lie.

I live in a house. Law and custom and truth say: "Your house is your castle." You have the right to protect it with your blood and life. Well, your country is just a bigger house. Let nobody, here nor abroad, take your house from you. Abe Lincoln told you that. Tom Jefferson told you that. The Supreme Court of the United States tells you that.

Maybe the Indian can say: "This is the Red Man's country." The Indian was here first. The White Man robbed him. But the

Indian has too much sense to say that today that this is a Red Man's country!

Victory at Home and Abroad

What is the trouble with the Negro in America? He has let the Fascist Whites tell him that his is a White Man's country. Whose country is it? I answer the question in my poem "Rendezvous with America":

> Into the matrix of the Republic poured:
> White gulf streams of Europe
> Black tidal waves of Africa,
> Yellow neap tides of Asia,
> Niagaras of the little peoples.
>   America?
> America is the Black Man's Country,
> The Red Man's, the Yellow Man's,
> The Brown Man's, the White Man's.

Yes, America is the motherland of *all races of men*. Crispus Attucks, a black man, was the first man to die for our country in the Revolutionary War. Two black men first stood in the presence of the Emperor of Japan, when Admiral Perry opened Japan to Western civilization. I am now looking at the autographed picture of Mat Hensen, a black man, who was the first man to plant the Stars and Stripes at the North Pole.

Sambo, read your history. Then you will fight harder to keep the Bilbos from taking your country away from you. It would be a foolish father who would let somebody take his house from him and then say tauntingly: "This is my house." America is the Black Man's house. Fight for that house—at Home and Abroad!

Will the Colored Race Rule the World?
October 30, 1943

An article in the Southern newspapers caused me to think about this subject. It is nothing new, in either schoolbooks or the barbershop. Around 1900, Dr. W. E. B. Du Bois wrote something like this: "The chief problem of the Twentieth Century is the problem of Color."

White Americans facing yellow Japanese, in the jungles of the South Pacific, will say: "Amen! Amen!"

Of course, I say the chief problem of this century is the American dollar, the German mark, the French franc, the English pound, and the Japanese yen.

What is the root of evil? Answer: $$$$$

A few years ago, Dr. Lothrop Stoddard, whom Harvard University miseducated, wrote a book called *The Rising Tide of Color*. In this book he saw the colored races conquering the world—or about to do so—after the white races had killed themselves off, as they are doing so efficiently now. Many white people still think like Dr. Stoddard!

A Noted Columnist Speaks

Robert Quillen, who is widely read in Southern newspapers, is all excited by this business of white people killing each other. He lets his mind run away with him. He views the future of a hundred years hence.

A visitor from another planet comes to a city on Earth. He can find only an old man in the street. The buildings are empty. The factories are rusty. The old man says the whites are paying tribute to the dark-skinned masters.

Yes, the whites used to be masters. The whites had knowledge. Knowledge is power. Knowledge rules the world. That's the reason Gandhi is in jail. The British have the knowledge of bombers and tanks.

But the old man says that whites had blundered. They killed off each other with tanks and bombers. Then they taught the dark races how to make tanks and bombers. Of course, the colored races outnumbered the whites four to one. So now the whites, in this parable, had become the slaves, and the darker races had become the masters.

Now, this is that day that some Negroes dream about. Like Lothrop Stoddard, they see a rising tide of color. Of course, this is pure bunk.

For myself, I don't want either Sambos or Bilbos ruling me. Big fish eat little fish, and the color of the fish doesn't count. A big black fish will eat a little black fish as quickly as a big white fish will eat a little black fish!

All Colors Have Messed Up in History!

At one time the colored races ruled the world. Read my long poem, "Babylon," which ought to be out soon in the *Atlantic Monthly*.

When the Big Colored Boys had the world in a jug, the little boys caught hell—both the little whites and little blacks.

For 2,000 years now the Big White Boys have had the world in a jug—still the little whites and the little blacks catch hell.

Now some Sambos and Aunt Hagars want to put the Big Colored Boys on top again. Ain't that something! Today we're fighting so there won't be any Big Boys at all.

Jesus said: "He who is greatest among you, let him be the servant of all!"

The big man of the future, whether he is black or white will be the man who can wash the biggest number of feet. Tomorrow we are not going to have any race ruling another race.

Tomorrow we are going to have a world of the races by the races and for the races!

NAACP Unites 20 National Organizations
February 5, 1944

I am glad to see the work that Walter White and the NAACP are doing on the United Front. In unity there is a clenched fist against Negrophobia. Too long has the Negro race split itself into conflicting, petty organizations—all of whose voices were lost in the White Man's Wilderness.

This is an age of big business, big organizations, big This and That. We see it clearly in economics. The little businessman cannot compete with corporations. That's the reason the little businessmen have organized to meet the giant monopolies. That is the reason we see the growth of cooperatives.

Only a big nation can wage a successful war. It is said that only four nations in the world can do that. They are Germany, Russia, Japan, and the United States. But our ancestors saw this. That's the reason they sang: "Walk together, children!"

The Big 20

So the NAACP, realizing modern trends, has called the Big 20 of Negro organizations together. What is the purpose? To get ready for the coming election. And this election is the most crucial one since Lincoln's time.

The Bilbos of the South and the Big Boys of the Republican party are cleaning their guns. They are after the big game. Who will boss the United States during the next four years? This period may decide our national destiny for the next one thousand years!

The Negro vote will play a big role in this election. It may be the deciding vote. So the NAACP is right in calling the brothers and sisters together. A yardstick must be found to measure political parties and candidates. We aren't going to throw away our golden opportunity this time. I am glad to say that we don't have any national Uncle Toms to divide us this time. If one raised his head, I am satisfied that our watch-dog Negro Press will see that he is religiously liquidated.

The slogan of this New Negro is: ''A new world is a-coming, and damned be him who standeth in the way!''

The Yardstick of the New Negro

So these big organizations of the race have laid down a yardstick for all candidates and parties. Their morality is not the white man's morality. It will cause the Bilbos to froth at the mouth and sweat in the loins. What are our planks?

I. We demand of any political party desiring the support of Negroes a vigorous prosecution of the war. Victory must crush Hitlerism, both at home and abroad.

II. We insist on the right to vote in every state, unrestricted by poll taxes and white democratic primaries.

III. National administration must legislate against lynching and also violence against Negroes in the armed services.

IV. Republican and Democratic members of the Senate will be judged on their voting for cloture or their failure to vote against it. The Negro wants the abolition of the filibuster.

V. The program of the FEPC to protect the right to work without racial or religious discrimination must be continued and expanded.

VI. Segregation and discrimination in the armed forces must go.

VII. This war must bring to an end imperialism and colonial exploitation.

VIII. The Negro vote will vigorously oppose any candidate for President or Vice-President who is of a vacillating or reactionary character.

III
World War II

Drama: "The Tragedy of Ethiopia"

May 28, 1938

Drama: "The Tragedy of Ethiopia." Setting: Geneva. Characters: Representatives of the League of Nations. Time: the year of our Lord 1938. Author: $$$$$$

Haile Selassie, sick mentally and physically, arrived on the scene in a dramatic 11th hour appeal to the conscience of nations, before the final curtain fell upon the last official act in the tragedy of the King of Kings.

The dark little man was not alone in his heroic fight for the freedom of his people. Negroes should not forget those courageous statesmen who stood shoulder to shoulder with Haile Selassie. They were Dr. V. L. Koo of China, Julio Alvarez Del Vayo of Loyalist Spain, the envoy from New Zealand, and that master diplomat Litvinov of Russia. The most vigorous defender that Haile Selassie found among the "Christian" statesmen gathered at Geneva was the atheistic Maxim Litvinov from Godless Russia! What irony! What inconsistency!

If old William Shakespeare had been there he would have written a tragedy greater than *Hamlet,* greater than *King Lear,* greater than *Macbeth,* and it would have been called *The Tragedy of Ethiopia.*

Imperialism Marches On

When Mussolini's savage hordes invaded Ethiopia to spread civilization with machine guns and high-powered rifles and syphilis, I was sitting in a Negro drug store near the courthouse square of a Southern town. Several professional men were in the place when the announcement came over the radio.

A prominent physician got to his feet and exclaimed: "Mussolini will never take Ethiopia!"

The gentleman became eloquent. He said the country was too rugged, too mountainous. I told him quietly that bombing planes eliminate mountains. That poisonous gas seeks out the hiding places of guerilla warriors. That spears and old-fashioned guns are no match for mechanized modern warfare.

The doctor became very angry, like most persons who try to make facts out of wishes. In a recent debate with the University of Southern California, we had discussed the munitions question. I had discovered the armed strength in Italy. I had reasons to believe that no first-rate military power could afford to challenge Mussolini. Not then. And not now.

Imperialism marches on! Great Britain knew it was almost suicidal to let Mussolini take Ethiopia. Get down your map and look at it. Mussolini's fist in the Mediterranean Sea is like a blow to the solar plexus of the British Empire. Great Britain bluffed and bluffed. Mussolini called her bluff. He knew Great Britain could not go to war!

The Octopus of Capitalism

Capitalism grows fat on profits. Capitalism must have profits. That's common sense. A good businessman is a man who makes money. Capitalistic nations have always exploited weaker nations. The sugar magnates needed Cuba; so we had the Spanish-American War. Uncle Sam, under the dictates of Big Business, barred up the Chamber of Deputies in black Haiti and ran the legislators out of the windows.

Capitalism needed workers in the nineteenth century; so millions of Negro slaves were torn from Mother Africa and dragged into the Americas, leaving their blood in swamps and valleys, or mountains and hillsides. The living and the dead were chained together, and the sickening odor of a slave ship could be smelled for five miles even when the hatches were closed. It was capitalism that cut your check last week!

Capitalism is an octopus that feeds on the weak. No lie. Ask thinkers like John Dewey and Einstein, Dr. Laski of the University of London and Professor Charles A. Beard.

A Negro who believes in capitalism is a Negro who believes in the rape of Ethiopia, the peonage system in Georgia, and the infamous exploitation of all weaker peoples.

Capitalism must have profits. It sucks profits from the people at home; then it reaches into foreign countries and wraps its tentacles about China and Ethiopia sucking profits!

Ethiopia was the victim of capitalism in the form of imperialism; Mussolini was put in power by the financiers of Italy. He sold out the Italian people. Today they groan under financial and psychical burdens.

White Civilization Goes Downhill

The Unholy Three, England and France and Italy, sold out the League of Nations for thirty pieces of filthy silver. This caused the breakdown of international law that required centuries and centuries to build.

The world cried out in disgust and anger when Germany made a scrap of paper out of the neutrality of Belgium. Of course, people forgot that little Belgium had cut off the hands of black natives in the Congo because they could not bring enough rubber for the white capitalists. My mother used to sing after father had preached in his little church on Sunday morning: "You will reap just what you sow."

England and France and Italy now exploit 500,000,000 colored peoples. For what? For dollars. For profits in gold and oil and rubber and agricultural products. But at home the masses of the population in these countries tear out their lives against economic injustices. That's the cancer that will eat away these dishonorable governments.

White civilization is sliding downhill. International law today is a scrap of paper. Therefore, Mexico slaps England in the face and gives a belly laugh. The Japanese take a shot at the British ambassador.

Perhaps René Maran, winner of the Goncourt Prize, was right when he declared, in his introduction to the novel *Batouala,* that civilization was a scourge, a conflagration. The white man—I mean the big white man—has messed up the world. He's had two thousand years to make good. He's had the best soil of the earth at his command. Nature and fortune have smiled upon him. But he started out wrong. Because he started out to exploit. He has always believed that might made right. For a while, he walked the earth like a god. For a while, the blacks and yellows and browns thought he was a god. Even today some mediocre Negro A.M.s and Ph.D.s think he's a god.

I have read many books and newspapers and magazines put out by big white men. They make me laugh. They make me want to cry. Yes, the white man is lost in the wilderness of capitalism. Franklin Roosevelt tells him that when he talks about the sixty families that control ninety percent of the national wealth.

Laugh, Black Man, Laugh!

Mr. Black Man, the white folk said you were dumb. They wrote thousands of books and hundreds of laws to prove to themselves that you were dumb. We're in the worst of all possible worlds. Who made it that way? Our good white friends who said they had a monopoly on intelligence, brains, literature, art, science, and religion. Yes, the White Man messed up the world. Laugh, Mr. Black Man, laugh!

Two Madmen and Two Damn Fools!
April 22, 1939

Every intelligent Negro has his eye on Europe and his ear against the United States. Every intelligent Negro is reading some fearless Negro newspaper in order to keep up with the drift of current events. The Atlantic Ocean of Teddy Roosevelt's day no longer exists. Figure it out for yourself. In order for a Negro to interpret the race problem in America, he must know the history of the world, yesterday and today. The race problem in the United States is a pimple on the diseased elephant of civilization.

So put your finger on Florina, Greece. On April 9, 1939, Zog I, the fugitive king of Albania, issued a powerful statement to the United Press:

"There are two madmen who are disturbing the entire world—Hitler and Mussolini. There are in Europe two damn fools who sleep—Chamberlain and Daladier."

Strong words from ex-King Zog I. Millions of common folk and thousands of intellectuals will agree with the ex-ruler of helpless Albania. Among them exiled Beneš of the Czechs and Selassie of the Ethiopians.

I cannot agree with these gentlemen. Hitler and Mussolini are not mad. Hitler and Mussolini are bad. The first is an international Al Capone; the second is a John Dillinger. They are after glory; they are after territory. They came upon the scene late in history. France and Britain had hogged most of the world. The hands of France and Britain are bloody with profits. What your sixty families did in America, these two countries did on the five continents. The professors at Harvard and Columbia admit these sordid facts, but gloss them over with sweet words like the laws of supply and demand, imperialism, markets of the world, territorial expansions, etc.

Be not deceived, Black Boy. Sambo steals a chicken, and he goes to jail. A businessman steals bonds, and he goes to Congress. Great Britain steals from 400,000,000 innocent people, and she goes down in history as a "colonizer" and "diplomat."

Your multimillionaires stole when it was "legal and right" to steal. France and Britain stole entire continents when it was "legal and right" to steal. Since I may be either a dumbbell or a liar, you had better read for yourself *Robber Barons* and the *Sixty Families* and the *Shame of Cities*. These books cite millions of facts. If you can find a single error, then you can become a millionaire through a libel suit.

Hitler and Mussolini came upon the scene late, like John Dillinger and Al Capone. After thieves have fattened themselves, they always say: "Thou shalt not steal." Dollars make conservatives; old age makes profligates gentlemen.

The good old days of capitalism are gone forever. Thank God! I realize that we still have a host of capitalists without capital, but death will soon be their Santa Claus.

Today millions and millions of people are stoutly opposed to domestic and international robbery. We have a better conception of justice than our forefathers. Hitler and Mussolini are a throwback to the Robber Barons. Hitler and Mussolini want dollars and lands just like the Vanderbilts and Fords and Insulls. Since France and England have gobbled up most of the riches and lands, Hitler and Mussolini have decided to get theirs with bombing planes and machine guns.

The premiers of France and England are not "damn fools." They are crooks and Judases. A college fraternity will often sacrifice the college in order to advance the interests of the fraternity. Well, rich men and rulers will sell their country in order to keep their class in power. Supreme examples of this are Chamberlain and Daladier.

Hitler and Mussolini are crooks. Chamberlain and Daladier have been their accomplices. Now, crooks often double-cross each other. That's what happened after Munich. I told you months ago in this column that Chamberlain was a Judas shedding crocodile tears in Parliament. Will Duranty of the *New York Times* and Walter Winchell are now telling millions of readers the same thing. Since the lowdown has been spilled, I can hold up my head.

I say with Christian humility: "I told you so!"

A White Uncle Tom of 1939

If a Negro keeps his eyes and ears open, he can pick up many things that are similar to the things in his own life. Words change their meanings. Uncle Tom today is a word full of shame and unmanliness. Centuries ago, to call a man a Christian was like calling a man a Red today at Chitling Switch, Miss.

All races have their Uncle Toms. Albania has hers. Uncle Toms are usually found in high places, among the Black Cabal and the nobility, for examples.

On April 12, 1939, in Tirana, Albania, Italian Foreign Minister Count Ciano abolished the old Albanian government and set up a flunky state. He also organized a flunky constitutional assembly.

Now Djafer Ypi, a famous Albanian, was made the head of the administrative committee. When the assembly opened, he delivered the chief address before the robber Italians. Now can you imagine a man who has been more unprincipled than this flunky when he uttered these words before the rapers of his people?:

"Mussolini is a greater man than either Caesar or Hannibal. As a strong character, he will never permit our small but old nation to lose itself."

A barefaced lie. Albania lost itself as a nation when Mussolini's legions crossed the border. All the Uncle Toms are not in the Negro race. Beware of these so-called leaders who are ready to bargain away human rights to secure a lap-dog peace. Djafer Ypi has a soft job under the Italians. They will do all the thinking. As their Uncle Tom, he will be used to feed his people the dope of underdog citizenship. Djafer Ypi will live in a big house, drive big cars, eat big dinners—and make speeches to his benighted Albanian brothers on the goodness of Duce, who is greater than Caesar and Hannibal! In time the Albanians will think and act like the peons in Alabama.

Black Boy, snap out of it! Haven't you seen black Djafer Ypi's bowing and scraping before white Mussolinis in America? Black Boy, on such occasions, didn't you feel like tearing up the stage with a thousand alley-apples?

Student Hangs Himself with Book-Strap

This tragedy was flashed across the United States from Los Angeles. It is a severe indictment of American education and European civilization.

We are informed that a fear of war and a haunting dream that he was forced to kill his fellowman drove this 17-year-old boy to suicide. The mother of little Buddy Merrill found his body swaying from the end of his book-strap in the family garage.

I am wondering about the books he carried in that book-strap. Did those books give the boy the facts of life? Did they shoot him a lot of bunk about idealistic platitudes? Did they let him know who made wars? Did they tell little Buddy about the profits big men derive from patriotism? Did they tell him about our dollar democracy?

When I look back at all the bunk they gave me in schools and colleges, I can sympathize with Buddy, who has now answered the eternal riddle of eternity. Buddy's mother says he was scared by the radio broadcasts and the headlines in the papers. War! War! War!

A news commentator quoted the President thus: "If a general war comes between the democracies and the dictators, the United States will be forced to take a stand with the democracies."

It is said that Buddy's teachers were stunned. Why? Since they had failed to tell the boy the truth about the economic basis of civilization and the challenge that meets every honest man to change that civilization—why should his teachers have been stunned? As teachers, they will never suspect that they are to blame for the boy's suicide. No. They are good. They will blame a corpse.

His teachers will look back at the boy's career and discover little things that pointed toward Buddy's abnormality. He will be held up as a bad example for other little boys.

The fact is some natures are finer than others. Some souls are more soulful. Some spirits are more spiritual. Most of us adults have lied to ourselves so much that brutality does not move us. Of course, if we get caught, we raise heaven and earth with lamentations.

Buddy had a fine soul. He could not stand to shoot down other boys. He did not know why men shot down each other. His teachers never told him that. Today I asked several boys and girls why soldiers kill each other. Not one knew the logical reason. They were in Buddy's shoes. So was I. The elders lied to me. Now, can you blame me for not believing ninety-nine-hundreths of the things I see and hear?

Buddy made the mistake of bumping off himself. He should have bumped off those who made the world a hell for the sensitive boy. Since we poor men and women have to do the fighting, we should contend for the constitutional right to declare war. The making of war should be taken out of the hands of the war makers, in Europe and in America.

The Second World War:
International Crooks
September 9, 1939

Sunday, September 3, at 11 A.M. London time (5 A.M., EST) Prime Minister Chamberlain declared: "We are at war with Germany." Readers of this column will remember that I predicted eleven months ago that this very thing would happen. This Second World War, like the first one, is the result of a long chain of crooked dealings. I place the blame of this war squarely on the shoulders of Great Britain. Let us review the events of the past years. We should find the painful facts that made this conflict inevitable.

Do not be deceived by the fine phrases that these international crooks will use. Chamberlain has already told the ignorant English people that God is on the side of the English. Herr Hitler has already declared to the ignorant German people that God is on the side of Germany. To cover up their dirt men use the garment of religion in many, many cases.

The Battle for World Markets

The love of money is the root of all evil. These nations have gone to war to get the dirty dollars. I hear some folk say that men love to fight and kill. It's human nature. That's a lie. How many men do you know who want their bodies filled with lead and twisted by poisonous gasses? You can only make people fight by whipping their emotions with propaganda. Then, in wartime you have to draft men. Men, generally, do not want to fight.

Now, look at England and France. They are great imperialistic nations. They cornered the best of the world markets. They have exploited the richest parts of Africa and Asia. They have used the gangster methods of Al Capone and Jack Legs Diamond. Now, Hitler, a very sharp crook, came upon the scene rather late.

But he wanted his share of the dough. Naturally, France and England wanted peace after they had stolen most of the earth; you can see how a guy who has seized the loot would say to another robber: "Thou shalt not steal."

So this is a war for the markets of the world. Hitler is not mad, as you hear people say. He has laid his plans well. An old monkey-faced Chamberlain has helped him. In fact, without Chamberlain's assistance, Hitler would have been stopped years ago. Then we would not have this present war.

England's Double-crossing

Hitler and Mussolini could have been stopped. England and France did not want to stop them. First came the sacrifice of helpless Ethiopia. England did nothing. Then Austria, China, Spain, Czechoslovakia, and Albania were given to the fascists.

England and France did nothing. They didn't give a tinker's dam about the freedom of those small countries. Yes, they bargained away the rights of the weaker nations. England and France could have preserved the peace of the world by supporting the League of Nations, which they themselves created.

The Russo-German Peace Pact

People who won't face the facts fail to blame England for Russia's failure to become an ally of the so-called democracies. Why did the negotiations break down? This is the reason: France, England, and Poland wanted Russia to fight for them; but they didn't want to fight for Russia if she were attacked. Again, Poland didn't want Russian soldiers on her soil in case of a war.

Thus, it is obvious that the so-called democracies had no intention of making a Soviet alliance. They wanted another Munich. Yes, forty-eight hours after Hitler had invaded Poland, Chamberlain was angling for another Munich, a sellout of a smaller nation whom he had sworn to protect.

All along, Chamberlain had favored Hitler. Chamberlain hated Russia. He did not want an alliance with Russia. He was doing all he could to prepare Hitler for an attack on Russia. Stalin knew that. Scholars all over the world knew that.

When Hitler took over Czechoslovakia, he secured 3,000 bombing planes, equipment for fifty infantry divisions, more gold than there was in Germany, and the Skoda munitions factory, the second largest in the world. Why did Chamberlain arm Hitler thus? Chamberlain thought Hitler was getting ready to attack Russia.

All this time the English and French representatives were delaying the negotiations in Moscow. Yes, the English and French commissions had no authority to sign a treaty. Can you imagine that? Then, like a bolt from the blue, came the announcement of the Russo-German pact.

Old monkey-faced Chamberlain threw up his hands in terror. While he was trying to double-cross Stalin, Stalin had double-crossed him and Hitler had become a Brutus. There is no game so dirty as the game of international politics.

No Problem Is Settled Until It's Settled Right

This second World War proves that no problem is settled until it is settled right. Big nations have preyed upon the smaller nations. Big nations have made treaties scraps of paper. If England and France had protected Ethiopia and China and the other weaker countries, there would have been no war. Hitler and Mussolini are the products of the crookedness of the big nations.

I hope the United States does not enter this war. But I am afraid she will. Our international banking system and our economic loyalties link us with England. Already our press is drumming up sentiment for the so-called democracies. Big men can make huge profits out of our entry into this conflict. I have no illusions.

A few minutes ago I listened to a radio announcement. It said that Germans had dropped bombs upon the American embassy in Warsaw. Get this: the American officials said that the bombing was intentional. And, too, it was announced that a German submarine had sunk an English ship carrying Americans. This is the kind of propaganda that caused the United States to enter the First World War.

Prime Minister Chamberlain said in his ultimatum to Germany: "We have a clear conscience."

How in the name of common sense can Chamberlain have a clear conscience? He—more than any other man—laid the foundation for the present conflict. If Mussolini had been stopped when he invaded Ethiopia, fascism would have been stopped. But Chamberlain was playing a big game. He lost the game. He will go down in history either as a crook or an ignoramus. Perhaps—as both.

We Americans must stay out of this war. We must not listen to the siren of the war lords. We Negroes certainly have nothing to gain in a war. Too many Negro soldiers have already served as cannon fodder for the big white boys. Keep up with the European developments. This war is going to change the world. I'm looking for uprising in India and in other colonies. I predict that Chamberlain will be the last imperialistic premier of England.

Paul Robeson Looks at
the Second World War
December 9, 1939

In his interview with Ben Davis, the eminent Negro baritone asked a question of the highest importance. It reminded me of Cicero's query about Cataline before the Roman Senate. Mr. Robeson inquired: "If Chamberlain believes in democracy for small nations, why did he hand so many over to Hitler and Mussolini?"

Dr. Maxwell in his recent *History of Europe* gives us step by step the way in which Chamberlain sanctioned the brutal attacks of Hitler. Every military strategist in Europe and America knows that the combined air and naval and land forces of France, England, Czechoslovakia, Poland, and Russia could have stopped Hitler at Munich.

Hitler, then, would have been compelled to fight on three fronts at the same time. The wise German military staff told Hitler that it was impossible to fight on two fronts at the same time.

Scissors Movement in Warfare

Napoleon Bonaparte himself was unable to win on two fronts. The battlefield of Waterloo—according to Carlyle, in his *French Revolution*—was shaped like a huge A. The English and the Germans caught Napoleon in the pocket of that A. They used the scissors movement. Germany used it on Poland. Russia is now using it on Finland. An enemy with superior numbers always tries to scissor its way through.

Now, Chamberlain knew that the combined forces of France, England, Czechoslovakia, and Russia could have used a double scissors movement on Hitler in the military sense. Look at a map showing pre-Munich Europe. Then count the combined number of airplanes, ships, guns, men, and economic factors at the command of those allies. Nothing in the world could have stopped them.

From the foregoing facts we must conclude that Chamberlain was either drunk or crooked—or both dumb and crooked. From my reading of scores of impartial militarists, economists, and diplomats, I've concluded that Chamberlain was both dumb and crooked.

This is not a popular thing to say. Propaganda is trying to get us into this war. The truth would keep us out. But there are bankers who will make millions out of this war, while mothers' sons give their bodies to the maggots. And for what? To make the world safe for British exploitation.

But Mr. Robeson says: "The Negro people will not soon forget Spain, Czechoslovakia, Austria—and certainly not Ethopia."

Aftermath of Munich

Since the breakdown of Chamberlain's diabolical policy of appeasement, fear has seized every nation. This is something most commentators have overlooked. Haile Selassie said this would happen. He was right. He said it, however, five years before it happened.

After Munich, every small nation got the jitters. Yes, every large nation said: "There can be no peace."

What was the result? You see it in today's newspapers. The huge Russian army moves into Poland and Finland. Why? To take up militarily strategic positions. Against whom? Against England. Against Germany. Fear has seized the nations. It's every dog for himself, and the devil take the hindmost.

Most Americans are morally indignant. So am I. But I am fighting mad because the fascists were not stopped when they could have been stopped so easily. The things that are happening now are inevitable.

When a mad dog is let loose, it is needless to denounce people who get out their guns to kill him. In the wild firing, somebody who is innocent may be killed. That is our present situation. Chamberlain could have muzzled the mad dog of fascism. He didn't. He had selfish reasons.

Robeson Hits at France

You can give Paul Robeson credit for one thing: he does not bite his tongue; he is not afraid, like most big Negroes, to tell the truth.

Mr. Robeson says: "The terrible irony of it all is that there are about one million Senegalese troops being used by Daladier now to make French imperialism richer and more ruthless against the colonies.

This is indeed a tragedy. Black slaves are fighting to keep themselves in slavery. Robeson has studied in Africa. He knows several African languages. He knows what it is for Africans to be under French "democracy." If you want to read a book that will make you cry, then read the black René Maran's story, *Batouala*. Yes, rotgut whiskey and syphilis have been used to "civilize the savages."

What Shall Negroes Do in the United States?

Mr. Robeson has the answer: "I know that our energies should be directed toward building the labor movement—based on Negro and white equality."

Most big Negroes haven't seen that yet. The Negro's salvation lies in just one thing: the CIO—the white-and-black labor union. The race problem will not be solved in sororities and fraternities, bridge parties and little Negro businesses. The race problem will be solved at the BOTTOM—and not the TOP. Tomorrow belongs to the UNDERDOG and not the TOPDOG.

Paul Robeson, a topdog, sees that. Paul Robeson has greater wealth and fame and social standing than millions of little Negroes who are trying to be big. Paul Robeson has the economic security that most middle-class Negroes would give their souls to possess.

I know Negroes who are sickening snobs without a fraction of Mr. Robeson's attainments. Mr. Robeson is an honored guest in the luxurious drawing rooms of Fifth Avenue. He does not think himself superior to them. Therein lies his greatness.

White people often try to buy off brilliant Negroes by telling them they are "different." Mr. Robeson is one Negro who cannot be bought.

Freud Has the Answer

Now, here is a puzzle. Why is it that Negro geniuses like Paul Robeson, Richard Wright, and Langston Hughes—whom I know personally are welcomed into the most exclusive white circles in America—are at the same time the most modest and race-loving men? On the other hand, I know little 2x4 social-climbers whose snobbery will make any sensible person vomit. They crave flattery as a hog craves slop. Dr. Sigmund Freud has the answer.

Paul Robeson knows that race is a myth. He knows that class exploitation and snobbery are the enemies of man. He is a genius with a message. He has all the qualifications of a Black Moses. I am glad he has returned to this country. We need him.

A Negro is a misleader until he sees that the race problem must be solved at the BOTTOM. It is time for white-collar Negroes to take off their white collars and get down in the ranks of the black-collar workers.

Radicals and Liberals Lost in a Fog
February 3, 1940

I still believe that a Negro who is *not* a radical is crooked, ignorant, or yellow. How times have changed during the last six months! Last June even the moss-backed Sambo professors got on the band-wagon of radicalism. You had to be a liberal to keep the students from calling you a *nut*. Every dark thinker was going either *pink* or *red*. Now they are going *yellow*.

Reaction comes to the little old USA. The Red hunt starts. Of course, the Black hunt has been going on for 77 years. Where are the radicals and liberals of 1939? I'll tell you. Most of the scared brothers have wrapped themselves in an American flag. With tears of patriotism in their eyes and their pockets stuffed with handkerchiefs, they now strike a pose and say: "Give me democracy or give me democracy!"

I admit that this is a foolish question, for only God knows where democracy is. It's certainly not in Waycross, Ga., or in the District of Columbia.

I've always been a radical. You see, I started thinking for myself young. I was born in Moberly, Missouri. But I didn't like the town. So I left it when I was three months old.

I've always had the spirit of that Negro hero, John Henry, the spike-driving man. The night that John Henry was born his mammy made him mad. So John Henry kicked down the bed. Ask Sterling Brown to tell you about John Henry!

Two-Bit Radicals and 2x4 Liberals!

I've never had much faith in those who take up with popular causes and flirt with new isms. I am speaking now of so-called intellectuals. I think a man should be a man of principles. He should acquire those principles through hard and vigorous study. Then he should be ready to die for his principles. A principle that a man isn't willing to die for may be a great principle; but that man isn't worth a tinker's dam.

Your two-bit radicals and 2x4 liberals change with every shift of the wind. They never think for themselves. They have no guts. Many of them defended the underdog in the past because it was popular to defend the underdog. They also dreamed of Utopia because that was popular. Those same two-bit radicals and 2x4 liberals now quake in their boots at the mere mentioning of the word—Radicalism.

117

They now steer clear of everything that smacks of agitation. Some of them have dropped their real radical friends as if they were hot coals.

I still believe that a Negro who is not radical is crooked, ignorant, or yellow.

The Defense of England and France

Whenever I hear a Negro whooping it up for England and France, I yearn for the good right fist of Joe Louis. Yes, murder swells in my heart and I see black. This, in spite of the fact that I've never killed a louse, though lice have killed some of my best friends.

You see, I'm afraid that this country is going to war. The two-bit radicals and 2x4 liberals who've deserted the vanguard of thought are assisting the Big Boys. The Big Boys want to make billions out of flesh and blood on the battlefields of Europe.

My heart bleeds when I think of poor Ethiopia, China, Spain, Czechoslovakia, Memel, and Austria. I know that all of them could have been saved if it had not been for the selfish rulers of Great Britain and France. Poland and Finland are but the aftermath of Munich. Remove the causes and you remove the tragic effects.

This war will settle nothing. It will produce other wars and rumors of wars. Uncle Sam has no business in that European mess. Europe is playing a crooked game. Until Europe decides to give economic justice to all men there can be no peace. Money is the root of the present war. It is not a battle of isms—of ideologies. It is a battle of pounds and francs and marks. It is a battle of the haves and have-nots.

If the verbal democracies want peace, let them give up their exploitation of white men and brown men, of black men and yellow men. That they will not do. Fascism is a sore on the diseased body of civilization. Take the profits out of war, and there will be no war. Let the bankers do the fighting, and there will be no fighting.

Whooping It Up for Democracy!

If Jesus Christ preached in a white church tonight—you'd find his body swinging from a telephone post tomorrow morning. If Thomas Jefferson stood before Congress and made a speech on the Constitution—Congressman Dies would drag him before his un-American Committee on American Idiocies.

Get out the brass band, Sambo. Swing out on the theme song, Democracy. Dr. Doolittle, from the Citadel of Negro Education, put on your cap and gown and whoop it up for 100 percent Americanism whatever that mixture is.

Everybody's doing it. Doing what? The Democracy Trot. It's too bad that Houdini died so soon. If old Houdini were here he could show the boys some fine democratic stunts. Houdini had novelty. He didn't bore you to death with old tricks. Most of these whoopers for democracy pull gags that had whiskers when George Washington was a baby.

The other night I heard a white man from Little Rock, Ark., speaking on the glories of democracy—freedom of speech, freedom of thought, freedom of action—and I jumped from my chair, ran to the mirror, and looked at my face to see if my complexion had changed.

You talk about the Utopians. Lord, Lord, Lord! the Utopians in their brightest days never had a thing on these boys who whoop it up for Democracy in 1940. No lie. If by some miracle democracy should materialize all at once, fifty million Americans would fall dead. If democracy came to the United States, Congressman Dies and his fellow Southerners, who were not elected by ALL THE PEOPLE, would be kicked out of Congress.

Little Man, What Now?
The Bunk about Finland
March 9, 1940

Is the white man dumb? Or does the white man think the colored races are dumb? Trying to solve that problem, I've scratched my head until my fingers are full of splinters.

Magazines, from the liberal *Nation* and *New Republic* to the yellow-journalistic *Collier's* and *Liberty,* shed crocodile tears over the invasion of Finland. The *New York Times* and the *Chittling Switch Offender* denounce the bloodthirsty Reds. The illustrated *Life* and *Look* carry pictures of the blond heroes of the Far North. Many of our preachers and professors have become weeping Jeremiahs. Several of our Negro newspapers have beome wet sheets instead of yellow sheets. All because of the invasion of Finland!

Mr. Hoover to the Rescue

Having failed to rescue 11,000,000 hungry and jobless Americans right under their noses, President Roosevelt and Congress have sent $30,000,000 to rescue the hungry Finns, five thousand miles away. Does charity begin at home? Sez you! Did the President say anything about the anti-lynch bill?

Now Mr. Hoover comes upon the scene, with his Finnish Relief.

When the Bonus Army marched on the capitol Mr. Hoover's motto was "Bullets instead of bread!"

There is some rotten inside dope that the newspapers have not revealed about Finland, Russia, and Mr. Hoover. It involves an exchange of dollars—the root of evil.

Mr. Hoover was Chairman of the American Relief in 1918. Mr. Hoover was also dealing in gold, silver, copper, timber, iron, and lead properties in the Inter-Russian Syndicate.

That brings in a Mr. Urquhart and the London Stock Exchange. Also the Banque du Commerce Privée of Paris. Also the crooked Emile Franqui, probably the richest man in Belgium. And that drags in the grabbing of the Chinese Engineering and Mining Company of the Orient. Then the minister Boris Bakhmetief, ex-ambassador of the Czar's court to Washington, glides upon the scene. I am quoting Dr. Walter Liggett.

To understand the invasion of Finland, you have to go back twenty years. You have to trace a web of conspiracy stretching from Tokyo to Helsinki to Paris to London to our own State Department. Dr. Eugene Rosenstock-Huessy can help us here.

A Big Man Jumping on a Little Man

We are told that the world is aroused because we see a little man attacked by a big man. This half-truth is more dangerous than a black lie. Consider these facts. Weak races and weak nations and weak minorities have been oppressed—yes, they are now oppressed by powerful enemies. Christian nations have had two thousand years to stop the exploitation and massacres of defenseless peoples; and they have done little.

I got hot in the collar when a certain professor of history brought me the argument about the big fellow beating up the little fellow.

The English and the Little Fellows!

Powerful England has been exploiting small peoples and killing them for five hundred years. Look at the bloody records. Read the works of Sir John Hammerton, if you please.

Dr. Robert Briffault, the famous English historian and anthropologist, says that the democratic Englishman killed off the natives of New Zealand with rat poison! Did you hear about that?

Because the East Indians wanted their freedom, the English shot tens of thousands of them down like dogs. Their George Washingtons and Thomas Jeffersons have rotted in filthy jails. Today, England rules India with machine guns. Twenty years ago England promised India her freedom. India gave two million men and shiploads of money to make the world safe for democracy. India was paid in machine-gun bullets.

Even while Chamberlain cries democracy, patriotic Irishmen die in Dublin to free their country from the tyranny of Mr. Chamberlain's Great Britain.

In Palestine, the crooked English promised Palestine to the Arabs and also to the Jews. This black lie has caused Jews and Arabs to shoot each other down.

I need not say anything about how the English rob the natives of South Africa and Egypt. The story is familiar.

The U.S. and the Little Fellows

I could tell you about the other Christian nations. How Belgium cut off the hands of Congo natives when they failed to bring in enough rubber. How Italy machine-gunned Ethiopians armed with harmless spears. Italian bombers flew over Haile Selassie, dropping death, while the Ethiopian ruler bowed with a Bible in his hand!

Mussolini's son called it a great sport. Did the President and Congress rush arms and supplies to the helpless Ethiopians? Did England send a single gun?

Everybody knows we stole Texas from Mexico. The steal was so rotten that it made honest Americans vomit. American marines shot up the Haitians—barred up the doors and windows of the legislature.

Panama once belonged to Colombia. The United States wanted to build the canal. Colombia refused to sign on the dotted line. Therefore, the Big Boys engineered a revolution and put over the crooked deal with Panama. Countless revolutions in South America have been engineered by American businessmen. Was anybody perturbed?

Now, we come to Uncle Sam and the Negro. For over seventy years Negroes have been jimcrowed, exploited, hounded like criminals, and burned at the stake. Negro women have been raped and lynched. Negro churches have been riddled with machine-gun bullets.

The Negroes and the Finns

The Finns have airplanes and huge fortifications to protect themselves. Military strategists say the Mannerheim Line is as strong as the Maginot Line. Finland has hundreds of machine guns and tanks.

The Negro doesn't have one machine gun, one airplane, one

fort. The Negro has proved his patriotism from 1776 to 1940. The Negro's blood and labor have been tremendous assets in building America.

Now, since America is so much interested in helping the helpless little fellows, why in the hell doesn't she help the helpless little Negro? The Finns have been democratic for twenty years. Okay. The Negro has been democratic for three hundred years!

Hitler Blitzkrieg Strikes Near White House!
Home Sweet Home—Death Trap in a Democracy
May 4, 1940

Did you see that page 1 picture in the *Washington Tribune* for April 20, 1940? I was glad the editor captioned it: "Not a Scene in Norway, but the Results of a 'Bombing Raid' in Washington." Otherwise, I'd have thought that lowdown, dirty Hitler had let loose another blitzkrieg on innocent women and children.

Things are getting pretty lousy when a public school teacher, in the Capital of our great Democracy, can't go to church without having her home bombed.

It seems that Hitler has nothing on the anti-Negro fascists in the Land of the Spree and the Home of Burma Shave. In fact, Hitler said on Tuesday, April 16, to President Roosevelt:

> In dealing with our racial problems, we are following the same principles America uses in handling the Negro problem. Mr. Roosevelt should stop meddling in European affairs, and look in front of his own front door.

Hitler's words are not a slap in the President's face—they are devastating blows to the solarplexus. The truth hurts, even if it comes from a scoundrel like Hitler. Now, in front of Mr. Roosevelt's own front door is a hellish blitzkrieg of Americans, by Americans, and for Americans.

While American Citizens Slept

Under the Stars and Stripes, a huge bomb tore through an American home, blew the front door off its hinges, and shattered windows in 500 homes. The explosion was heard for five miles.

I wonder if this teriffic explosion woke up the President, his White Cabinet, his Black Cabinet, the Congress, the Supreme Court, and the Dies Committee on Un-American Activities? These groups, paid by the taxpayers, have been snoozing too long. That's the reason anti-Negro fascists can bomb American citizens at midnight.

From the latest reports to reach me, the Washington cops acted the ancient role of cops in such cases: the cops heard nothing, saw nothing, did nothing.

Now, a word to the Sambos and Aunt Hagars: Keep your ears cocked to see if a tiny whisper of indignation comes from the Administrative, Executive, or Judicial groups in the Capital. Remember, Sambos and Aunt Hagars, the national election is not a hundred years off. You can vote in our Democracy without getting bumped off—in some places, at least.

Your Columnist on Verge of Nervous Breakdown

No lie. And this is the cause of it. Over the radio, in the pulpit, in the newspapers—the good white folk whoop it up for Democracy. Some of you cynics will say: "You oughta put wax in your ears."

I've tried that, Sambos. I've even retired to the woods. But I found no peace. The good white folk yelled louder: "Democracy! We have the greatest Democracy on the earth, in the sky, or on the sea."

Now, Joe Louis doesn't go around yelling: "Look at me! I'm champion of the world!"

Now, Jesse Owens doesn't bore you to death shouting: "I, Jesse Owens, am the world's fastest runner!"

Yes, as these good white folk whoop it up for Democracy, they jangle my nerves. If the sun is shining, why yell at the world the sun is shining? You make people think something is wrong.

If Shakespeare were living, I'm sure he wouldn't shout 777 times a day: "Will Shakespeare is the greatest writer in the world."

If a man is a Christian, he does not have to go around telling everybody: "I'm a Christian. I'm a Christian."

Jesus said: "By their fruits ye shall know them."

The good white folk should think over that. Perhaps they have thought. That's the reason they yell everlastingly: "We have the greatest Democracy in the world."

They have to yell Democracy to keep the world from hearing the explosion of bombs near the White House. They have to talk loud to drown out the cries of burning black men and of babies crying for milk.

You Can't Fool All the People All the Time

That sentence should be proclaimed in the White House, in Congress, and before the Supreme Court. Abe Lincoln was right.

Our politicians quote Lincoln—but they don't quote the things they should quote. Lincoln's words are a boomerang. The Big Boys know that.

Our politicians are like the old Negro preacher who said: "Brother, since I is what I is, there's some texts in the Bible I don't monkey with."

The other evening I went out to hear Madame Kamaladeeri, the eminent Hindu scholar. She had travelled all over the world several times. She made it clear that other nations and peoples are not fooled by our shouts of Democracy.

Madame Kamaladeeri said that when white Americans talk about Democracy, fascists and Communists and subjected peoples point to the hellish lynchings in America. When Americans talk about the persecutions of the Jews in Germany, the Germans point to jim crowism and disfranchisement of Negroes in America.

We love America? Okay, let us clean it up. Then we won't have to make fools of ourselves before civilized peoples. One example of Democracy is worth a million words.

Reason with me. Let your lawgivers reason with me. Let common sense have a chance. Let Justice speak. A bald-headed man shouldn't try to sell a hairgrower. A stinking bum wouldn't make a good salesman of perfume. You can understand that.

I get sick and tired of having Germans and Russians and Japanese telling the President to clean up his own front yard. If there are skeletons in the nation's closet, then Uncle Sam should clean out the closet. Or keep his mouth shut. That's common sense. I don't like the tragic spectacle of my country's being a laughingstock before the world. If the President can hear the explosion of a bomb in Helsinki and Oslo, he should hear better the bombing of a law-abiding citizen's house at 1324 Harvard Street, Northwest, in Washington, D.C.

If the President can denounce German fascists 5,000 miles away, he can denounce anti-Negro fascists in Congress and the United States. Democracy begins at home. Otherwise, our righteous proclamations of Democracy are as empty as sounding brass and tinkling cymbals.

Frankenstein and the Monster
May 25, 1940

The white man is scared to death. He has a right to be. His dollar madness has messed up himself and the world. Now he wants black men and yellow men to die horrible deaths to save a world they never made. The Pope tells the nations to pray for peace. Then the Pope builds a bomb shelter under the Vatican. Mr. Roosevelt tells us that God is with us. Then Mr. Roosevelt asks Congress for 50,000 bombing planes.

Once I had a neighbor. He used to curse and beat up his wife. But one night I heard my neighbor calling on God. I discovered that his wife had knocked the hell out of him with a skillet.

Another example. In the novel of the same name, Frankenstein constructed a monster and gave it life. Then the monster inflicted the most terrible retribution upon his creator. Frankenstein stands for one who is destroyed by his own works.

The white man is a Frankenstein who created the monster, POWER. This monster was made out of dollars and francs and guineas. That monster has devoured the darker races all over the world. Today that monster has turned upon his creator in a Second World War.

Behind the Scenes in London, Paris, and Rome

You have to read the newspapers with 777 grains of salt. And then some. Let us go back to July, 1935. Haile Selassie was then Emperor of Ethiopia. The white man's monster, Power, wanted that rich country. Power eats money. You cannot imagine Power fighting a World War for the Sahara Desert. Power fights in Cuba, the Dutch East Indies, South Africa, China.

Great Britain is the Frankenstein who created Hitler and Mussolini. Read back five years. Haile Selassie said to the League of Nations—which was deaf: "The conquest of Ethiopia means the conquest of Europe by the fascists."

On another occasion, Haile Selassie said to British newspapermen: "Belgium, France, Czechoslovakia, and Denmark now refuse to sell Ethiopia arms at any price, in obvious collusion with Benito Mussolini."

Haile Selassie, a black man, wanted to stop fascism in July, 1935. He pleaded with the nations for justice and democracy. They wouldn't sell Selassie a gun.

So the Emperor of Ethiopia said: "I shall march to battle with my arch-bishop carrying the Ark of the Covenant before me."

[*Tribune* Editor's Note: Actually Selassie became a victim of his own victimization. When Il Duce's legions began to close in on Addis Ababa the Lion of Judah packed up his gold and silver (power) and fled to England with his royal family.]

Now, these same nations want the world to come to their assistance. Those "low-down dirty Reds in Russia" were the only ones who wanted to fight for Ethiopia. Anthony Eden of the British Foreign Office had a talk with Mussolini in Rome. When he came out of the Dictator's den, the foreign press announced: "British agree to let Il Duce rule Ethiopia!" Read *Time,* July 8, 1935.

England and Hitler Double-Crossed France

When Woodrow Wilson went to Europe, he discovered things in a mess because of secret treaties. So much dirty work went on behind closed doors that a Houdini couldn't set things straight. Wheels within wheels. Plots within plots. Power politics. Double-crosses. Triple-crosses. Quintuple-crosses. International Al Capones at work in every capital of Europe.

The same thing preceded the Second World War. And the same thing will follow it. The monster, Power, is hungry. Dr. Harry Elmer Barnes has proved this in his 1,100-page *History of the World*.

Now, in 1935, Mussolini held the center of the stage. Like a small villain in a melodrama, he rattled his sword and prepared the scene for the entrance of the arch villain, Herr Hitler. Hitler fooled the Big Boys by making them believe he was after the Jews and the Reds. Mussolini had the signal to get the blacks. Of course, nobody would fight to keep the big bad wolf from getting the Jews and Reds and blacks.

Without the knowledge of France, Great Britain "not only gave Germany a blank check to violate the Treaty of Versailles but made a further and secret agreement with the Reich." France got hot in the collar and sent Ambassador Charles Corbin to clean up the crooked deal. Mister François Pietri said: "This may cause us to doubt not the friendship of Britain but her prudence." This is the way diplomats call each other fools, dumbells, crooks, liars, etc.

The Parliament of Man

I belong to no political party. So the only axe I grind is the axe of truth. When I chop wood, I never look to see where the chips fall.

I've never honored a political candidate by giving him my vote—being a black man in a white democracy.

Therefore, the good white folk who've messed up themselves and the world can't blame me. I've listened to the speeches of presidents and premiers—and I've learned how not to make a speech. I tried to play football in my college days. I did my best to run a broken field. I got tackled every time. Since that day I've studied the action of big white statesmen. They can run around facts and sidestep truth without being tackled.

We've had World War I. We're in World War II. This will be followed by World War III and IV and V. In each case the Big Boys will make the war, and the little boys will fight it. The cry of the Big Boys in each war will be: "Make the world safe for This or That." The battles for dollars and francs and marks will go on.

How can we stop wars? How can we blot out the big evil? The Apostle Paul said in a letter to Timothy: "The love of money is the root of all evil." Paul had the lowdown. Take the lousy profits out of war, and there will be no wars? Man's love of money created a Frankenstein named Power. There can be no peace until we get rid of "the root of all evil."

The poet Tennyson dreamed of a Parliament of Man, a Federation of the World. I cast my vote for that. The Big Boys don't want that. They want to pile up "treasures on earth." That means an everlasting series of wars between the Haves and the Have-Nots. In a Parliament of Man, the whites and yellows and blacks would be equal. In a Parliament of Man, a man would be a man for a' that!

Congressman "I" Mitchell:
A Case of Bighead Phobia
August 24, 1940

Ever since Brother Congressman "I." Mitchell came to the Capitol, from a 'Bama cotton patch, via the Loop of the Big White Boys, he has cut more monkey shines than His Highness of Monkeyshinedom, Senator Bilbo. Balaam's jackass did have sense enough to bray at the right moment. Brother Mitchell is always braying the wrong thing at the wrong time.

Last year I put Brother Mitchell's case in the hands of God. You remember, Sambo, how this courteous gentleman of color banged the telephone receiver in the ear of a *Tribune* reporter. Maybe God won't have anything to do with Brother Mitchell's monkey business in Congress. Anyway, Brother Mitchell continues his jackass tactics by slamming the door in the faces of Negro Youth.

Some Negro citizens have asked me what is wrong with Congressman "I." Mitchell. I don't know what in the hell is wrong! Maybe his high position has gone to his head. Some Big Negroes get the big head when the Big White Boys (accidentally) push them upstairs. Perhaps the crackers in 'Bama taught Brother Mitchell how to slam doors in the faces of black folk. Give the devil his due: even Major Brown had sense enough to listen to Negro representatives.

The Cottonpatch "Etiquette" of Brother Mitchell

You can take a man out of the cottonpatch, but it's easier for a camel to pass through the eye of a needle than to take the cottonpatch out of him. The only difference between Congressman Mitchell and Senator Bilbo is Brother Mitchell's dark physiognomy. If a biological accident had made Brother Mitchell white, he'd make a fine Ku Klux Klan kleagle.

Twelve million Negroes ought to pool their pennies and present Brother Mitchell with Emily Post's book in etiquette. The delegation representing the National Youth Congress, the NAACP Student Conference, and the Emergency Peace Mobilization never had a chance to state their case.

Brother Mitchell lectured them with the same discourtesy and fanaticism that the crackers used in lecturing Brother Mitchell in the cottonpatch. Professor A. Hunton, the learned scholar from Howard University, was helpless as the Ethiopians under Mussolini's blitzkrieg. Brother Mitchell learned from the 'Bama white folk that no Negro scholar is worth listening to.

Abraham Lincoln listened to unlettered backwoodsmen. Congressman "I." Mitchell didn't have time to hear the arguments of educated members of his own race. Of course, Brother Mitchell isn't worthy to unlace Lincoln's shoes. We've had many distinguished Negro Congressmen. None has disrespected his race like Brother "I." Mitchell. He has set a miserable precedent for white Southerners in the Capitol.

If my foot were long enough I'd set a precedent by kicking Brother Mitchell back into the cottonpatch from which he came.

Hints That His Visitors Are Pinks and Reds

Every time a Negro stands up for his manhood rights the good white folk say he's a dangerous Negro or crazy. Cottonpatch "I." Mitchell imitated his white masters in the interview on conscription. Without a bit of evidence the size of a mosquito's eye, Cottonpatch Mitchell, the Charlie McCarthy of the Big White Boys, insinuated that those upstanding members of his own race were Pinks and Reds. That was a dirty trick.

Suffering from the phobia of bigheadedness, Brother Mitchell must've thought that the group were after the 10,000 bucks Mitchell receives for saying "Amen" to everything the Big Boys say.

Brother Mitchell may sincerely believe that Negro youth should be conscripted into a jim-crow army and navy. He has a right to his opinion, though his opinion may stamp him as a dumbbell. I am not arguing that point. I am concerned with his back-alley discourtesy. How can we expect the whites to respect Negro delegations when our only Negro Congressman acts like a barroom bouncer in the Brazos Bottoms Nite Club on Beale Street? I bet old Bilbo is bellylaughing.

I bet the crackers at Waycross, Georgia, are kicking up the heels over this insult to the Negro by a Negro Congressman.

When a Negro says he doesn't want to be lynched, our cracker Congressmen can say now: "He's a Red!"

Brother "I." Mitchell Becomes a Prophet

Yes, false prophets shall arise. During this barbarian interview, Brother Mitchell saw things. He saw the Nazi forces gobbling up Haiti and Liberia within 60 days. Ain't that something! Brother Mitchell's prophecy is as full of bunk as his discourtesy. Although Hitler is having a hell of a time invading England, which is only 20 miles away, Brother Mitchell can see him gobbling up Haiti, 4,000 miles away—in spite of the Monroe Doctrine and the 21 Pan-American republics! All this is to happen in 60 days! Brother Mitchell thinks like a crawfish—backwards.

Why doesn't Brother Mitchell study Negro history, while he's waiting for the Big White Boys to tell him when to say "Amen" to some bill? Liberia and Haiti are already gobbled up. George Schuyler went to Liberia and studied that country firsthand. I recommend to Brother Mitchell, "Slaves Today," by this distinguished Negro writer. Brother Mitchell will learn how innocent African boys are brought to the rubber plantations by white Americans and Englishmen; how they die in three years' time from overwork and social disease. Why not make a speech on that in Congress, Brother Mitchell, since you're interested suddenly and mysteriously in the welfare of Liberia?

As far as Haiti is concerned, Brother Mitchell may get off his ask-me-no-questions and read his own *Congressional Records*.

Read the *Crisis* files of Dr. W. E. B. Du Bois. Read the report of
the late Dr. James Weldon Johnson, who investigated the unspeak-
able conditions in Haiti during its occupation by the American
marines. Read also the recent reports on the massacre of
thousands of Haitians by the imperialists of the Western Hemi-
sphere. Brother Mitchell, you don't have enough knowledge about
Haiti and Liberia to fill the belly of a prenatal bedbug.

Furthermore, Brother Mitchell, to prove your ignorance, I'll
make a bet. If the Nazis gobble up Haiti and Liberia in 60 days, I
shall eat this column.

The Weapon of the Weak to
Curb the Power of the Strong
September 7, 1940

When Solomon, who uttered 5,000 proverbs, got ready to teach
morality, he said, "Go to the ant, thou sluggard, and learn his
ways."

A Harvard professor in a remarkable book, *Of Ants and Men,*
has proved that Solomon knew his stuff. The ant has more virtues
than Man, who disgraces God continually by boasting that Man
was created "in the image of God."

Today we hear a great deal about the moral principles of justice,
democracy, and liberty. And there is a reason for that. And of all
things, it has been explained best by an old German philosopher
who would pat Hitler on the back if he lived today!

Jesus said the highest morality lies in charity, in kindness to the
weak. Of course, Jesus was crucified for saying and living that
philosophy. And for 2,000 years mouth-Christians have crucified
the Gospel of Jesus on a Cross of Dollars.

Plato said beauty and harmony and justice were the Trinity of
Morality. Nobody paid any attention to that but some old learned
scholar in the twilight zone of education. Nobody but a fool would
expect beauty and harmony and justice in a capitalistic world.
Reason with me, Sambo.

What Is Morality in the Modern World?

And now I come to that hateful German, Friedrich Nietzsche.
This brutal old philosopher was brutally frank. He saw beneath our
hypocrisy. He believed in the Superman. He looked upon life as a
struggle in which the fittest and the slickest survived. He saw that

money-getting used the teaching of the lowly Jesus to hide the brutalities and rascalities of money-getting. Of course, mouth-Christians have a thousand excuses for this. They say: "You must be practical!" Oh yeah?

I hate the teachings of Nietzsche; but if the Devil tells the truth, I say: "Amen." Truth is still truth if the Devil tells the truth. I accept the truth whether it comes from a friend or an enemy. It took me a long time to get that way!

So listen to Nietzsche: "Morality is the weapon of the weak to curb the power of the strong."

Chew that and digest it. What does Nietzsche mean by this? He means that only the weak are moral. Strong men and strong races do what they want to do without thought of right or wrong. The strong believe Might makes right, if they ever think about right. When a nation is strong, it boasts of its strength.

Like Napoleon Bonaparte, at the height of his power, the strong believe "God is on the side of the heaviest battalion." When a strong nation overrides a weak nation, it is the weak nation that cries: "Give me liberty or give me death." It is the weak nation that cries: "All men are created equal." The stronger knows that the strength of its arms makes nations unequal. So the weak try to curb the power of the strong by using the weapon of morality—the only weapon that the weak can use.

Examples from Everyday Life

Suppose that Sambo and Joe Louis get into a fight. Who would be the first to cry: "Oh, Lord, deliver me from this wicked brute"? Who would cry first for justice and mercy. The answer is obvious. When Joe Louis's two fists crashed against Sambo's chin, Sambo would shake heaven and earth with appeals to Man and God. Why? Because Sambo would know that the only weapon Sambo could use to curb the power of Joe Louis is the weapon of morality. If Sambo got the "drop" on Joe Louis with a forty-five, Sambo wouldn't even think about appealing to morality.

Take the Negro. The Negro is always appealing to the Constitution. Yes, Sambo is always telling the bad white folk about "the brotherhood of man and the fatherhood of God." People wonder why Negroes wear pants ragged at the knees. It's because Negroes stay on their knees begging for Democracy. Negroes sing spirituals to keep the white folk from lynching Negroes.

Do you know why Negroes sing "You Shall Reap Just What You Sow"? Well, the Negroes hope this song will scare the white folk. If Negroes had the power to knock the hell out of bad white folk, then the Negroes wouldn't sing "You Shall Reap Just What You Sow." If Negroes had the power to conquer the world they wouldn't sing "You Can Have All This World, Give Me Jesus." If Negroes had a powerful army, they wouldn't sing "Ain't Gonna Study War No More." Since the white man has the army and the navy, there's nothing for the Negro to do but say: "I ain't gonna study war no more."

Hitler and His Enemies

Read the newspapers of today and those of a year ago. Today Hitler boasts of his bombing planes and tanks. Today the English make frantic appeals to justice and democracy. The Negroes in the chain gang at Buzzard's Roost, Georgia, are not more "religious" than the once-proud conquering Englishmen. England, fearing the power of German armies, is doing exactly what poor Haile Selassie did five years ago: appealing to the conscience of the world for help.

When men are weak, they become moral. When men and nations are strong, they don't give a damn about morality. Fear makes men righteous. The Jew and the Negro are the world's most moral peoples, because they are the most persecuted. The Jew has given the world the profoundest moral principles.

Proud England, who walked the earth as conqueror for centuries, exploiting weaker peoples, is today appealing to justice and democracy. We Negroes can understand that. I'm wondering if Englishmen understand the pleas and prayers of black men in Africa and brown men in India.

Belgium cut off the hands of Africans in the Belgian Congo, when the Africans didn't bring in enough rubber. But when the Kaiser's armies overran Belgium in World War I, the Belgians cried for justice and mercy! Today, white Americans are talking frantically about democracy. Why? Because the white folk are scared. For seventy-five years black men begged for democracy, and the majority of whites paid no attention to the appeals of black men.

Maybe that old Negro mammy is wiser than our Big White Folk when she sings in the cotton patch: "You shall reap just what you sow!"

The One Man in the World
That Hitler Fears
September 14, 1940

When a columnist crawls out on a limb, every dumbbell belly laughs if the limb is sawed off. If you don't gamble, you never lose and never win. Thanks to Lady Luck, my guesses on international affairs give me a batting average of zero. Check back over your old *Tribunes*. In 1935, as a delegate to the International Exposition, at San Diego, I predicted the conquest of continental Europe by fascism, when the League of Nations let Mussolini gobble up Ethiopia.

I may be wrong this time; but I want to say a few things about Herr Hitler, the International Al Capone who was admired at the time by the Cliveden Elite of London.

In fact, if you've read Hitler's autobiography, *Mein Kampf,* and Dr. Eugeon Rosenstock-Huessy's *Out of Revolution,* and Kurt G. Ludecke's *I Knew Hitler*—well, you get a pretty good picture of Hitler and his aims. Most people see Hitler as the introvert. If Chamberlain and Daladier had read thoughtfully the above-mentioned books, there would've been no Munich and no war. Hitlerism would have been stopped dead.

The Man Hitler Fears

There is but one man in the world that Hitler fears. Hitler's cunning brain used Hitler's fears of that man to ruin nine European countries. A few men in England saw through Hitler's trick. Those men were H. G. Wells, Winston Churchill, and Dr. Briffault. Now the whole world knows the man whom Hitler fears. That man is Stalin. Since Hitler's fear of Stalin is greater than Hitler's hatred of Stalin, Hitler now appeases Stalin as Chamberlain appeased Hitler.

But let us go back to Hitler's book. Hitler gives Mr. Roosevelt a nightmare. But Stalin gives Hitler a dozen nightmares.

These are Hitler's own words from *Mein Kampf:* "The present rulers of Russia do not at all think of entering an alliance sincerely or of keeping one. We must never forget that the present regents of Russia are common bloodstained criminals . . . a rare mixture of bestial horror with an inconceivable gift of lying . . . advocates of lying, deceit, theft, rapine, and plundering. But one does not conclude a treaty with someone whose sole interest is the destruction of his partner.''

Hitler talked like that for ten years against Stalin; then, out of fear. While Hitler was plotting the downfall of France and England, he tricked the democracies by making them believe that Germany was arming herself to destroy Russian Communism. France and England fell for Hitler's big lie!

"Alone with Hitler"

This is the title of Chapter XXIV in Ludecke's book, *I Knew Hitler*. It gives you a keyhole peep into the mind of Hitler. The scene is at 10:30, September 12, 1932, in the famous Kaiserhof Hotel, in Berlin. There, Ludecke talked with his master, Hitler. They talked on the conquests of the future. If the statesmen of Europe had read seriously this chapter, the history of the world would have been different.

Again we see Hitler's fear of Stalin; also the trick Hitler used to fool the democracies. But let me give you Hitler's own words uttered so prophetically in 1932.

''I've got to play ball with England by holding aloft the bogey of Bolshevism—make them believe that a Nazi Germany is the last bulwark against the Red flood. That's the only way . . . to get rid of Versailles and re-arm. I talk peace, but mean war. . . . And if it's going to take bombs to show these gentlemen in London, Paris, and New York that I mean business, well, they can have them. . . . Suppose I came to an agreement with Stalin and proceeded accordingly. What if I were attacked . . . and Stalin should betray me— instead of helping us, should line up with our enemies?''

There you have the inside fears of Hitler. While his armies are spread out over western Europe, Hitler is scared that Stalin will stab him in the back. Hitler is a Nazi. Stalin is a Red. They are now strange bedfellows—and they lie awake, each with a knife in his hand for the other.

Why didn't Hitler attack Stalin, his arch enemy, instead of the democracies? Hitler told Ludecke this: If Hitler attacked Stalin, there might be two funerals instead of one. That's the all-in-all of the Russo-German Pact that shocked those timid minds that failed to read the facts. Sometimes I shall give the reports of the Japanese, Russian, French, and German military staffs on their estimates of the leading armies. Nobody in the democracies paid any attention to these reports which appeared before the war began. They are indeed illuminating.

Hitler's Fears Increase!

Read between the lines of your newspapers. Nobody knows just what move Stalin will make next. But Hitler knows Stalin will make any move that Stalin thinks will protect Russia.

B. C. Forbes said in his syndicated column on July 18: "There have been multiplying indications that Stalin is giving Hitler—and Mussolini—disturbing moments."

That's no lie. On the day before this, Josef Stalin, who rarely receives foreign envoys, was reported by the Associated Press to have had "a long talk with Sir Stafford Cripps, the Leftist British ambassador."

You can bet your boots that Premier Winston Churchill, who wanted to make a pact with Stalin before the war, had his hand in that particular piece of pie. Churchill is a realist. Churchill knows that things would look brighter for England, if Stalin set in motion, against Hitler, twelve million Red soldiers, ten thousand Red airplanes, and ten thousand Red tanks.

Hitler knows that, too. That's the reason he's so nice to Stalin. Nations, like individuals, follow their economic interests. The locomotive of history will make many a sudden and sharp turn before we get to heaven. So sit tight and act right. Hitler is watching Stalin more closely than Hitler is watching Churchill!

While Britain Is Getting Bundles
Let Sambo Get BVDs
March 15, 1941

All I don't know, I see in the newspapers. On the birthday of George Washington, a big headline appeared in the *Tribune*: "H.U. professor maintains Race faces peril. Dr. R. J. Bunche says Nazi victory would mean enslavement."

To face peril means to be exposed to danger. Now, it's impossible *to expose* my Race to danger. Every day in every year, including Leap Year, Negroes *catch* hell in the 48 States. The Negro is like the pickaninny in the story. The pickaninny did not *Face the peril* of the crocodile, because the pickaninny was already in the belly of the crocodile. A Nazi victory would not mean enslavement of the Negro, for the Negro is already enslaved. I know a *few* Big Negroes who enjoy a *few* privileges—accidentally. But that is not true of a few Jews in Germany!

Now, the Negro-hater in the United States is a rattlesnake. Hitler is a cobra. But I'm more afraid of the rattlesnake at home than I am of the cobra 5,000 miles across the Atlantic! I'm more afraid of the fascism of Senator Bilbo than of the fascism of Herr Hitler. I'm more afraid of the cops in Washington than of the gestapo in Berlin. No lie! Sambo, listen to this:

> Them Berlin cops knock the hell out of you;
> But them D.C. cops will do it too.

The History of the Big Boys in a Jam

Dr. Bunche will agree with me here. Whenever the Big Boys get in a jam, they always tell the little fellow this: "If we go down, you go down!"

I tell a story with a moral. A bulldog and a little cur lived in the same yard. The cur was skinny and hungry, because the fat bulldog ate the meat and left the cur the bone. One day the bulldog got into a fight with a German Police dog. The bulldog yelped for the cur to help him.

The bulldog said: "Cur, if this *mean* old German Police gets me, he'll get you next!"

So the cur went to the rescue. In the struggle, the little cur got his throat cut. You see, Sambo, so far as the cur was concerned, it didn't matter a damn which Big Dog won. The cur wasn't going to get anything but a bone anyway! Maybe, if the cur had had sense, he'd got a piece of meat for himself while the Big Dogs were fighting! Instead of looking after his *own* business, the cur was looking after the business of the bulldog! Ain't that something!

When the Germans had colonies in Africa, the black man caught hell. Then the English took over the German colonies with the help of Negroes, and the black man still caught hell!

> So it don't mean a thing
> If you ain't white like the King!

Instead of getting bundles for Britain, you black folk had better get BVDs for Sambo. Winston Churchill hasn't promised the Negro anything! Every time the Big Boys get in a jam, they always say to the little fellows: "If we go down, you go down!" How can the Negro *go* down when he's already down? The masses of Negroes are so far down in ignorance and illiteracy, poverty and jim crowism, that they don't know there is a Constitution in D.C.

Yes, Lord, the White Folk Are Scared!

Why shouldn't they be? The big white man has the world in a jug, and the stopper in his hand. No lie. He eats his pie NOW, and wants me to wait until I'm dead to get mine. The big Englishman and the big American strut up and down the earth like De Lawd in *The Green Pastures!* Hitler is after the dough. But I ain't got none. My pa and grandpa never had none!

Dr. Bunche is scared. I am, too. I'm scared of jim crowism and lynching. I get scared every time Churchill says *Democracy* over the radio. I knew a man, once, who choked to death on a lie!

Columnist George Schuyler says: "One of the strangest creatures tossed up by the current crisis is the pro-British Negro. He baffles anthropologists and psychologists alike."

Columnist Joseph D. Bibb says: "We have been dying too much for glory and patriotism. After the last World War many of our overseas veterans were beaten up in the South because they wore the uniform of this great Democracy."

Columnist J. A. Rogers says: "Of course, I'd rather deal with Hitler than with such antediluvian race-haters as Cotton Ed Smith, Bilbo, and Byrnes. Hitler, at least, is not a Bible spouter, like these Congressional renegades."

We Shall Live under Bilbos—Not Hitler

Will Great Britain win? I don't know. And you don't know. I love my native land. I believe if we get in that European hell we'll get messed up. George Washington told us to stay out of "entangling alliances abroad." Walter Winchell says Washington made an alliance with France during the Revolutionary War! True. But French soldiers came over here. George Washington had sense enough not to send American soldiers "Over There." And George Washington warned us years *after* our alliance with France—and America was free! Mr. Winchell overlooked *that*. George Washington used France; he didn't let France use America!

Negroes must fight on the American Front. Not the European Front. We'll never live under Adolf Hitler. We shall live under the Bilbos. A Nazi army will never invade the United States. That is a geographical and military impossibility. Russia has far more to fear from Germany than the United States. Proletarian Communism and capitalistic fascism are eternal enemies. Yet Russia is not rushing into that European war. After the war, revolutions are going to sweep all over Europe. Chaos will prevail.

The United States should remain out of the conflict so that she will be ready for the aftermath. Why should we disrupt our country? We have enough problems to solve as it is. Europe will have to save herself. Remember the tragedy of Woodrow Wilson. If the Big Boys in Europe had really wanted Democracy, they would not

have created a Frankenstein monster like Hitler. Let us build
Democracy at home. Then, by our splendid example, all the continents will imitate us. An ounce of practice is worth a million tons of
theory. While Britain is getting bundles, let Sambo get BVDs!

The Man Who Was Chained to a Corpse
March 22, 1941

Take a good look at the man. He is condemned to die. The death
cart is ready. In the bottom of the cart is a dead body. The guards
are ready. It is a hot day. The journey is long and dusty. Suddenly
the silence is rent by the screams of a woman. She is the wife of the
criminal. Her companions hold her back as she struggles hyster-
ically to go to the rescue of the condemned man.

Then the death cart moves away. It moves beyond the walls of
the city. Beyond even the last habitation of living men. Hours later
the guards get out of the death cart. Before them is a massive pillar.
And near it human skeletons. The criminal is sullen and speechless, as the guards chain him to the pillar. Then the guards take the
corpse and chain it to the man. Finally, the guards get into the cart
and drive off. Soon the air is split by the unearthly screams of the
criminal. The guards look back and see the condemned man in-
sanely struggling against the chains. Above the naked criminal and
the naked corpse, circle the huge vultures of the desert. That's the
way justice was served in an Oriental city 2,000 years ago!

While Millions Listened In

It is March 15, 1941. The scene is the ballroom of the Willard
Hotel in the Nation's Capital. It is the annual dinner of the White
House Correspondents' Association. President Roosevelt stands
between two flags: the Stars and Stripes and the blue flag that
symbolizes the highest office in the Republic.

Seated just in front of and below the President are Wendell L.
Willkie and Lord Halifax, the British Ambassador. Mr.
Roosevelt's appeal for the preservation of Democracy goes out
over the big networks and by short wave in fourteen languages,
including those of all the German occupied nations.

The President says in a strong voice: "The British people and
their Greek allies need ships. From America, they will get ships.
They need food. From America, they will get food."

The President's words cross the oceans. In a London bomb
shelter, a poverty-stricken Englishman, his wife, and his children

clap their hands violently. In a Greek dugout, the soldiers kick up their heels and shout for joy.

The President continues in a strong voice: "We believe the rallying cry of the dictators, their boasting about a master race, will prove to be pure stuff and nonsense. There never has been, there isn't now and never will be any race of people fit to serve as masters over their fellowmen."

When the President utters these words, they enter a brokendown cabin in Mississippi. About the radio sit a black sharecropper and his poverty-stricken family.

The oldest child says: "Dad, is President Roosevelt talking about Senator Bilbo and the white folks in Vicksburg?"

The father replies sadly: "No, son, Mr. Roosevelt is talking about Hitler and the Nazis. He ain't thinking about us black folks on Major Doolittle's plantation."

Democracy Chained to the Corpse of Jim Crowism!

In America, we have revived the old Oriental custom of chaining a man to a corpse until both rot away! While the President is making his brave speech to the nations, in the famous Willard Hotel, Democracy is chained to the rotten corpse of jim crowism!

The President says in a strong voice: "A few weeks ago I spoke of four freedoms—freedom of speech and expression, freedom of every person to worship God in his own way, freedom from want, freedom from fear."

And even while the President utters these fine phrases, Democracy struggles to free herself from the chains of segregation and lynching. Democracy clutches in her hand the Bill of Rights. Democracy cries to Justice and humanity to deliver her. And, above outraged Democracy, circle the vultures of Hitler and Bilbo. They are waiting for the great feast of fascism.

Democracy cries: "All men are created equal!"

But the cry of Democracy is lost in the platitudes of the President and in the victorious squawks of the vultures of Hitler and Bilbo.

Democracy sees black men who are taxed and disfranchised, and Democracy shouts: "Taxation without representation is tyranny!"

A group of Southern Senators pass by, on the other side—and laugh. Democracy is left to die and rot, chained to the stinking corpse of jim crowism!

While Rome Burns

The legend goes that, while Rome burned, Nero fiddled. While

Democracy was chained to the rotten corpse of jim crowism, the Big Boys in the Willard Hotel had a movie. It was called—of all things—*It Ain't Necessarily So*. But get this. The movie was shown just before Mr. Roosevelt delivered his speech! The movie had two titles, however. As you know, the picture was made by the White House Correspondents' Association. Its other title was this: *All We Know Is What They Let Us Write in the Papers*. Ain't that something—coming from newspapermen!

I wonder what passed through the mind of the President as he looked at that movie with its ironical titles. As the President thought about his fine phrases on Democracy, did he think: "It ain't necessarily so?"

I doubt it. Democracy is still chained to the corpse of jim crowism. Do big white men want to loose Democracy and let her go? I doubt it. Why? They are scared of the corpse of jim crowism. They are scared of being called Negro-lovers. They want the profits of racial prejudice. Hitler and Bilbo know this. That's the reason they squawk about race superiority. That's the reason they tramp upon minority groups.

As Negroes, we might as well get this in our heads. The masses of Negroes and the masses of poor whites will have to cut the corpse of jim crowism from Democracy. The Negroes' salvation lies with the masses of the Labor movement. There is no other way. Any other way is a way that seems right to man but the end thereof is death.

A Story That the White Folk Wouldn't Publish
May 3, 1941

Sambo had just got off from work. Tired and hungry, he was on his way to his tumbledown shack across town. He fingered the nickels and pennies in his pocket, wondering how he'd be able to buy his kid a pair of shoes for the closing of school. His feet dragged. Those twelve hours on the job!

As he neared the White House, he saw a huge crowd of white folk. He heard curses and profanity. In the mob he recognized several Congressmen from the South. Their faces were distorted with rage.

The crowd surrounded a giant of a man, the object of their violence. Sambo was shocked. He couldn't believe his eyes. Yes, he knew the victim. He'd often heard white folk talk about the blond giant. His name was Democracy! And the white folks were beating him up! But Democracy had plenty of guts. He struck vicious blows right and left. Sambo got hot in the collar. He started to go to the help of Democracy; then he thought about that huge mob of white folk. What could he do against a world of white folk?

Democracy Goes Down Under the Attack

Suddenly, Senator Bilbo stepped forward. He delivered a battery of brutal uppercuts at Democracy's face. Democracy tried to cover, but he couldn't ward off the sizzling attack of the gentleman from Mississippi. Democracy's eyes were now swollen and bleeding.

Then Mr. Jim Crow launched his trip-hammer blows. Democracy retreated under this furious onslaught. The crowd of whites laughed and jeered as Jim Crow slammed his iron fists below Democracy's beltline and delivered the illegal rabbit-punch in close exchanges. Sambo saw the helpless appeal in the face of the blond giant, and his sympathy went out to him.

Then a miracle happened. Democracy, on the verge of collapse, suddenly began to gather nerve and strength from some hidden source. He took the lead away from Jim Crow. He lashed out with rights and lefts, toe-to-toe. The white faces went pale.

Sambo yelled, "Give 'im hell, Democracy! Give Jim Crow hell!"

The white mob turned in astonishment and gazed at the little black man. Then they threatened him and cursed him and told him to stay in his place. Fear put its icy fingers around Sambo's heart. He wanted to leave. But something held him to the spot. Perhaps it was the way that Democracy was volleying shots to every portion of Jim Crow's body. Jim Crow was holding on now, trying to save himself.

At that moment Judge Lynch strode forward. He began beating Democracy over the head with the butt of his forty-five. The mob screamed its delight. Judge Lynch struck Democracy in the temple, whipped the weapon against his skull, and then hammered his chin. Democracy dropped to his knees in a bloody heap. Sambo saw an elderly white gentleman bend over the blond giant. Sambo thought he looked like a picture he'd seen of Thomas Jefferson.

The Coming of Hitler!

Then came a terrifying confusion of mixed sounds. It rent the distant horizon. The crowd grew still. Sambo heard the awful groans of Democracy and gazed fearfully at the battered figure of the blond giant. Afar off he heard the roar of powerful bombing planes and the rumble of tanks.

A bleeding Englishman staggered up the street crying: "Hitler! Hitler! Holland and Belgium and France and Greece have fallen! We must stop Hitler! We must save civilization!"

The fires of burning cities flared along the horizon. The earth shook from distant explosions. Sambo heard the tramp of mighty armies. Sambo looked at Democracy. The crowd of white faces looked at Democracy.

Somebody cried frantically, "Democracy, you must save us!"

Democracy rubbed a huge hand across his bloody and battered face. He seemed to be trying to remember something. Yes, he'd heard that appeal before—at Bunker Hill, at the Bastille, at Gettysburg, at Verdun. It was the same old story.

The Englishman was on his knees beside Democracy. Agony was in the Englishman's voice: "You alone can save us."

Democracy said, "I'm weak. You fellows have weakened me. I tried to save you in Spain and Ethiopia and Manchuria. But you fellows double-crossed me. When I get you fellows upstairs, you kick me downstairs. It's been going on for a long time. You fellows won't play fair. I've lost a lot of blood."

Sambo and Democracy

As Democracy lay there in agony, Sambo felt a big wave of courage surging up in his heart. Tears were in the eyes of the little black man. He'd heard a great deal about Democracy, but he'd never seen the giant who'd always fought for justice and freedom. Sambo knelt by the side of the bloody hero, *his* hero—the hero of Thomas Jefferson and L'Ouverture and Fred Douglass and John Brown.

Sambo put his head close to the lips of Democracy, and he heard the words: "Those who should've defended me have betrayed me. A house divided against itself cannot stand."

"I ain't never betrayed you!" cried Sambo. "I've been fighting for you a long, long time."

Democracy looked up in surprise. His dazed eyes focused on the worn black face.

Sambo was still talking: "Democracy, we got just one more chance."

Democracy inquired painfully: "What's that, Sambo?"

Sambo thought fast: "Listen, Democracy. We gotta get rid of these Judases in our ranks. We got to rub out old Jim Crow and Judge Lynch. Hitler can't do nothing with us if we get rid of them double-crossers."

Suddenly a change came over Democracy. He stood up. He shook himself. A strange fire came into his eyes.

Democracy said: "Sambo, you know your stuff. It's those Fifth Columnists, Jim Crow and Judge Lynch, that are messing up things. We can't have a national defense with those rattlesnakes poisoning the blood of America."

"Okay," said Sambo. "Democracy, let's get going!"

"Are You Digging on My Grave?"
May 31, 1941

Most of the people I meet are scared to death. There is wailing in the land. During the last month, I've visited seven states. Darkness covers the land, like midnight in a jungle swamp. The monster of Nazism has filled the people with a terrible awe.

Yet, I'm an optimist. I'm not scared, because I saw chaos coming six years ago. Then, I've certain principles that Hitler can't defeat. Truth crushed to earth will rise again and knock the hell out of you!

Nazism has been coming for One Hundred Years. Its seeds were planted during the Industrial Revolution. For fifty years, men had been losing faith in men. Cut-throat competition had reduced men to predatory animals. In the 20's our everyday philosophy had been reduced to "the survival of the slickest." Dishonesty became the best policy. An honest man was an uncaught crook. A virtuous woman was a woman who knew "how to take care of herself." We said you had to do the other fellow before he did you.

The scientist reduced God to $qp - pq = ih/2''$. Everybody looked out for himself. $$s spelled success. We started worshiping titles and degrees instead of brains and character. The wise guys told us that Big Business could save humanity. Of course, I wasn't fool enough to believe that. A fine house was supposed to make a home. Now, even Senator Bilbo admits we're in a mess.

The Reign of the Graveyard Boys

After the first World War, the graveyard boys came into power. These cynics said: "Eat, drink, and be merry, for tomorrow we die." Of course, they didn't tell us what to do if we ate and drank everything today and didn't die tomorrow. This was the Booze Era of the Lost Generation.

And now we come to the poet, Thomas Hardy, who saw men and women as pawns in a losing game. He voided the pessimism of the English countryside, towns, and cities. Let us look at that poem,

"Ah, Are You Digging on My Grave?" Old man Hardy had a graveyard philosophy. No lie!

If Hardy lived today, he would say, in the words of the song: "It ain't what you do, and it ain't how you do it."

So Hardy went to a woman's grave. The dead sister heard somebody digging on her grave. She thought it was her sweetheart. But it wasn't. He'd married a dame with the bucks.

Who was it, then? Her closest relative? No. Her dearest kin had decided that there wasn't any need of planting flowers on the grave, because the dead don't know anything about flowers anyway.

Then, was it her enemy? No. Her enemy no longer thought her worth a lifetime of hate. In fact, her enemy didn't care where she was buried, since death had put her out of the way! You see, we can't get much of a kick out of hating the dead! Yet, I think it's better to hate the dead than the living. Of course, mouth-Christians won't agree with me on this.

"Then Who Is Digging on My Grave?"

For the fourth time the dead woman asked the question. If it wasn't her lover, her dearest relative, her enemy—then who could it be? In that moment her little dog answered. It was he digging on his mistress's grave. He hoped his movements hadn't disturbed her.

The dead mistress was overcome with joy. At least, her little dog hadn't forgotten her! Why hadn't she remembered? So the dead lady began to bless the little dog. He was more loyal than human beings. Dogs are such faithful animals!

Then the little dog began to explain to his mistress why he was digging on her grave:

> Mistress, I dug upon your grave
>   To bury a bone, in case
> I should be hungry near this spot
> When passing on my daily trot.
> I am sorry, but I quite forgot
>   It was your resting-place.

Even the dog was thinking about his belly. He'd forgot all about his dead mistress. Well, Sambo, it seems to me that this poem by old Thomas Hardy just about sums up the graveyard philosophy of the world. Just as the little dog was hiding his bone from the other dogs, men were hiding their filthy dollars.

Digging on the Grave of Humanity

Seeing how our dollar philosophy has led to war and imperialism, I come to the awful conclusion that the Big Boys are digging on the grave of humanity. Yes, they've buried the bones of their exploitation in graveyards. Nazism is a grave robber. You get what I mean.

Now, if we had spent as much time cultivating the brotherhood of man, the world would be different. But we were wise guys. Altruistic thinkers couldn't tell us anything. The way of human exploitation, which seemed right to us, has led to destruction.

Now, in this crisis we're scared to death. We had a chance to drive the moneylenders from the temple; but we didn't have the guts to do that. We had a chance to practice economic equality, social justice, and racial tolerance; but we scorned the virtues of democracy. Now, we're scared.

Now, the monster, Hitler, is digging on the graves of Europe and Africa. He's hiding his dead bones of Nazism. He's even digging up the bones hidden by the English bulldog. We betrayed humanity and democracy in Ethiopia, China, Spain, and Czechoslovakia. Now, we're scared. Men do crazy things when they get scared.

This is a time for sanity. This is a time for housecleaning. This is a time for truth to speak. Away with hysteria! Away with the graveyard philosophy of cynicism and defeatism and compromises! If you stick to your principles, you won't be forgotten in Life or in Death. I know plenty of dead men who are alive! And I know plenty of live men who are dead!

A Red Russian Made History,
Sunday, July 19, 1942
July 25, 1942

If you don't throw a bouquet at the Red Russians today, you're a Fifth Columnist. With General MacArthur calling the Reds the greatest fighters in history, there is nothing Sambo can say but "Amen!" I thought, in the very beginning and said so, that Hitler would catch hell in Russia. But the Russians have shocked me. They sure have the big stuff.

I knew they'd made, in twenty years, progress 1,000 times more rapid than any other people. I knew there is no such thing as a race problem in the "Godless country." Yes, there're 200 races over

there, varying from white to black. Of course, as a black man I ain't
kicking off nobody who gets rid of a race problem.

But I'm writing this week about a Russian composer. Yes, the
greatest composer in the world today is a doggone Red! (O Lord
Jesus, help Uncle Joe Stalin to hold Hitler until Uncle Sam gets his
gun loaded!)

Sunday afternoon, at 3:15, I sat beside my neighbor's radio. My
own radio is like the Defense Program: it suffers from *bottlenecks*.
Toscanini, the world's greatest conductor, was directing Comrade
Dimitri Shostakovich's "Seventh Symphony." Don't try to call
that name, Sambo; just say, "Comrade DS."

The Fighting Composer of Leningrad

Now, in order to understand the Reds, you have to have imagination. No lie. Of course, if the League of Nations had understood the Reds five years ago, Hitler would have been stopped five
years ago. But we live and learn—I hope.

Now, this man Comrade DS writes the world's greatest symphony with the German bombs falling around, and he serves as a
soldier fire fighter in Leningrad! Then, the Red novelist, Eugene
Petrov, writes a novel while the Germans are bombing the hell out
of Sevastopol, and he's serving as a colonel!

Now, one thing I know: a Christian is not scared to die. Only
infidels are scared to die, because they're going to hell. I wonder
how many Christians would write a symphony or a novel with
bombs falling around their heads and feet!

So Comrade DS wrote his masterpiece, and stopped Hitler's
roughnecks at the same time! Some guts! The music was reduced
to microfilm and put in 200 frames. It came to America by way of
Cairo. Now, what I don't know about music would fill the universe. But I got sense enough to read what the critics say and then
try to learn. Of course, the time is coming when every child in
America will understand the masterpieces of music and art. Russian peasants discuss Shakespeare like Harvard professors. Russians believe in culture for everybody. That's right!

So I sat at my radio and tried to understand what Comrade DS
was saying to the world through music. I understand "Minnie the
Moocher" and "The Delta Stomp." I understand how Joe Louis
yearns for an education. So do I yearn for music culture.

The Ideas of the Seventh Symphony

Now, what makes Comrade DS great is what he makes notes
say. His music ushers in a New World.

John Rosenfield, the famous critic of the *Dallas Morning News,* says: "Psychologically this indicates a clamorously revolutionary spirit that breaks the bonds of musical convention as the workers of the world loose their chains with a shout and blow."

This critic reminds us that Beethoven also produced his master-pieces "in a revolution that had as its central idea the notion that a man was a man."

Toscanini, admirer of our own Marian Anderson, was anxious to direct this symphony of a New World. I am sure that, as an Italian, he is sick of the Old World of Sawdust Caesar Mussolini and the exploiters of mankind.

Comrade DS's symphony was heard round the world. I'm sure that in the conquered countries of Europe, where the people know more about great music than we do, this broadcast symphony was a herald of the new freedom.

I believe this war will do more to blot out racial, denominational, political, social, and economic lines than any other in history. True, it started out as just another war. However, today, it is becoming a people's war. Of course, there are some old fogies who're still trying to hold on to their class and racial prejudices. But the nails are now being put in their coffins.

For one thing, you cannot scare the average man by crying "Red" or "Radical" or "Infidel" everytime a sensible man advo-cates a change. Of course, I've never been able to understand how a Negro with bedbug sense could object to a change in things.

An Open Letter to
Senator Bankhead of Alabama
August 8, 1942

On Northern Negro Soldiers in Southern Camps

Dear Fifth Columnist:

This is the first time I've ever written to one of Hitler's buddies. As an American citizen, I hate the guts of fascists, both at home and abroad. Soon our Commander-in-Chief, President Roosevelt, will announce his decision on the eight Nazi agents. If justice were done, you'd be the ninth member of that treacherous group. You're trying, by subversive hell-tactics, to do the dirty job these eight Nazis attempted.

You're more dangerous than they, because you're boring from within. A rattlesnake in the bosom of our democracy is more dangerous than one imported from Nazi-land. You have no more right to sit in the U.S. Senate than the chief gangster of the gestapo. The speeches you make to the poor benighted whites of Alabama are pages taken from Hitler's bible, *Mein Kampf.* You are a disgrace to decency.

The Associated Press reports that you suggested to Gen. George C. Marshall, Army chief-of-staff, that Northern Negro soldiers should not be quartered in the South. That is none of your damned business. Uncle Sam puts Negro patriots where he wants to put them. You two-bit cracker cottonfield demagogs from 'Bam' are always trying to dictate national policies.

This very barbarous suggestion shows that you should've been named *Blankhead* instead of Bankhead! Nobody with as much sense as an Alabama boll weevil would have made such a crazy suggestion at such a critical time.

Senator Blankhead, why are you scared of Northern Negro soldiers? Ain't you living right? Is something rotten in the cottonfields and courthouses of Alabama? Are you big crackers fleecing the poor whites and the poor Negroes? Are the Negroes down there discussing the poll tax? Is it that you white folk are violating the Bill of Rights and the Constitution?

Why should any Americans who respect and uphold the Constitution object to other Americans coming into their State? If the books are clean and white in Alabam, why object to their being examined by fellow citizens?

Is Senator Blankhead scared Northern Negro soldiers will mistake Alabam for Hitler's Germany? The wicked fleeth when no man pursueth. Amen! Is Senator Blankhead scared that Northern soldiers will resent gestapo methods in Alabam?

Victory at Home and Abroad

Senator Blankhead, in this crisis of our nation, we have to get down to brass tacks. Therefore, two questions face every American. First, do you know what Democracy is? Second, do you believe in Democracy?

If you are not too blank, you know what Democracy is. If you are against Hitler, you believe in Democracy. If you believe in Democracy, then you will eat those undemocratic words you vomited against Northern soldiers.

You cannot serve two masters—Democracy and Negrophobia, Christianity and Race-prejudice, the Constitution and crackerism, Americanism and jim crowism.

You say Northern soldiers will cause trouble in the South.

That's a lie, a monkey-faced lie, as big as any Hitler ever told. It is thoughtless men like you who cause trouble in Alabama and in Congress.

There are progressive white Americans in the South who believe in Democracy, fair play, and winning the war. Senator Blankhead, you are as far from these true Americans as heaven is from hell.

American soldiers should be treated like American soldiers. Anybody who insults a soldier in the uniform of our country should be treated as a Hitlerite. On this policy no true American will budge a fraction of an inch.

Your suggestion to General Marshall was an insult. When you made that infamous suggestion, you stabbed America in the back with an Alabam jackknife. Why should Uncle Sam disrupt our war program to soothe the racial prejudices of cottonfield crackers and two-bit demagogs? If Uncle Sam has to quarter soldiers in our homes to win the war, let him do it!

White Men among Yellow
and Brown and Black Women
October 3, 1942

As a nation, the Russians are the only white men who respect yellow and brown and black women. But more of that later. Of course, color doesn't mean a damned thing to me. But it is a matter of life and death to most whites—yes, and to most Sambos who blindly imitate whites. I agree with the anthropologists, Dr. Boas and Paul Radin, that race is a Zero. *Man* is important. Men are big when they see *Man*.

Today we are fighting for the Four Freedoms. At least, the white radios in Dallas, Birmingham, Atlanta, and Chitterling Switch tell me that, when it's sleepy time down South.

So let us grant that the whites are fighting to make the world safe for the Four Freedoms. Now, you Sambos and Aunt Hagars stop squawking: "It ain't necessarily so."

This is a global war. We mean by that, Sambo, there ain't no place on Mother Earth where we ain't fighting for the Four Freedoms.

White Men in Foreign Countries

Now, millions of white soldiers will find themselves in the four corners of the world. In a military way they will be the best equipped soldiers in the world. But that will not be the most important thing. We cannot win this war without the United Nations. To get their help we must be the best propagandists in the world. Read that sentence a hundred times. Tell it to the President, to Congress, to the whites. We cannot win without the support of a billion of yellows and browns and blacks.

The war cannot be won unless white soldiers know how to treat the women of other races. White men have been taught for generations that whiteness is a sign of superiority. Soldiers take their women where they find them. How will white soldiers mix with yellow and brown and black women? Will these Caucasians treat the darker women with contempt, as cheap playthings? If they do, these whites will create an Atlantic Ocean of resentment and hate among both sexes of the darker races. Do our statesmen realize this?

Today, white soldiers are unprepared for this job. As fighters for Democracy, they haven't been taught Democracy at Home. Therefore, they are taking their hellish racial prejudices to Africa, South America, China, India, and the islands of the seas. We cannot win the war by killing a few hundred Japanese and making thousands of enemies among colored peoples through racial prejudices.

England discovered that fact in Burma and India. Our most effective propaganda is the practice of Democracy among the colored races.

Walter White and the NAACP

Mr. White has suggested that Secretary Stimson create a bureau of interracial good will for the army and navy. No better program has been suggested for winning the war. We cannot win the war without the good will of millions of yellows and browns and blacks.

I shall quote from a white Southerner, whose letter appears in the *Shreveport Times* (Louisiana). Maurice Tatum graduated from Louisiana Tech, where he was vice-president of the International Relations Club. He is now a soldier in India.

Mr. Tatum writes: "There are some white women here (at least two), but they are afraid of American soldiers. The Indian women (there are plenty of them) think we are wild men from a circus. . . ."

This needs no comment. It bears out Mr. White's suggestion. In Louisiana and Georgia and Mississippi, white men are not taught HOW to behave among dark women. Yet these men are sent abroad as representatives of Democracy! Yes, we need the VV here and in India.

There is no racial prejudice in Russia. The Russian soldier is taught (in the army and out) to respect the women and men of all races. The soldiers of many nations fought with the Chinese army. But an American reporter said the Russian soldiers alone treated Chinese women as women. This reporter said the Russians didn't even visit the whorehouses. Of course, there are no whorehouses in Russia itself. I suspect the Russians are going to teach us mouth-Christians a lot of things before this war is over.

Remember Africa at the Peace Table
November 21, 1942

Before me lies a picture of black troops, under the French flag, that defend Tunisia, in northern Africa. They are magnificent men, tall, broad-shouldered, as brave as any soldiers in the world today. The paper wants to know if these soldiers will oppose the Americans. That is a big question. European nations have often used black soldiers in Africa to fight for white men in Europe.

Mr. Churchill said: "The Allied nations have no wish but to see France free and strong."

We Negroes have no wish but to see Africa free and strong. Too long has Africa been the football of Europeans. I hope the United Nations take the Four Freedoms to the peace table. We have the Atlantic Charter. The Chinese are asking for a Pacific Charter. But I never hear any of the white mouth-Christians talking about the Africa Charter.

Africa: The Bloody Question Mark of Centuries

I once heard Dr. Aggrey, the black South African, call Africa the question mark of the centuries. This bloody question mark has faced every civilized nation. No white nation has been moral enough to answer the Africans with justice and democracy.

Every world conquerer has tried to conquer Africa. But in time Africa has swallowed them all. If I were a Shakespeare, I would write a tragedy greater than *Hamlet,* greater than *King Lear,* greater than *Macbeth*. It would be called *The Tragedy of Africa*.

Out of Greece came Alexander the Great. He took the phalanx, developed by his father, and ran through the famous Persian Empire like Joe Louis's fist going through tissue paper. He built Alexandria, in Egypt, as a monument to his power. It is said that Alexander wept because he couldn't find any more worlds to conquer. Then he went to the foot of Mt. Olympus, where the gods of the Greeks lived, and told the gods to march forth and he'd take "heaven" by storm. But Africa swallowed the armies of the Greeks.

Napoleon, master of strategists, invaded Africa. He stood in front of the pyramids and said to his soldiers: "Twenty centuries look down upon you." But the African sands swallowed Napoleon's army.

And now the armies of Hitler and Mussolini are being swallowed in the African sands. Yes, Black Boy, Africa will swallow many a white army after we are dead and gone.

The African Charter

I do not like the words of Mr. Churchill when he says: "We mean to hold our own. I have not become the King's first Minister in order to preside over the liquidation of the British Empire."

I am sorry Mr. Churchill lost his head and uttered those words. Vice-President Wallace has told us that this is the Century of the Common Man. Mr. Roosevelt has told us we are fighting for the Four Freedoms of Mankind. Now Mr. Churchill tells us we are fighting to preserve the British Empire. That's exactly what the millions of India have been saying. How will these unfortunate words of Mr. Churchill affect the smaller members of the United Nations?

Every nation should rule itself. As old Abe Lincoln said: "No man is good enough to be the master of another."

We want an Africa Charter. I see now that the Atlantic Charter doesn't cover everything. I see why the Chinese and Hindus are doubting Thomases. In this World War II we must clean the Germans and Italians out of Africa. Then at the peace table the English and French must be told to take their little suitcases and leave. We want Africa for the Africans. Come on with the Africa Charter.

The Buzzards in the Senate of the U.S.A.
November 28, 1942

Hitler and Mussolini and Tojo lost battles this week in North Africa and the Pacific. A wave of enthusiasm swept over the United Nations. While the peoples shouted with joy, they could still hear the hammer blows of the Russians at Stalingrad, putting nails in the coffins of the Fascists.

Then came a big noise on Capitol Hill. It was the fight over the Anti-Poll Tax Bill, which would free the white and black masses in the Bible Belt. In the Senate of the United States, Hitler and Mussolini and Tojo won a big battle for fascism. Yes, senatorial buzzards, like Bilbo, feasted on the rot in our Democracy. While these buzzards devoured the hand that fed them, Hitler and Mussolini and Tojo gave the belly laugh in Berlin and Rome and Tokyo.

Millions of American citizens ground their teeth in impotent rage. The United Nations watched the horrible spectacle. Democracy—what infamy is committed in thy name?

Bilbo and Connally and George

We are told that Senators, paid by the people, had to be arrested and brought to the Senate to do their duty. This is a shame before God and Man. No wonder the enemies of mankind are always shouting about inefficiency of democracies! While our young men die for Freedom on desert sands and in jungle wastes, Bilbo of Mississippi and Connally of Texas and George of Georgia gut the heart and suck the blood of Democracy.

Bilbo, who is alleged to be after the Devil's position as the Father of Lies, said that "educated" Negroes were with him. If he will name those black Uncle Toms, Black America will take care of them!

George added to the filibuster by saying: "There might be a lot of misplaced commas in the *Journal* that require correction and debate."

O'Daniel of Texas tried to stall by bringing up the question of voting on a dead man's bill concerning dry zones around army camps.

McKellar of Kentucky attacked his old friend and colleague, Senator Barkley, who may go to the Supreme Court.

While the world looked on, the buzzards from the South gorged themselves and created a stench in the nostrils of free men. A billion colored peoples of the world will discuss this tragic scene in our Democracy. Already they look at us with eyes of doubt.

What This Filibuster Means to Americans

This filibuster means that we must fight the enemies within as never before. The solid South means to remain solid and defeat Democracy.

Here is a lesson for Negroes and their friends. I've always said that the biggest enemy of the Race is the Big White Man. Not the little ones. Bilbo and Connally and George represent the ruling class of the South. They are the descendants of the antebellum Cotton Empire. They are the heirs of the Ku Klux Klan. They control the schools and churches and newspapers. They spread the lies about race superiority and social equality.

These buzzards will die before they let the Negro get Justice. They are like the copperheads that opposed Abe Lincoln. They are the Lavals and Quislings in our midst. They would rather see the fascists win than see the Negro with Democracy! So be not deceived. Know them.

Now is the time for the Negro and all true Americans to gird their loins for battle. We shall not retreat one step from the goal of Justice. These cracker Senators believe keeping the Negro down is more important than winning the war. Through this hellish filibuster, they have tied up the whole War effort. How shall we answer them?

We shall answer in the words of Macbeth: "Lay on, Macduff, and damned be him who first cries, 'Hold, enough?' "

Don't Count on Miracles in This War
February 2, 1943

Mr. Franklin D. Roosevelt's speech, on the night of February 22, was a masterpiece of realism and common sense. We Americans—and the good white folks, especially—have not got down to the dirty business of blood and sweat and tears. The Big Boys are still trying to crush the little fellows. The Bilbos are still trying to crush the Negro.

Mr. Roosevelt sang the praises of the big Red army. Of course, that's like saying, "The sun is shining," a bright noonday. Yes, the Reds have proved the world a world of liars and dumbbells—at least when it came to judging the Reds. Of course, I did more watching the Reds than kicking them off—so I don't have anything to swallow now. In fact, as a black man, I have too much sense to kick off anybody who practices "racial democracy."

So let us look at some high points in Mr. Roosevelt's speech. He said a mouthful, if you ask me. I hope the Big Boys upstairs got an earful. Maybe, then, they'll stop some of their monkey business and return to the Constitution. Of course, I doubt this.

The Walls of Jericho

Listen to Mr. Roosevelt: "Others among us believe in the age of miracles. They forget that there is no Joshua in our midst. We cannot count on great walls crumbling and falling when the trumpets blow and the people shout."

Mr. Roosevelt summed up the attitudes of great numbers of Americans. We want Nazism crushed; but we still want to drive the old car to the ball game. We want Nazism crushed; but we still want to squeeze the dirty profits out of Labor and the Public. We want Nazism crushed; but we want to keep the Negro in the white folk's kitchen.

We want to eat our cake—and have it too!

Yes, that is the good old American way! So we lie to ourselves. We expect God to strike Hitler dead. Or the Russians to bleed their way into Berlin. Or an earthquake to blow up Tokyo. Or the conquered peoples to topple the gestapo.

In other words, we want to go back to the good old days of Joshua. We want to blow the horn and shout. Then the walls of the Jericho of fascism will come tumbling down. Ain't that something?

Wolves in Sheep's Clothing

Mr. Roosevelt took a rap at the Peglers and Dies and Bilbos. Our President reminded us that, during the American Revolution, there were Benedict Arnolds who sold out the country.

At that same time, there were wolves in sheep's clothing—men who sneered at the Declaration of Independence. Those liars said the brotherhood of man was impractical. I almost hate the words *practical* and *impractical*. They cover up a multitude of evils.

Those cynics of the American Revolution booed at the phrase *all men are created equal*. They considered it idealistic. Of course, the Old South used the same argument against the freedom of the Negroes. The Old South said the monkey and the Negro had two things in common: lack of intelligence and lack of a soul.

Today, the liars are shouting again: "Impractical! Idealistic!"

Every time a good man advocates improvements, some idiot hollers: "It's agin human nature!"

We are out to make a better world. Mr. Roosevelt, in spite of the traitors around him, shows that he has not lost his ideals. Our destiny as a race and as a country is bound with the destinies of China and Russia. We are going to build a World Charter. We shall not let either hell or Martin Dies keep us from building a World Charter!

The Four Freedoms of Mrs. Roosevelt
September 11, 1943

The New Threshold is a new magazine put out by the United States Student Assembly. It is a journal of student opinion. It seeks to present the vital currents in the thought and action of American students. It has the determination to say that out of this war must come a peace that is (1) just; (2) durable; (3) democratic.

These are worthy aims. But I cannot say that the anti-Labor boys and the anti-Negro boys with the big clubs have these worthy aims in their ungodly skulls.

In this, I seem to agree with Mrs. Roosevelt. And no woman has ever sat in the White House who was worthy to hem Eleanor Roosevelt's skirt.

In *New Threshold* Mrs. Roosevelt proclaims her Four Freedoms for the Home Front. She believes in Victory at Home and Victory Abroad. She believes in Victory on the Negro Front. Many good white mouth-Christians believe in Victory on the Western Front and the Eastern Front. But they would go to hell before seeing a Victory on the Southern Front!

Abolish Jim Crow!

That's a bold title in the little old USA. Who wants to abolish Jim Crow? I'll tell you. Only those who have been washed in the blood of the Constitution. Only those who can say with Patrick Henry: "Give me liberty, or give me death." Only those who would have followed Tom Jefferson, Abe Lincoln, Garibaldi, and Sojourner Truth!

On the other hand, if we should abolish Jim Crow—as Mrs. Roosevelt advocates boldly—certain "representatives" of the People in Congress would drop dead. Yes, Sambo, it would take all the funeral parlors in the District of Columbia to handle the corpses, if either Christianity or Democracy came to the District.

With this in mind, then, you can see how bold Mrs. Roosevelt must be, when she heads her article with the unmistakable words: "Abolish Jim Crow!"

In this magazine for Youth, Mrs. Roosevelt speaks to both Youth and Old Age. As you know, Old Age is a stumbling block in the path of Youth. That's the reason God calls so many of the old heads home!

The Four Freedoms on the Southern Front

Mrs. Roosevelt takes some healthy blows at the theory of social equality. I hope all the Big Boys from the South read these words of the First Lady: "Down through the ages, it has been proved over and over again that this is one of the questions which people settle for themselves, and no amount of legislation will keep them from doing so. We would not have so many shades of color in this country today if this were not so."

My God, the First Lady has a punch like Joe Louis. Pardon me, for the comparison, but it's all I can think of, at the moment.

Mrs. Roosevelt knows that social equality is not the real issue. It is a red flag waved at the bull of race hate. In all history, the men of no minority group have ever taken the women of a majority group. So let us get down to brass tacks, with Mrs. Roosevelt.

What does the Negro want?

(1) Equality before the Law.
(2) Equality of Education.
(3) Equality in the Economic Field.
(4) Equality of Expression.

I believe these Four Freedoms on the Home Front may be taken by Negroes as their War Aims. I am glad Mrs. Roosevelt has bearded the lion of race hate in his den. I think every Negro ought to write Mrs. Roosevelt a letter of thanks.

Sex in Congress
October 16, 1943

The pork-faced men from the South are always dragging sex into Congress. Why they do this is something of a mystery. We are certainly fighting for our lives. Nobody with any sense wants anything that Hitler and Tojo have—but their heads. But it's hard to get united effort when a congressman waves step-ins instead of the Stars and Stripes.

The Congress of the United States is the only legislature where the law-makers froth at the mouth while they discuss sex. Rape seems the only subject that some of our pork-faced legislators can wax eloquent on. That is indeed funny. It is also pathological.

Of course, some white Southerners, like Caldwell and Faulkner, have given us revelations in the sex psychology of pork-faces. So we know a great deal about the secret passions of the Big Boys down South. But I still maintain and assert and declare that the floor of Congress is no place for pork-faces to waste the taxpayers' money talking about bedroom equality and happenings in the bushes.

A Man from Alabama!

In the U.S. Congress, there is a mossback by the name of Frank Boykin. He is the Man from Alabama. While the white boys and black boys from his state are dying in Italy and the Solomons, this pork-faced Judas raves about Mrs. Roosevelt and the Detroit riot.

Says this pork-face from Alabama: "It is blood on your hands, Mrs. Roosevelt. More than any other person, you are morally responsible for those race riots. You have been personally proclaiming and practicing social equality at the White House and wherever you go, Mrs. Roosevelt."

Now, I have been to Alabam. I have seen those high-yellow babies in Alabam. I have seen those half-white men and women in Alabam. Now, Congressman Boykin, somebody has been practicing not only social equality but bedroom equality in Alabam. There are no virgin births in Alabam.

A white novelist from Florence, Alabam, by the name of T. S. Stribling, has told the world all about bedroom equality in Alabam. For doing this, he received America's highest literary award—the Pulitzer Prize.

Congressman Boykin, yellow babies have come out of the House of Alabam. But only white babies have come out of the White House.

The Man from Mississip

A Southern pork-face can't talk about the race problem without getting low-down. Why is that? If a Negro or white liberal discusses economic or political questions, it isn't long before the pork-face drops the question below the navel. Why is that? Is it that the pork-face is woman-crazy?

Now, take that mossback from Mississip, by the name of John Rankin. He's in Congress, too. He got all heated up because some whites and Negroes came to the House restaurant. Now, people go to a cafe to eat—I suppose.

But ranting Rankin saw Communists who "go around here and hug and kiss these Negroes, dance with them, intermarry them." These words were uttered on the floor of the House, July 1, 1943.

Finally the Man from Mississip saw "many innocent, unprotected white girls, who have been raped by vicious Negroes."

Thus ranting Rankin's lustful mind ran from the bedroom to the bushes. A man who talks like that should be put under observation. He's goofy. He's like a guy in a poolroom who belly laughs as he tells sex stories, in filthy details.

With our country's destiny at stake, a congressman should have something to talk about besides hugging and kissing and raping. Even the flunkies of Hitler and Tojo have more decency than to descend to tales of the bedroom and bushes in legislative halls.

The Big Boys at the Peace Table
February 12, 1944

Everybody is now talking about the Peace Table. What will happen there? Who will be there? Will the Haves or the Have-Nots boss things? Will the little boys take their cue from the Big Boys? Mrs. Roosevelt has already said (quote) that the Negro should sit down with the others! (unquote).

What will happen at the Peace Table? I don't know. Neither do you. We all have hopes. Some will have despairs—maybe. Will another war come out of the peace? Well, I can tell you about that. Of course, I see you sneer, "Oh, yeah?"

How did I get the low down? Well, you can get it too. Patrick Henry said: "I can only judge the future by the past." So true! Now, let us look at the past. Let us go back twenty-five years. Lincoln Steffens, who loved black men and white men, tells the story. He was in Paris at the Versailles Peace Conference.

Behind Closed Doors

We little fellows don't always know what happens behind closed doors. That is, when the Big Boys put their heads together in the secret chambers. Sometimes, of course, things leak out through the keyhole. Sometimes, they don't. Well, at Versailles this leaked out, and old Lincoln Steffens got it.

Clemenceau, the big man from France; Lloyd George, the big man from England; Woodrow Wilson, the big man from the USA— the Big Three talked together about Peace behind closed doors.

Clemenceau, the Tiger, said: "One moment, gentlemen, I desire before we go further to be made clear on one essential point."

Lloyd George and Wilson wanted to know what it was.

Clemenceau said: "I hear talk about a permanent peace, a peace to end war forever. Do you really mean that, Mr. Wilson?"

Woodrow Wilson said yes.

Then turning to Lloyd George, old Clemenceau said: "Do you really mean that, Mr. George?"

Lloyd George said yes.

Clemenceau said: "Very important, very important. We can do this; we can remove all the causes of war. But have you counted the cost of such peace?"

Lloyd George and Woodrow Wilson asked together: "What costs?"

Then old Clemenceau, the Tiger, said: "Well, we must give up our empires and all hopes of empires. You, Lloyd George, you English will have to come out of India, we French out of North Africa, you Americans out of the Philippines and Puerto Rico, and leave Cuba and Mexico alone. We must give up our spheres of influence.

"And yes, we shall have to tear down tariff walls and establish free trade in all the world. This is the cost of permanent peace; there are other sacrifices. It is very expensive, this peace. Are you willing to pay the price, all these costs of no more war in the world?"

Astounded, Mr. Wilson and Mr. George protested that Clemenceau was covering too much ground; they had not meant all of these things as the price of peace.

"Then," old Clemenceau shouted, "you don't mean peace. You mean war!"

So again we are at war. The Second World War! Now, when we sit down at the Peace Table after this war, the ghost of old Clemenceau will put these questions to the Big Nations again. Are you willing to give up your colonies? Are you willing to give the Four Freedoms to the Africans, Indians, Negroes, Chinese?

If the Big Boys at the Peace Table fail again to give justice to all nations and races, then we shall have the Third World War!

IV
Random Shots

Ghosts
October 9, 1937

Do you believe in ghosts? Ghosts! Well, during the last month every newspaper in the Land of the Spree and the Home of Burma Shave has carried a thrilling ghost story. Believe it or not! I like ghost stories . . . but not ghosts. I've seen many a one rise in this worst of all possible worlds. My boyhood days in the small towns of Iowa and Missouri were haunted with ghost stories. I used to go to church because I was afraid to stay at home by myself. Why? Ghosts, y'know. Since Julius Caesar published the first daily newspaper in Gaul, people have shivered over tales of spectres.

Henrik Ibsen, the Norwegian dramatist and poet, wrote the world's greatest ghost story in a play called *Ghosts,* in which that divine actress, Nazimova, of Crimea, Russia, has appeared on Broadway over a period of years. I shall never forget that heart-touching scene in which Mrs. Alving and Pastor Manders overheard her artist-son Osvald making love to his half-sister, Regina, in the conservatory, and the hysterical mother cries: "Ghosts! They have risen again!"

Shakespeare liked ghost stories and told some good ones. Every school boy has heard *Macbeth.* Shakespeare had his nerve, all right. Ghosts usually hang around old abandoned houses. And they like to plague us at midnight. Shakespeare had one appear in the middle of a king's banquet. Of course, Shakespeare can get away with anything! Just as Macbeth raised his cup to drink to the "health" of the man he had murdered, in stalked the mocking ghost of Banquo. Wasn't that something! But Macbeth was no coward. Why should he be? Did he not think he could not be killed by a "man of woman born?" Macbeth was not afraid to fight a Russian bear, a rhinoceros, nor a Hyrean [*sic*] tiger. But what can the sword of the best swordsman do against a ghost?

Men who come to power over the dead bones of other men fear
ghosts. Hitler cannot sleep at night. Mussolini is afraid of a
skeleton hand that might clutch his throat from out the treacherous
past.

And now we come to that ghost story that has appeared in every
newspaper in the United States. One night in September, 1923,
U.S. Supreme Court Justice Hugo L. Black, surrounded by
hooded members of the Invisible Empire, Knights of the Ku Klux
Klan, sealed with his blood and took the oath to uphold White
Supremacy. At that time Mr. Black did not know that fortune
would smile on him and a President would place him among the
Nine Immortals. Mr. Black will tell you that ghosts do arise in a
man's life . . . just as Ibsen and Shakespeare demonstrated on the
stage. The black ghost of that oath to the Ku Klux Klan may shunt
Mr. Black into political oblivion. I can imagine Justice Black
soliloquizing in his secret chamber as he faces that ghost of
yesterday:

> The Moving Finger writes; and having writ,
> Moves on: nor all your Piety nor Wit
> Shall lure it back to cancel half a Line.
> Nor all your Tears wash out a Word of it.

Does Human Nature Change?
We Are Not Born Human Beings
April 1, 1939

An elderly woman in San Francisco asked me this question. Her
club associates had discussed it. It faces you and me today in the
home, the school, the marketplace, and the church. Yes, human
nature changes. If it did not, I would go to the top of the Empire
State Building and jump off.

Heraclitus, the famous Greek philosopher, said: "Everything is
in a state of change; and the only thing that does not change is the
law that everything changes."

While a man talks about the old-time religion, religion is changing. Ask the eminent divine, Dr. Fosdick. While a lover is swearing
his eternal love, his love is changing. Ask Shakespeare. Every
seven years a wife gets a new husband, and a husband gets a new
wife. Why? My biologist colleague tells me that every cell in the
human body changes every seven years!

Copernicus, the Polish astronomer, overthrew the theory of the universe proclaimed by Ptolemaeus, the Greco-Egyptian geographer. And in our own day, Einstein upsets the Newtonian theory of the universe.

I stood in the huge room at the California Institute of Technology, where the greatest telescope in the world was to be placed. A learned physicist explained to me the millions of miles that he would look into the unexplored worlds above. I staggered out of the chamber, reduced to nothingness. Change. Change. Why, ancient priests told their ignorant followers that the sky was only five miles above the earth!

No wonder a wise man in the Bible cried: "Vanity of vanities! All, all is vanity under the sun!"

No wonder Abe Lincoln sadly repeated the poem: "Oh, why should the spirit of mortals be proud!"

Change is the law of the universe. Worlds that would make our own world look like a peanut change into ashes and are scattered a million miles away.

Then puny man, lost in a universe of change, questions: "Does human nature change?"

Emerson, that profound American scholar, says: "There's a crack in everything God made."

Well, if that is true, why can't there be a crack in man's thinking? Of course, this question is ridiculous. Truth is in front of us. We puny men are trying to catch up with it. Some of those who most ardently shout that they have the truth have only a belief with a crack in it.

Why Do Men Oppose Change?

Since we live in a changing universe, why do men oppose change? Perhaps there are many reasons. If a rock is in the way, the root of a tree will change its direction. The dumbest animals try to adapt themselves to changed conditions. Even a rat will change its tactics to get a piece of cheese. But you have observed that a man will close his eyes and ears to a truth that is new.

One time I was lecturing to a white audience in Wisconsin. A Southerner and his wife were sitting on the front seat. I remarked that the famous novel, *The Count of Monte Cristo,* was written by a Negro. The film was showing in town and everybody was talking about it. Most of those present did not know that Dumas was a Negro. The Southerner's wife asked him if it were true. He shook his head vigorously in denial. Yet, he had never investigated the fact!

The mind that is open to new truths is a rare mind. We read those books that sanction what we already believe. We like those persons who agree with us. We are not truth-seekers. Opposing new ideas, if we had lived in the past, we would have helped the lynchers crucify Jesus when He brought in a new religion. We would have opposed the Revolutionary War just as we oppose the Russian Revolution now. Why? We are afraid of change. We sanction only that which has the sanction of time and respectability. If you are honest with yourself, you will admit that the challenge of a new belief gives you a brainstorm. I pity you. If you were a truth-seeker, you would gladly examine the new belief.

Now, why do men oppose change? Do they have money to lose? Do they have prestige to lose? Do they have their pride to sustain? Fundamentally, the old belief gives security often when there is no security. In a world of change, people want to hold on to something. They hate to admit to themselves that they are like a ship without a rudder or compass. The volcanic changes in finance and politics and religion fill them with helplessness and fear. They become panicky. They are terrified by the modern Noahs talking about a flood. They don't want to listen to the modern Daniels translating the handwriting on the walls of their ancient beliefs. In other words, they want none of the truth–seekers.

In a Louisiana town I once talked on the race problem. Both the whites and the Negroes knew I was telling the truth. The whites were amazed and the Negroes were scared to death. They missed half my speech because they were watching the faces of the whites. As the whites rose and passed out first, the silence was awful. The black chairman apologized to his white friends by saying he didn't know what kind of man I was when he invited me to speak. As he told me good-bye, there was an awful silence.

The Chief of the G-Men Is Wrong

Last year Mr. Hoover, chief of the G-men, and I delivered commencement addresses in the same Oklahoma town. I took issue with Mr. Hoover on the question of crime. Mr. Hoover thinks his G-men can stop crime with the cooperation of our citizens. Crime was here before the G-men came upon the scene, and it will be here when they are gone.

Our dollar-mad society produces criminals. Slums are breeding places for criminals. Unemployment increases crimes. The Negro leads other racial groups in burglary. Why? Because the Negro is sunk lowest in the economic abyss. Jesus would not say to a starving man: "Thou shalt not steal."

Man is an animal first. Feed a dog well if you want him to stay out of the meat platter on the table. Last week a child came to my house begging for food. I stepped out of the room a minute. When I returned the child was wolfing with both of its skinny hands the scraps left on the dinner table. The child's little eyes had the same savage look that I've seen in the eyes of a hungry rat gnawing a bone. Our dollar-crazy civilization made that child what it was. There are dogs in Washington that are more cultivated than little black children picked up by the capital police. Why? The dogs have received better training than the so-called human beings. The dogs live in fine houses. Those children live in fire-trap tenements. The dogs take shower baths. The helpless children don't know how a bathtub feels. The dogs live on beautiful streets. The children live in nauseating alleys. Twenty years from now the police will shoot those children down as dangerous criminals. And over the radio the Crime Busters will dramatize the lives of those criminals to warn other children in dark alleys that crime doesn't pay.

Human nature. Society produces human nature. Therefore, society is responsible for human nature. The potter is to blame, and not the pot, if there is a crack in the pot. That's the reason that sensible people everywhere are interested in changing society. A white boy from my hometown saw this and wrote a fine novel called *A World to Win*.

Change. Change. The equator is changing. Suns burn to ashes, and new suns are born. Rivers dry up. Forests disappear. Whole species vanish from the face of the earth. Kingdoms rise and fall. Religions flourish and die. Mighty kings—Kublai Khan, Attila, Ibrahim Pasha—reign for a season and slip into oblivion.

Love blooms and dies. Timbuctoo and Troy, seats of colossal civilization, are only names in the story books of writers whose very bones have been devoured by the hungry jaws of time. Men who thought they had monopolized the truth have their mouths stopped with dirt. Their dust comes up in a weed on a lonely grave. A cow eats the weed. A man eats the cow. Then death eats the man. It has happened a hundred billion times. It will happen another hundred billion times. Change. Change. Everything changes but the law that everything changes. I have changed even as I wrote this article on change.

What Is The Root of All Evil?
November 18, 1939

Do You Take Dope?

Don't get angry because I ask this question. Neither say *Yes* or *No*. Just wait awhile. Sambo has been waiting a long time for the rights of Life and the Pursuit of Happiness.

As one who has taken several kinds of dope, I feel that I am an expert on the subject. Then I've given much study to the dopes used in different countries. The worst thing you can do if you expect to get through a college or university is to pattern your reading after mine. I have reading sprees. I may get to thinking about snakes and spend weeks studying rattlers, cobras, pythons, Gilas, and chameleons.

Snakes have many habits peculiar to men. Or I may start on a reading spree that covers the history of undertakers. By the way, that's a good racket for some of you black boys if you look up the racketeering stunts of the Egyptian undertakers! Again, you will find it interesting to compare the initiations of our sorors and fraters on our intellectual campuses with those of the African witch doctors. But let us get back to the question of dopes.

Savannah, Georgia, and the Dope Ship

Savannah harbor was the scene of the capture of a dope ship. Savannah made the front page at once. Of course this was not the first time. In December, 1778, a British army, accompanied by American traitors, entered the city; and 200 years ago the great Polish General Pulaski was killed there.

Black Boy, I get sick below the belt when I hear white men whooping it up for the Declaration of Independence and the Constitution, when many of their ancestors fought against George Washington and Thomas Jefferson, especially in the South. Ask the professors at Harvard and Yale and Columbia. No. Don't do that. When it comes to the treason of white Americans, the Big Boys have told the professors that mum is the word!

You aren't supposed to know that white Americans, in the British army shot foreigners who were fighting to free America! The first Civil War in the United States was not fought between 1861 and 1865. It was fought in the Carolinas and in Georgia, where good white Americans did their utmost to keep the British flag waving over the Bible Belt. Professor David Saville Muzzey, Ph.D., let that out by accident!

So when you hear white Americans whooping it up for the

Constitution you can give them the good old Negro belly laugh. Be patient. I'm trying my best to get to that dope ship at Savannah.

A Very Peculiar Christmas Gift!

Old General William T. Sherman's March to the Sea broke the backbone of the South. It was then that the South sang the world's most mournful blues. And the South has been singing *Gone with the Wind* ever since. Old Sherman was like Joe Louis. He had a knockout blow in either hand. Old Sherman said: "Stop monkeying around. Let 'em have it in the bread basket!"

You've had all kinds of Christmas gifts. But I think Old Sherman sent Lincoln the most peculiar one and the greatest one of all. No lie, Black Boy. I almost jump up from this punch-drunk typewriter when I think about it, and give my teasing brown-skinned heels a half-dozen clicks.

This is the telegram that Old Sherman sent to Abe Lincoln on Christmas night. "As a Christmas gift the city of Savannah, with 150 heavy guns, plenty of ammunition, and about 25,000 bales of cotton."

That Christmas gift sent the South skidding downhill like a horse's tail going over Niagara Falls. On February 3, Vice-President Stephens of the Confederacy—like Nicodemus coming to Jesus when all the boys were abed snoring—came to meet Mr. Lincoln at Hampton Roads to discuss terms of peace. Mr. Lincoln held the ace of trumps.

So he told Stephens to fork up or shut up. Stephens left, with his head hanging down like Nicodemus. Old General Grant took a long puff on his cigar when Mr. Lincoln told him how stubborn Mr. Stephens was. Then old Grant, in his tent, took a long drink of first-class booze, pepped himself up, and knocked on the gates of Richmond. President Jefferson Davis asked who was there, grabbed his papers, and beat it. So General Lee was left holding the empty basket. General Lee knew when enough of anything is enough. So he surrendered.

Stop Taking Dope, Black Men!

Now that dope ship set me thinking. The incident was sociologically significant as well as psychologically illuminating. I have just finished reading some reports from the Government at Washington about the widespread use of dope in the United States. Depressions make people, old and young, dope-eaters.

However, I am more intensely interested in the kinds of dope that this narcotic bureau does not mention. I am interested in the dopes of sophistry, the dopes of rugged individualism, the dopes of prejudice, the dopes of snobbery, the dopes of mysticism, the dopes of you-can-make-it-if-you-know-your-stuff.

America's most deadly dope is not the reefer, cocaine, or opium. America's most dangerous dope is the dope of false propaganda. This dope comes from high places. This dope is put out by two types of people: those who don't know and don't know that they don't know; and those who know the truth, but for malicious reasons tell lies.

Black men, stop taking the dope of Big White Men and Big Negroes. Do your own thinking. Before you start thinking, spend considerable time reading. Go into the byways and hedges of reading. Get off the beaten trail. Get down to the root of evil. What is the root of evil? I'll give you the best explanation in the whole world.

The Bible says: "The love of money is the root of ALL evil."

Ask your preacher to come out of the clouds and deliver a sermon on the text next Sunday. I wish I had the power to make every minister in America preach on that text for fifty-two Sundays straight. There are millions of facts to prove that the dollar is the root of all evil. Man is not bad by NATURE. NURTURE has made Man bad. NURTURE, not NATURE, has made the dollar the root of all evil. I shall discuss this some day.

I should like for some minister in Washington to write a sermonette in the *Tribune* on this all-important text mentioned above. The Bible has given you the source of ALL evil. Now prove that the Bible is right.

The love of money is the root of ALL evil is a good physic for anyone who is suffering from the constipation of dopey ideas.

Take the dollar-profits out of race prejudice, religion, wars, matrimony, crime, prostitution, hyprocrisy, sins,—get rid of the love of money and you will solve most of the problems of Man.

But the boys don't want to do that. They want to have the Golden Rule, and Mammon too. That's impossible!

The Biggest Question in the World:
When Is a Man Dead?
December 23, 1939

"When shall I die?" is the question that plagues most people. I can see that this is very important. The death of a man is no more than dropping a pebble into the middle of the Atlantic at midnight during a storm.

Another flood could come and wipe out everybody but a male and female: a thousand years from now you'd have a big nation. Nature loves the species—not the individual

Edgar Allan Poe thought that the most tragic thing in the world is the death of a beautiful woman. He put that idea in a poem and called it "The Raven." Of course, Poe didn't know that beauty is simply an illusion Nature uses to bring babies into the world. When a man and woman have a child, Nature is through with them, whether they're beautiful or ugly.

I think it's awful to see a genius die. After all, it's the genius that makes human beings better. I realize that nobody suffers like the genius. He is so far ahead of us. We businessmen and Ph.D.s and scrubwomen have to catch up with genius. Sometimes it takes generations.

When Shall I Die?

Every man would like to have the answer to that question, if he is a Christian. You see, a Christian is not afraid to die! He is going to a better world. There he will find eternal happiness. Therefore, a man who is going to Heaven is anxious to leave these low grounds of sorrow. I can understand why the infidel is afraid to die. Nobody wants to roast in hell millions and millions of years!

I have faced death about twelve times. Once I was very scared. But then, as I think about it, I was very selfish at that time. Since I've made my peace with Truth, I do not fear to die.

Now, the Old Year is dying. Millions of men and women who knew the smile of the sun a year ago are no longer with us. Before some of them were shoveled into the earth, they had become living ghosts. Thousands of them died without having lived. Some of them, like the Ancient Mariner of a classic poem, walked the shadow-land of life-and-death.

I remember the old song my mother used to sing, in a little red

church by the side of a river in Iowa, many years ago: "Before this
time another year, I may be gone." She is gone now. But she was
not afraid to go. She gave her final directions to the family and
smiled and left us standing about the bed.

When Is a Man Dead?

This is the important question. It doesn't matter much when you
die or where you die. World-famous physicians are interested in
one big question: When is a man dead?" Some have staked their
reputation on the solution of that question. I've never seen a
physician puzzled over the query: "When did he die? When the
doctor and the coroner and preacher come together, they want to
know one thing: "Is this brother dead?" That's the last question
and the most important one.

Only a detective wants to know: "When did he die?" And the
dick does not ask the question because he is interested in the dead
man. The dick is trying to check upon a living man. He wants to
find out who did the dirty work. When is a man dead?

I have the impudence to think I have stumbled upon the answer.
In 1915, Sinclair Lewis, a Nobel Prize winner, wrote a novel called
The Trail of the Hawk. The hero is a boy named Hawk, an ambitious dreamer, who becomes manager of an automobile corpora-
tion in South America. As a boy Hawk admires the village
freethinker Bone Stillman, who has learned a world of things from
men and Nature and forbidden books. Old Stillman urges the boy
to go ahead to bigger and better things.

This is the advice old Stillman gives the young man: "Anybody
or anything that doesn't pack any surprises—get that?—surprises,
for you, is dead, and you want to slough it like a snake does its
skin."

There is the answer in a nutshell. A man is dead when he doesn't
pack any surprises. Of course, you have sense enough to get the
profound philosophy of old Bone Stillman. A living organism is full
of surprises. The higher the organism, the harder it is to predict its
reactions. The biologist, looking for a surprise, calls it a mutation.
The genius is continually surprising us. Every great man in a sense,
is a sort of sleight-of-hand performer. A woman who holds a man's
interest longest is full of surprises that bring out her personality.

Mediocre people are minus the surprise. They follow the herd,
the status quo, the thing that is proper. They are victims of
pandemic psychosis. Their theme song is this: "Everybody's
Doing It." They are slaves of conventions. They are intellectually
and spiritually dead.

Old Bone Stillman was right; a person who has no surprises is dead. You can tell a thinker when you meet one: his ideas are packed full of surprises. His conclusions are different. What respectable people call a virtue, a thinker calls vice. What "good" people call a vice, the thinker calls a virtue.

Parents often murder a child because it is different. Such a child requires the highest specialized training. Harvard University is not for geniuses. It is for average students. Our schools are factories that grind out T-model personalities that talk alike, write alike, dress alike, think alike, act alike. Their teachers are dead.

The untutored Negro is full of fresh surprises. As a rule education ruins him. He becomes a black Caruso, a black John Dewey, a black Theodore Dreiser. Richard Wright, however, is Richard Wright. Marian Anderson is Marian Anderson. Paul Robeson is Paul Robeson. That is as it should be. When you hear Marian Anderson sing, you are surprised. When you read a story by Richard Wright, you are surprised. When you see a Robeson act, you are surprised. These artists are alive.

As a teacher, I can say that my profession has more dead men and women in it than any other. When the average learned professor walks into the classroom, the students are like condemned prisoners waiting to walk the Last Mile. And, of course, since the Sabbath is a day of rest, most people go to church to get a good snooze. When the preacher announces his text, everybody settles back comfortably because he knows all the Bible stories by heart. I know one clergyman who had cots put in his church. This was a surprise, and thus he increased his attendance and the dimes in his collection box.

If you want to live, stay in the company of people who are packed with surprises. If you want to grow intellectually, contact people who think differently. Dead ideas are like dead bodies, they carry a stench. Why is it we like to meet people who are well traveled and well-read? They are alive. If you want to live, mix with all types and all classes and all races of men. You will never suffer from boredom. See good plays on the legitimate stage. Prowl in old book stalls.

Dead bodies or stiffs have no surprises. Only the living do the unexpected. Adults must cultivate the curiosity of children. Children are always looking for the unconventional, the extraordinary. Its surprises are behind. Thus, old men dream dreams, and young men see visions. Get off the beaten path: you will find wonderful things in life. A man is dead when he doesn't pack a surprise. This is a surprise.

In the *Washington Tribune*
I Write as I Please
January 6, 1940

At the beginning of the New Year, I ought to say something about my relations with the *Washington Tribune*. My contacts with editors and publishers, white and black, are very extensive. I know what they preach . . . and what they practice. I know what gets to the readers and what does not for political, social, and economic reasons.

When dumbbells talk about "the freedom of the press," I know they are dumbbells. When I hear idealists denouncing the dictatorship of the press in foreign countries, I smile cynically.

Those who know me know that I think for myself and write as I please. Of course, I am not interested in scandals. I am tremendously interested in ideas and principles. I cut wood and let the chips fall where they will. I don't evade issues. I'd as soon walk off the road as walk in the middle.

I never attack a man unless he is standing in the way of a principle. I don't know any man who is worth my attack as a man. And I don't like to waste my logic and facts in personal rebellions. My pals are aristocrats and scrubwomen, scholars and dumbbells, millionaires and tramps.

I am at home in a penthouse on Fifth Avenue or a boxcar on the C. & A. I don't believe in cliques and classes. I can "walk with crowds and keep my virtue, or dine with kings, nor lose the common touch." You see, I am a truth-seeker. I have no apology to make for my belief. I'm always getting new beliefs.

What Will People Say?

What people will say makes cowards of most of us. That doesn't bother me, when you're seeking truth, you don't have time to think about what people will say. Especially Big People. I think I can protect myself when I advance an argument. If I fail, I confess my ignorance and get on the side of truth.

Once I delivered an address at Howard University. A gentleman came forward and said, "Mr. Tolson, I disagree with you."

I said: "Sir, I didn't come 1,500 miles to get you to agree with me. You overestimate your importance and mine. I'm interested in but one thing: What is your objection to my argument."

You see, truth has nothing to do with what I believe or what you believe. Or what scholars believe or a billion common folk. Truth is objective, not subjective.

172

What Makes Me Angry

I used to hate men. Now I hate certain ideas of certain men. A man is important only as he represents an idea. You see, I know now that a man is what he is and a man can't help what he is. I don't have time to prove that now. A rattler is a rattler, and it can't be a lamb. In the same way a man is the product of nature and nurture.

I believe in biological and environmental predestination. A man gets his ideas from his contacts. Those give him a point of view. My point of view is the result of getting a little bit of truth here and there consciously and unconsciously from thousands and thousands of personalities in books and every walk of life.

One blow of a hammer may drive a nail home. Then it may take a dozen blows of the hammer to do the same thing. This is also true of an idea. A certain stimulus of a certain idea may hit the human consciousness a hundred times before the idea enters the mind. The effect of a stimulus depends on its size and the number of its repetitions. When you learn that simple fact, you've traveled a long way on the road of life.

Take the late Dean Kelly Miller, for example; some readers have wondered about the vast difference between his ideas and mine. It was impossible for the venerable dean and me to think alike. He had met one set of influences; I had met another. He was sincere. So am I. But sincerity is no test of truth. The African mother is sincere when she throws her child to the crocodiles in her religious worship. So men don't make me angry. I know how men are made. Ideas make me angry. Ideas rise from economic conditions. It may take you a hundred years to get that through your skull. Perhaps you'll have to tumble into the gutter or the breadline to learn that. An empty belly is the best teacher of economics.

Where the *Tribune* Comes In

Now in the *Washington Tribune,* I write as I please. When my articles come out, I can recognize them. In some other papers and magazines I've been compelled to ask the editors if I wrote articles bearing my name.

There is a sabotage of ideas in America. Read Dr. Beard's *America in Midpassage.* There is a malicious attempt to keep Americans ignorant. The news is twisted. Important things are kept out. Trivialities are magnified. Truth is hidden. Hard-hitting writers don't get a hearing.

I had the manuscript of a book turned down because I wouldn't rewrite it the way the editor wanted it rewritten. I refused to pervert the truth. We were sitting above Fifth Avenue in his luxurious office. He passed me a huge cigarette box of beaten gold and asked me to smoke. His wife was a popular actress in Hollywood. Yes, he couldn't understand how a poor Negro would-be writer would turn down possible wealth and fame, when all he had to do was to change his slant on life and get his manuscript put out by a publisher who'd never put out a Negro book. While I sat there, the telephone rang. A professor from Harvard wanted to see Mr. ——— about getting his manuscript published. But the professor from Harvard didn't get in!

"What have you decided?" inquired the editor.

He stood up, indicating that the interview was over.

"I will not commit a literary abortion," I said.

Now that Fifth Avenue publisher can buy the *Washington Tribune* a thousand times; but I'd rather write for the *Tribune*.

Henpecked Husband: Comedy or Tragedy
January 20, 1940

Some day I hope to write a book on the henpecked husband. The subject has its comic and tragic aspects. Its economic basis. Its abnormal manifestations. Its dramatic relief. Its infinite varieties. Some husbands like henpecking as a fish likes water. Others hate it. Some are proud of nagging. Others rejoice in henpecking and spurn it by turns. It is clear that some men owe their success to henpecking. On the other hand, henpecking has ruined many potentially great men. Henpecking wives are miserable.

Henpecking is a woman's declaration of independence. The marriage license is an ancient survival of the bill of sale. It simply proves that a man owns a woman. If another man tries to steal a husband's piece of property the husband simply shoots the lover and appeals to the "unwritten law." Therefore, stealing a man's wife is a form of burglary.

Now, the henpecked husband would not exist in a real democracy. In our civilization the cards are stacked against a woman, except in singular cases. The frantic efforts of middle-aged women to look and act like girls of sixteen prove the economic and social insecurity of women in the 1940s. Middle-aged women are like old cars on the market: age depreciates their value. Men want up-to-date models.

Our civilization is competitive—heartlessly competitive. There-

fore, old cars must compete with new cars, old businesses with
new businesses, old women with young women.

If a man has a good income, he can buy old wines and young
women. Sometimes the woman reverses this rule by getting her
hands on some money or a profitable job. Then she can't tell if the
man married her or her income.

What Napoleon Thought about Henpecked Husbands

The Empress Josephine, who had some Negro blood in her
veins, certainly gave Napoleon the blues. She was extravagant and
fickle. Perhaps, if she'd had some babies, she would have been
different. Of course, that's a big IF. She two-timed Napoleon. Yes,
she four-timed him. She bought a thousand pair of shoes for her
dainty feet. Napoleon divorced her after Father Time had made
some changes in her face and figure. Napoleon gave a good reason
for the divorce. Of course, only Napoleon knew the real reason.

Napoleon said: "There is no greater misfortune for a man than to
allow himself to be governed by his wife."

I wonder if that was the reason for his divorce. Napoleon, like so
many henpecked husbands, did not get his divorce until he got
solidly on his feet, but I don't know of any rich folk who have left a
palace to find love in a cottage. Frank Harris says there is no
difference between a duchess and a chambermaid in the dark; but a
husband has to look at his wife in the daylight of the kitchen.

The Henpecking Wife

The henpecking wife is the result of economic and social maladjustments in a majority of cases. In the average case, men and
women are happy in the periods of courtship and the honeymoon.
Then, when they settle down to the business of making a living and
a home, violent reactions take place.

Most wives grumble about being neglected. Why? Well, most
men exhaust themselves mentally, in trying to make money. Dol-
lar-getting becomes an obsession. Fear of job haunts most men,
day and night. The wife becomes a piece of furniture in the home. I
have seen the misery in the faces of women with so-called successful husbands. The neglected wife is the price of success. When a
wife is neglected she gets religion or another man.

Since the lover does not have to support the wife, he has the
freedom necessary to make love.

A nagging woman is a bird beating her wings against the cage of
matrimony. Henpecking is her revenge for her marital misery. If

women want to be happy, they will have to work for a society in which there will be economic justice. Women have to vote to change things. I have more confidence in the humanitarianism of women than I do in the money-grabbing politics of men. I am a hard-headed thinker, but I believe the heart is a better guide to happiness than the head. Women have hearts. That's the reason they henpeck.

There Can Be No Democracy
without Dictatorship
February 10, 1940

In New York City, during the holidays, I found myself in a group of white intellectuals—writers, artists, and professors. They were whooping it up for democracy. That is a big pastime now. Since I was the only one present whose color gave color to the occasion, they wondered why I remained silent.

They had circled the globe in denouncing dictatorships, and I had said nothing. While it is true that I do my level best to keep up with what is going on abroad, I believe in cleaning up your own house before telling the neighbors to clean up theirs. An elderly gentleman asked for my point of view.

"There can be no democracy," I said, "without dictatorship."

Of course, this self-evident fact was like the explosion of a bomb. So I hastened to explain. You may rule out all the isms here, and get down to hard common sense. I could prove my case by going into the nature and philosophy of government. But that's unnecessary.

Away with the dialectics of Plato's *Republic*—which was not a republic. Historians like to boast about democratic Athens; yet in Athens "only 9,000 out of the population of 515,000 in 300 B.C. could marry or vote. The 506,000 were not property-owners." Athens had a dictatorship: but not the RIGHT KIND of dictatorship!

Judas Iscariot and the Money Bag

Perhaps you want to know why I bring Judas into this discussion. Well, Judas set out to be a smart guy. I don't know where Judas got the lowdown on dictatorship. But he had it. Of course he messed up. But all dictatorships mess up. That's the reason the history of man is the history of the rise and fall of governments. You can't have a government without having a dictatorship. Now disprove that! Government implies Law. And Law implies a Big Boss.

Who is that Big Boss? Judas knew. Yes, Judas knew that the Big Boss who holds the money bag dictates what the boys shall do and what the boys shall not do. So, while the other disciples listened to Jesus, Judas was counting the coins. Of course, Judas, and Al Capone, and Caesar messed up.

Why Mr. Roosevelt Was Called a Dictator

When Mr. Roosevelt went into office, he discovered a dictatorship of Big Business, by Big Business, and for Big Business. Mr. Roosevelt should have known that before he went into office. Thomas Jefferson discovered it 150 years ago. Dr. Charles A. Beard has told us all about it in his monumental book, *The Rise of American Civilization.*

Now when Mr. Roosevelt started putting the screws to the economic royalist dictators—they began calling the President a dictator! That let the cat out of the bag. Only poor Negroes and poor whites and Uncle Toms believe we have democracy! When democracy comes per se, there will be no government. So don't be fooled. Think it over.

Dictatorship in the South

We hear a great deal about those awful carpetbaggers who came South after the War. Lies, of course. Read Dr. Du Bois's *Black Revolution.* The South circulated these lies to justify the dictatorship of the master class of the South. And some Sambo professors have fallen for that bunk!

Why does the South defend to the death states' rights at this time? I'll tell you. To keep in power its white dictatorship. Read Cramer's *God Shakes Creation.*

Old Frederick Douglass said that if a Union army was not kept in the South for a long period, the Negro would be re-enslaved. And that has happened. Since the North was too chickenhearted to maintain a Northern dictatorship, we have now a cracker dictatorship. So long as we have a government, we shall have a dictatorship of some kind. The South fights the anti-lynching bill because the South fears the dictatorship of G-men. Nothing else.

Is a Dictatorship a Dictatorship?

It's funny how scholars, so-called, get confused on this. A dictatorship is brutal. All governments are brutal if you violate their laws . . . and get caught. Look at the Jews in Germany and the Negroes in the Capital of our verbal democracy.

Is a dictatorship a dictatorship? Is an animal an animal? Now, a bedbug is an animal; an elephant is also an animal. But does that make a begbug an elephant? What I am trying to say is that all dictatorships are not the same. Their methods may be identical; but their aims may be as wide apart as the poles. Two fathers spank their sons: one out of meanness, the other out of devotion.

At the present time in the history of the world, there can be no democracy without a dictatorship. What I want is the RIGHT KIND of dictatorship. I don't want a dictatorship of jim crowism as we have it today.

I believe Mr. Roosevelt is a man with a social conscience. I criticize him because he has listened too much to the economic royalists. It's going to take a great amount of dictating to straighten out things in this country. With millions starving and millions scared they'll starve, the President will have to use the whip hand. And the people will have to dictate to the President to make him dictate.

Once my father had a 500-pound hog. She would eat all she could and then lie in a trough so the other hogs and pigs couldn't get a thing. Pa had to take a club and beat her out of the trough. That was a dictatorship.

Now in the United States a few people are living on the fat of the land, while millions stand around crying for bread. That isn't right by any law of God or man. So Uncle Sam will have to do what Jesus did when He went into the temple among those money-lenders. That's dictatorship.

Give me more of it! I want Congress to dictate that every citizen shall enjoy the rights of life and the pursuit of happiness. I want Congress to dictate the abolition of poverty in a land of plenty. I want Congress to dictate the enforcement of the Constitution. Otherwise our boast of democracy is a joke before civilized peoples. But before we get the RIGHT KIND of dictatorship, nine-tenths of your present Congress will have to be kicked out of office.

The Ingratitude of Those Who Beg!
May 11, 1940

It was a cold day. The Poet was walking along a city street. The crowds swirled by. Every pedestrian was thinking about his petty business. The Poet watched their faces. He was reading them as he read the verses of the masters of today and yesterday.

And the Poet was sad. The heartlessness of the multitude was an ache in his heart. He'd dreamed of brotherhood. But here, in the city street, he saw the stark naked brutality of the crowd in its vast unconcern. He was seized with an unutterable loneliness. It is terrible to be alone in a crowd. The Sahara is not so desolate, so friendless.

And then the Poet saw a tramp. The Poet's mind lit up. His soul burned. Hours later, in his garret room, the Poet wrote the lines describing the unknown bum:

> The odds and ends of a ruined man
> With a face like dirty lime,
> He licked his ravaged lips and croaked:
> "Brother, can you spare a dime?"

The Split Ego of the Beggar

The Poet's eye looked into the soul of the Beggar and saw the man inside. Prophets have foresight. Scholars have hindsight. The Poet has insight. The merchant looks at a man. The aristocrat looks upon a man. The Poet looks into a man. That's the reason the ancient Romans called the Poet the man who sees.

So the Poet, on that cold day, in that crowded street saw beyond the rags and dirt and cowardice, struggling in the outcast. Hours later, in this garret room, the Poet wrote:

> And the beggar struggled hard
> Sir Galahad and knave,
> And in his ego one could sense
> The master and the slave.

The Beggar Is a Rapist

But not in the way we think. The Poet knew that there is a kind of spiritual rape more degrading than the physical. Society had reduced the Beggar to a human ruin. He was now in a class with Bigger Thomas of Wright's *Native Son*. Therefore, the Beggar's evil raped everything it saw. It raped virtue, beauty, honor. It degraded everything it looked upon.

Now, the Poet had made a mistake in the stanza given above. He had assumed falsely that all of us could sense in the Beggar "the master and the slave." Most of us are so unconsciously brutalized that we never take a second glance at a Beggar. To avoid our plain duty, we may lie to ourselves by saying the Beggar may have a thousand bucks hidden among his rags. Of course, Jesus told us to give to all Beggars, for angels may be among them. And if you have been a bum—as I have—you know that in a gang of bums you seldom find two bits.

The Poet decided to help the Beggar. Have you ever observed the awful anxiety in a Beggar's face as you prepare to give him a lousy dime? Hours later, in his garret room, the Poet wrote:

> His coat of rags was stark with grease.
> And gnarled and cracked his hand;
> And from the ruin a ravaged eye
> Raped everything it scanned.
> I paused to search my pocketbook;
> He squirmed from side to side
> With torturing anxiety
> No vanity could hide.

The Arrogance of Charity

Do you feel good when you give to a Beggar? That's a damnable thing. Millionaires often become philanthropists and get a big kick out of giving to the lame, the halt, and the blind. They thank God that they're not like the recipients of their charity.

The Poet also suffered from the arrogance of charity as he pictured himself in this stanza:

> And now puffed up by charity
> That gave me virtuous calm,
> I placed the arrogant coins upon
> The Beggar's crooked palm.

A Sudden Change Takes Place in the Beggar

Instead of thanking the Poet, the Beggar showed his hate. Unless society has robbed a jobless man of all pride, he resents the hand that feeds him. A man wants work—not charity. Begging crucifies the soul of man. The Poet had the insight to see this. A Beggar, rightfully, hates a giver who thanks God that he is not like the Beggar. Hours later, in his garret room, the Poet wrote:

> I saw the hatred in his face,
> The pride prohibitive,
> The soul that agonized to beg
> That a jobless man might live.

The Poet Begins to Push Back Barriers

The Poet looks deeper. The Beggar becomes a symbol. An awful picture haunts the Poet. He sees the guillotine of hate Society has erected, the dry bones of the dead, and a strange Judgment Day. The soul of the Poet grows bigger—big enough to embrace the Beggar as a brother. Together they march toward the New World's sun.

> The Last Mile that a beggar walks
> To grub a piece of bread
> Leads to the guillotine of hate,
> The dry bones of the dead.
> But from those bones the underdogs
> Shall take the Judgment Seat,
> When worlds shall tumble into ruin
> Beneath their rulers' feet.
> Flesh of my flesh, bone of my bone
> The Beggars and I are one;
> But we beg no longer as we march
> To meet the New World's sun!

My Apologies to the Graduates of 1940
June 1, 1940

I stood on a dock in New York harbor in 1933. I saw that giant greyhound of the sea, the *Europa,* glide toward the open Atlantic. A vast silence fell upon the multitude. White handkerchiefs fluttered from the dock and from the decks of the ship. The lights on the great liner swung across the night.

My two friends and I had shaken hands with that exaggerated good humor men assume to hide their deeper emotions. It was the last time we were to be together. The great actor had got off one of his Broadway jokes. The famous newspaperman had given him a playful poke in the ribs.

Being a man of sentiment, I'd turned away and said to the actor: "You'd better get going, you boob."

The actor had replied with a laugh: "Bringing the curtain down on me, eh?"

That happened on a spring evening in 1933. My two friends and I shall never chat again backstage in a Broadway theater. The actor is somewhere in war-sundered Europe tonight. The newspaper-man is dead. When a voyage begins, no man can tell where it will end. Commencement is a serious thing. The journey of a lifetime begins with a single step. Nobody knows what lies ahead.

On the Ignorance of Commencement Speakers

I have been one of them. A commencement speaker is an egotist. But he is more than that. Otherwise he'd not rush in where angels fear to tread. The faculty calls him in as a guy who has the lowdown on life. He is a guide standing at the crossroads. The faculty has done its best—or its worst.

A commencement speaker is called in to advise the graduates. This is a damning admission of the part of the faculty. It is like a doctor calling in a specialist. It means that after the faculty has exhausted its efforts the students still need something or other before commencing the journey.

The commencement speaker puts on his rose glasses, his black robe, his hood of learning. The graduates, giving final proof of their ignorance, look up at the commencement speaker with that faith and devotion found only in the faces of domesticated dogs. Man loves the dog because the dog is the only animal foolish enough to trust man.

The commencement speaker orates about Life. Ah, ah—the sweet mystery of Life! The commencement speaker, remembering the bucks he'll get for his physical effort, pays a magnificent tribute to the self-sacrificing faculty who're thinking about the bucks they'll have next year if they're lucky enough to get back their jobs.

"Ah," sobs the commencement speaker, "ah, Life is real. Life is earnest. You are facing the greatest crisis in the history of the world. New occasions teach new duties. For four years you've sat at the toes of this beloved faculty. The world calls for men and women! Yes. Yes. And again, yes!"

Go Out and Conquer, Graduates of 1940

Every commencement speaker says these words in one way or another. Whether he speaks at Harvard or the Chittling Switch High School. A man's reach should exceed his grasp—or what are the bucks for? However, if a commencement speaker is wiser than Balaam's ass, he will not tell the graduates to seek the dollars in these times. Indeed, he will emphasize the spiritual values, while everybody is double-crossing to get the bucks.

Again, the wiser-than-dumb speaker will season his address with statistics. Nobody remembers statistics anyway. Not even the orator. So the orator can impress the ignorant by quoting figures. This proves that the speaker is "factual and scholarly."

I suggest from wide experience that a speaker deluge the faculty and graduates with statistics—especially if he doesn't have a speech worth a tinker's dam. A stamp can secure from Uncle Sam billions and billions of statistics. I remind you that Mr. Franklin D. Roosevelt has solved the problem of unemployment with statistics.

From Poverty to Riches!

This is a trick that never fails to get the applause of graduates, the faculty, and the long-suffering parents. Everybody likes true stories that give a false impression of Life. For example: Honest Abe went from a log cabin to the White House. Of course, no commencement speaker is fool enough to mention the millions of poor boys who were born in log cabins and died in log cabins.

Only a Richard Wright or a John Steinbeck would tell the stories of those who had high hopes and got nowhere. A success story builds you up—for a big letdown. That's the reason thousands of young people go to the devil. I wish the readers of this column could see some of the letters I receive from time to time. They wring the heartstrings. They come from young people and their elders who've been victimized by success stories.

It is awful for a man to use the magic of words to lift people to the heights, only to have the hard facts of Life dash their hopes to the ground. It is like a doctor who diagnoses a case wrong.

On Facing the Unknown

I got this idea from a hobo in a boxcar. He was a philosopher. He asked this: "What can a man do when he can't do nothing?"

How many people have ever sat down to think on that? Facing the future is facing the unknown. If success comes your way, any dumbbell can tell you what to do. But did you ever try to advise a man when he was down and out? Didn't your words sound empty? Why? Because you knew words couldn't solve the man's problem. The other day a brilliant scholar asked me where he could find a job. I didn't know.

I could've said: "Where there's a will, there's a way." But I feared physical violence, since the man was so much bigger than I.

If any graduate of 1940 wants to mess up a commencement speaker, let him say: "Do you know where I can get a job?"

I apologize to the graduates of 1940. I have but one thought to leave with you. I believe this will help you, whatever lies ahead. Go into your room and bolt the door and ask yourself the question: "What can a man do when he can't do nothing?" Nobody can answer that but you yourself.

Are You a Fugitive in the Stratosphere?
July 20, 1940

The word *stratosphere* often appears in the daily news. When I was a student of physics in college, I never saw the word. Of course, that doesn't prove that the word didn't exist. Perhaps it simply proves my ignorance. What a man sees or doesn't see has nothing to do with truth. Every day I'm seeing things that I've never seen before.

Stratosphere? Let us look into the word. I'm afraid we spend too much time looking at things. You get what I mean, of course.

Now the scientists, who deal in hard words that're easy to scientists, say this: "Stratosphere is the upper portion of the atmosphere, above 11 kilometers, in which temperature changes but little with altitude, and clouds of water never form."

You have to take the word of the scientists, for they're closer to truth than the word-slingers. Scientists are interested in what IS. Non-scientists talk about what AIN'T. Scientists ask for the gall of facts. Non-scientists want the sugar of prejudices. Scientists went into the upper atmosphere only after they had conquered the lower atmosphere. Science works from the immediate to the distant. That's the sensible way to work.

Flights into the Stratosphere

Professor Picard's balloon made flights into the stratosphere. You read about that in all the papers. Why are scientists interested in the stratosphere? You must remember that scientists are always trying to solve practical problems, with the least waste of time and energy. Scientists will listen to anybody with anything new.

Science says: "Prove that This is better than That."

Now, science did not go into the stratosphere until it had conquered the lower atmosphere. Science is demonstrated and demonstrable common sense. You get what I mean, of course. Science solves the problems of Today before attempting to solve those of Tomorrow.

Science sent balloons up a mile before trying to send them up ten miles. Science made an engine run fifteen miles an hour before making a streamlined train go two miles a minute. Science built a wagon to run on the ground before it made an airplane.

Science has a hard time, because mouth-Christians and democracy-whoopers misuse the inventions of scientists to exploit their fellowmen. Science builds a railroad car. Violators of the Constitution convert the railroad car into a jim-crow car. Science increases production. Selfish non-scientists decrease the distribution. Thus we have starvation in a land of plenty. Science digs gold. Mouth-Christians bury gold.

Therefore, the scientists condemn us for taking flights into the stratosphere before conquering the ground. We meddle with God's business in heaven and make a hell out of earth. We fly into the stratosphere of democracy and ignore the economic and racial injustices right under our noses. We talk about spiritual mansions and let babies die in filthy shacks. We want those speakers and writers who'll give us rides in the stratosphere. We do this because we're too yellow and selfish to face scientifically the facts of life.

Escape from Reality!

Perhaps you know the lines of this poem better than I. I've never taken time to memorize them. I don't know who wrote them. At least, this is the thought:

> Two men looked through the iron bars:
> One saw the mud; the other, the stars.

Speakers quote this as a profound something. I think it's bunk. Why? Because the poet and the speakers and the listeners condemn the man who saw the mud. With the mud of poverty, unemployment, and disease all about us, it's about time for us to start cleaning up the ground. You have to live on the ground.

I don't think much of a housewife who spends her time stargazing, when her house is dirty. I don't think much of a cook who looks at the stars, while the cockroaches and flies contaminate the food.

Don't be a fugitive from reality. Don't escape from the facts of life. Your greatest poets and reformers—Shakespeare and Jesus, Walt Whitman and Abe Lincoln—didn't take refuge in the stratosphere of romance and unreality. They dealt with men and women working out their destinies on earth.

Faith and Dreams

I have faith. I like to dream. I have faith to believe that a man who says he loves God and hates his fellowman is a liar and the truth isn't in him. Yes, I dream of a new earth. I have faith in the ultimate triumph of justice, liberty, and equality. In the meantime, I have sense enough to work for these things.

My faith is so strong that I make no distinction between theory and practice. For example, you either believe in democracy or you don't believe in democracy. I ask no more for myself than I'd give to a washerwoman. I believe in the Golden Rule on Sunday; also on Monday.

I want freedom of speech for myself; therefore, I want it for every other man. My only prejudice is against prejudices. If a Holy Roller wants to roll, that's his business so long as he doesn't roll into me or block the traffic. Suicide is a private matter. Use your razor on your own throat—not on mine.

If it feeds your vanity to think you're better than I, then I don't give a tinker's dam. But if you try to embarrass me or inconvenience me with your prejudice, then you've violated the Constitution and I shall give you hell.

I'm not going to fly into the stratosphere of the imagination, to keep you from mistreating me. I shall stay on the right side of the road, like a good American. If you try to push me into the ditch, that means you're a Fifth Columnist and you want a brickbat thrown at your skull in the name of Constitutional liberty.

The earth is big enough for all of us. Democracy was made for the earth not for the stratosphere of politicians. I don't believe in postponing the Constitution. The Stars and Stripes should be in the heart as well as the buttonhole. Take democracy out of the stratosphere. When a man says democracy to me, I ask: "What are you doing to wipe out economic, political, and racial injustices?"

How Can You Tell an Intelligent Mind?
September 28, 1940

The schools and colleges have opened their doors. Millions will travel the highways of learning. Few will learn anything worth anything. We have the factory system of education without the efficiency of the factory. Everybody's doing it! Doing what? Lindy-hopping from high school to college. Doing what? Jitterbugging through the university. There was a time when a Ph.D. meant scholarship. Now it means a mealticket. Once an M.A. meant a Master of Arts. Now it means a hot dog.

I'd like to write about education, but the educators don't know what education is. Yes, I've consulted Dr. John Dewey, Dr. Nicholas Murray Butler, and other great magicians. When I was in college, the professors there proved me a moron with their intelligence tests. That also happened to Edison.

So I'll take up the question of intelligence. No, be not afraid. I shall not discuss the intelligence tests which do not test intelligence. Let not my detractors gloat.

Sunshine and Shadow

I don't know what intelligence is, but I know it when I encounter it. Neither do I know what electricity or life is. I know what intelligence can do. I can tell an intelligent mind when I encounter it. Sometimes I don't recognize one when I meet it. You have to encounter things to know them. Education is the result of encounters with men and books.

Paul Laurence Dunbar wrote a book called *Lyrics of Sunshine and Shadow*. This is a big title. Sunshine and shadow. It helps to explain things. An intelligent mind is a mind that thinks in terms of sunshine and shadow. It sees things in terms of antithesis—contrasts. You see now what I'm driving at.

I once wrote a little poem about two men who looked at the same house. One viewed it from the front; the other from the rear. Each saw different things, of course. Both got some facts about the house; but neither got the truth about the house.

> You look at the front of the house;
>   He looks at the back:
> You call him a charlatan,
>   He calls you a quack.

That's the way it goes when you fail to think in contrasts, in terms of sunshine and shadow. I'll try to quote from somebody else's poem:

> Two men looked through the iron bars:
> One saw the mud; the other the stars.

Both of these men were unintelligent. An intelligent man would've seen both the mud and the stars. You see what I mean.

The Faculty of Seeing the Whole

Have you talked with persons back from a trip? Have you asked them about their impressions of a city. What do you get usually?

Very little. Why? Because they saw only one aspect of things.
They didn't see the whole. An intelligent mind sees the whole, the
contrasts in environment and personalities, the mountain and val-
leys, the good and bad, the comedy and tragedy.

I have in mind Joe Sewall's trip to Goldsboro, N.C., that he
reported in his column "Your Stars and Mine." He saw the tumbledown shacks within a stone's throw of the beautiful Negro
homes. That's what I mean by seeing the whole.

Kipling, the poet, speaks of walking with crowds and keeping
your virtue; of dining with kings without losing the common touch.
He should've added—getting a big position without getting a big
head. Sambo can understand that. Especially in Washington
among the Big Negroes!

Life consists of caviar and cabbage. Plenty of cabbage. Somebody called Washington the City Beautiful. In spite of the Negro
tenements where the rats jitterbug all day and all night, and the lice
do the lindy hop!

Yes, the intelligent mind places opposite ideas in juxtaposition.
Therefore, it is good at epigram and irony. And above all, it easily
detects sham, fraud, and hypocrisy. The intelligent mind cares
little for conventions, traditions, precedents, authority, titles, and
fads. It is not overawed by pandemic psychosis. (Skip it, Sambo.)

The Underlying Identity of Things

In the second place, intelligence sees the underlying identity of
things. Biological evolution is nothing more than the theory of the
underlying identity of animals. A prejudiced white man thinks he is
different from the Negro. The bedbug has more sense than that.
Therefore, he sticks close to man; he identifies himself with man.
And lives. The white Southerner does not identify himself with his
Negro brother. Therefore, the white Southerner dies economically, culturally, and spiritually.

Benjamin Franklin saw the identity of lightning and electricity.
Tennyson saw the underlying unity of life in a flower and life in a
man. Isaac Newton saw the identity of movement in the vertical
falling of an apple and the elliptical falling of a heavenly body.

Dr. Hibben, the logician, once said that the great mind discovers
the unity of things beneath a diversity of phenomena. Okay. The
black Zulu and the blond Anglo-Saxon have a oneness, an identity
of I-ness. Human beings differ quantitatively but not qualitatively.
Most men die without discovering that fundamental of life.

So the intelligent mind thinks in contrasts; then it sees the
underlying identity in contrasts. Shakespeare and Al Capone are

different in many ways. They are also identical in many ways. In every man there is the saint and the sinner, the rattlesnake and the monkey, God and the devil. Accidents of environment bring out these identical and contrasted elements. Murder, rape, and suicide live in each one of us. The intelligent mind sees homogeneity in heterogeneity. Caviar and cabbage differ only in the arrangement of electrons.

The American Youth Congress
February 8, 1941

Can the Boys and Girls Save Their Elders from Hell?

An old educator told me at the Peace Mobilization in Chicago last summer: "The boys and girls of Today are going to Hell."

"That is impossible," I replied, "because Hell is overcrowded with their mamas and papas, their grandmas and grandpas."

The old educator left me in a huff. He couldn't take it. Anger is the refuge of those who can't face the truth. I have no defense for the elders. They have made the world a Hell in which to live. No wonder they get hot in the collar when challenged by Youth! The governments of cities and states are run by the "wise" elders.

What are the terrible results? Slums, child labor, gangsters, rotten politics, peonage, lynching, jim-crow laws, corrupt medical practices, unemployment, business racketeering, prostitution, residential bombing, police iniquities, rattlesnake hypocrisies, murderous wars. By their fruits ye shall know them! No wonder the elders get riled when Youth points the accusing finger at them. What else can they do?

What Great Men Have Thought of the Elders

The elders are always telling Youth to pattern their lives after the elders. I can think of nothing more terrible for humanity. It would mean stagnation and death. Jesus didn't do it. At twelve He was challenging the elders! During His three-year ministry He denounced the elders as hypocrites and vipers. The rich young man failed to follow Jesus, because he wanted to keep his riches as the elders had taught him! When Jesus got ready to picture the Kingdom, He didn't select the elders. He took the children, "for of such is the Kingdom of Heaven." Jesus was betrayed and crucified by the elders!

The elders corrupted the earth and it was destroyed by a flood—according to the Bible of the elders. And the only elders saved were Noah and Mrs. Noah. Remember—Sodom and Gomorrah were "wide open cities" run by the elders—not by the young folk.

If you wanted to build a better city what is the first thing you would do? Plato answered that question over 2,000 years ago.

Plato said: "We must begin by sending out into the country all the inhabitants of the city who are more than ten years old, and by taking possession of the children who will thus be protected from the habits of their parents."

Yes, whether we like it or not, the greatest corrupters of the boys and girls are their conceited elders! Instead of condemning themselves, the elders condemn their innocent victims. Dr. Watson, the great child psychologist, would not let the elders handle his children. He didn't want them polluted!

Youth Looks Forward: The Elders Look Backward

Have you read John Locke's *Essay on the Human Understanding?* Read it. Jonathan Edwards, the first American philosopher, chewed and digested Locke's book at thirteen years of age. Locke discovered in 1689 that a baby comes into the world with a mind spotless like a piece of white paper. Ideas are not inborn. The mind of the child is polluted after the "wise" elders have got through teaching the child! A white called me a "n———r." He got the word from his elders!

In spite of the fact that Jesus continually told the elders that they must become like a little child, the hardheaded elders tried to make the child like the elders!

What are the terrible results? Hitler tries to make German Youth murderers like Hitler. Senator Bilbo tries to make Southern Youth hate Negroes like Senator Bilbo. In textbooks, over the radios, and in the newspapers the elders hammer into the innocent minds of Youth the lessons that will mean the exploitation and damnation of humanity. The only elders worth a plugged penny are those with the vision of Youth.

The elders have had thousands of years to bring happiness to the world. They have failed miserably. The elders talk about Democracy; but they will crush any Youth who tries to make the world safe for Democracy. The elders, as mouth-Christians, preach the parts of the Bible that won't hurt the elders; and as followers of Jesus the elders are millions of miles and then thousands of years behind Jesus.

When the Youth try to make the world a fit place for human

beings, the elders can only slobber at the mouth and cry: "You're Reds and impractical idealists!" The elders have been doing this since they poisoned old Socrates for telling the truth to the Youth of Athens. The elders always look backward. Youth looks forward. Thank God for youth!

I Wish the Youth Could Run the World!

I'm tired of the elders. They're hypocrites and vipers! They're like the old woman who messed up a barrel of good flour trying to make a pan of biscuits! I can think of nothing better than the worldwide funerals of those who are over twenty-one. I'm against wars, because they kill off Youth and leave the elders to plot other wars. On the other hand, I'd support a total war in which all the elders would be the first to go over the top.

I criticize the American Youth Congress for permitting the elders to deliver their "wisdom" to Youth. Would you call in a doctor all of whose patients have died after his kind ministrations? I see no logic or common sense in seeking the advice of elders who have messed up the world from the time of Mr. and Mrs. Noah.

The elders are not interested in changing the world. There are rare exceptions, of course. I know some old men and women who have the viewpoint and courage of Youth. I'll tell you a story. "Once a garden contained a hundred rattlesnakes. Five of them were innocent snakes whose fangs had been 'milked' of poison. But, in order to play safe, the gardener had to kill the one hundred rattlesnakes." In other words, members of the Youth Congress, the elders are your class enemy.

When Will Death Come for You?
March 13, 1943

(Coincident: I just finished this article as a telegram came announcing the death of my old friend, Dr. J. E. Dibble, of Kansas City, Missouri.)

Life is a funny thing. Man is a bundle of contradictions. Life is a box of surprises. I think man is the only animal that is consistent in his inconsistencies.

So I never say: "Men do this."

So I never say: "Women do that."

Well, now I started out to write a little piece about that famous hard-boiled writer, Ernest Hemingway, who wrote the famous novel, soon to be a movie, on the Spanish Revolution—a book called *For Whom the Bell Tolls.*

Hemingway is a hard-boiled sinner. Is that okay? But when he got ready to get the title for this book, his greatest, he went back to a spiritual-hearted man, old John Donne, the preacher. Now the modern preachers, generally speaking, never heard of John Donne. However, English teachers can tell you a great deal about him. Ain't that inconsistent?

Now, Reverend John Donne lives today, though he died in 1631. That's what the books say. I don't know, Reverend John Donne lives, not because of what he preached about God, but what he said about Man. You see I am inconsistent in my consistency; but consistent in my inconsistency—like Man. I wanted to write about Hemingway, but I am writing mainly about Reverend John Donne!

For Whom the Bell Tolls

I quote Reverend Donne: "No man is an Iland, intire of it selfe; every man is a peace of the Continent, a part of the maine; if a Clod bee washed away by the Sea, Europe is the lesse, as well if a Promontorie were, as well as if a Mannor of thy friends or thine owne were; any mans death diminishes me, because I am involved in Mankinde; And therefore never send to know for whom the bell tolls; It tolls for thee."

(I hope the printer printed it as is.)

This sermon has not been equaled since the Sermon on the Mount, 2,000 odd years ago.

After you have read this a hundred times, you begin to see the Four Freedoms, the Great Charter, the Declaration of Independence, the Liberty and Equality and Fraternity of the French Revolution, the Declaration of Independence, the Century of the Common Man, and the Golden Rule.

What does Reverend Donne say? No man is an island. Most men think they are. The South tries to make an island of the Negro. Jim crowism is an attempt to cut the Negro off from the continent of man.

I Die When You Die!

If the sea washes away a small clod, you have a smaller continent. True. All of us can see that America would be less, if the Rocky Mountains were to tumble into the sea.

What does Reverend Donne mean? He means that if a Sambo dies in Chittling Switch, it is important—for Humanity is less. Not only that. If a man dies whom M. B. Tolson has never seen, M. B. Tolson is less. Why? I am a part of Humanity. I am involved in Human Destiny. This is also true of every man in the world—white or black, big or little.

I tell you, friends, even as I write about this sermon of old John Donne, I am overwhelmed by it. I wish every modern preacher and teacher would talk on it next Sunday, next Monday—in fact, as long as this war against fascism lasts.

Now, when the black bell tolls, don't we dumbbells ask: "For whom the bell tolls?"

We think it tolls for John Doe or Aunt Hagar. Reverend John Donne says every funeral bell tolls for me. It tolls for you. Every time a man dies, you die and I die.

That's a deep philosophy. I hope you see it. It means that Al Capone is part of me; Senator Bilbo is part of me; the whore in Paris is a part of me. Conclusion!

> I die in part, when you die,
> You die in part, when I die.

En Route to Washington
August 21, 1943

The Sunshine Special, the crack flier of the Texas and Pacific, leaves San Antonio, the Alamo City, and speeds across uplands and lowlands, to the hometown of the St. Louis Blues. Gone are the terrible Apaches, who used to kill white men with diamond rattlesnakes. Gone are the slave markets of East Texas, where the riverboats brought their cargoes up the Sabine and the Red River.

So at midnight, I find myself in a jim-crow car, with jim-crowed Negro soldiers, on my way past the Smith and Wesson Line. The coach is jammed with men, women, and children. Talk—sometimes bitter. Dark laughter. Tall tales about the Southland.

We are jammed in the vestibule. A Pullman-porter-preacher, dead-heading to Little Rock. He lets an odd character in—without a ticket and without the knowledge of the conductor. We learn that the lean-faced little man is the Arkansas Traveler. Yes, a Man of God, going into the highways and byways with the Gospel.

As the train rushes through the night, the little preacher says: "Repent ye, for the Kingdom is at hand!"

A black sailor takes a long drink from a black bottle, wipes his mouth, and says: "Preach it, Arkansas Traveler."

Everybody laughs.

A Fat Sister Comes In

As the hours wear on, the talk becomes louder. We talk about everything. Yes, in the jim-crow car, there is a democracy among the passengers: two preachers, two professors, three porters, a third cook, a sailor, two soldiers—all piled together talking about this and that. Freedom of Speech? Yes.

The Pullman-porter-preacher says: "Randolph is the greatest Negro leader in America."

"Reverend," says the black sailor, "you're crazy with the heat. This damn Jim Crow is got you all screwy. Walter White is the greatest Negro leader."

The preacher belly laughs: "Walter White ain't no Negro."

The sailor's eyes bulge. "What is he then?"

The preacher says: "Walter is white. He's just *passing.*"

The dark laughter in the vestibule almost blows out the sides of the car. Ain't that something? Boy, oh, boy! Walter White *passing* for a Negro! In barges a fat dark sister, warlike, gigantic, with a small red hat on her vast dome.

The Fat Sister says: "You-all stop that noise. Ain't you got no race pride? You oughta go somewheres and git an edjucation. I always says, 'Nothing hurts a n———r but his mouth!' "

The Harlem Riot

A porter says: "Wasn't that Harlem riot a shame before God?"

"Hell, naw!" says the sailor.

"Harlem is a godless city," says the Arkansas Traveler.

"How can you condemn Harlem and steal a train ride?" says the sailor. "The Negro is getting tired of the white folk's monkey business."

"You tell it, brother!" says the soldier. "I feel like smashing this jim-crow car. It wouldn't do no good—but I feel like smashing it. Ain't you ever got sore, preacher, and just kicked a chair that happened to be in your way?"

The preacher says: "That's sinful."

The soldier says stoutly: "That's human nature. They call the Harlem rioters hoodlums."

A porter says: "What makes a man a hoodlum?"

The young teacher from an Arkansas college says: "Did you ever read Richard Wright's *Native Son?* Well, that book tells you what makes a black man a hoodlum."

The Arkansas Traveler says: "I don't read no book writ by the hand of man. I read *the Word of God.*

The sailor says: "Men, I never reads—for when I reads, I gits confused."

Golden Rule and Dog-Eat-Dog Rule
February 19, 1944

Joe Louis fought some mighty battles against some mighty men. So did Jack Dempsey. I saw both men in some great battles. I believe that if the two men had met, it should have been the Battle of Ring History.

In such a battle Joe would have won. Not because he is a Negro. Some black folk think any black man can whip any white man, if the white man doesn't call in the cops! But let us leave this. I'm talking about a bigger and better fight.

It is the Golden Rule vs. the Dog-Eat-Dog Rule. These two rules have staged many battles during the ages. Who won? Well, you know which. Why? Well, which rule do you use in business, in the school, in the church?

Dog eat dog is the rule of the jungle. Darwin stated it well in the survival of the fittest. Just as a powerful animal kills off the weaker animal, a big business kills off a little business; and a big mouth-Christian kills off a little Christian. Yes, and the big nation kills off the little nation. Yes, and the white kills off the black.

Great Religious Teachers

Since all the great religious teachers knew that men used the Dog-Eat-Dog Rule in everyday life, every great teacher gave to his disciples a Golden Rule. A Southern newspaper, the *Houston Post,* opened its eyes and said:

"The Ten Commandments and all the other biblical teachings for the conduct of men toward each other could be dispensed with, if everyone would live up to the Golden Rule."

True, O Lord! But the Golden Rule, plus all the other biblical teachings in Houston, Texas, doesn't make the white folk clean up the ungodly slums and streets in Houston! That IF is as big as the Rocky Mountains!

Christ said: "Whatever ye would that men should do to you, so ye even do to them."

Hindu said: "The true rule is to do by the things of others as you do by your own."

Buddha said: "One should seek for others the happiness one desires for one's self."

Parsi said: "Do as you would be done by."

Confucious said: "What you would not wish done to yourself, do not to others."

Mohammed said: "Let none of you treat a brother in the way he himself would dislike to be treated."

All great teachers have given us a Golden Rule. Why? They saw the tragedies of the Dog-Eat-Dog Rule. They wanted people to be happy. Out of their great hearts poured a passion for human liberty!

Are Men Dogs?

One night in Harlem I dropped into an apartment on Sugar Hill, the dicty spot of the Black Belt. Six women were there with cocktail glasses. I found them discussing men.

A high-yellow sister was saying: "All men are dogs."

As a defender of men, I observed that I had encountered all kinds of dogs—alley dogs, Park Avenue dogs, big dogs, little dogs, uneducated dogs, intellectual dogs. Dogs differ in kind and training.

Let us become serious, now. Most people believe that men are dogs; and women are dogs, too. That is, most people believe that Man is selfish, sinful, evil, lustful, hypocritical by nature. If Man is evil by nature—if human nature is evil— then it is right for men to practice the Dog-Eat-Dog Rule instead of the Golden Rule.

Is Man born good and does he become bad? Or is Man born bad? This is a deep question. Socrates debated it in Athens. Paul heard it debated on Mars Hill. Modern scholars have not the answer. Is Man good or bad or neutral? Will the Golden Rule work in society, or must it be left where it is—in Church on Sunday?

Maybe we shall find an answer to some of these questions by next week. In the meantime, you do a little thinking. So will I.

The Word *Freedom* in the Wolf's Dictionary
February 26, 1944

Let us continue our little discourse on the Golden Rule versus the Dog-Eat-Dog Rule. I believe this discussion a basic thing in our world today. We must all choose either the one or the other. The issue will face the gentlemen who sit at the peace table.

Out of these two rules, forever clashing, grow two different definitions of freedom. Let us not be dogmatic. While we utter the Golden Rule with our lips, we may—like Senator Bilbo—practice the Dog-Eat-Dog philosophy.

Freedom? Men have suffered for it; starved for it; died for it. Freedom has a double meaning. All four-legged animals do not mean the same thing by it; neither do all two-legged ones. So let us explain.

In the midst of the Civil War, Abe Lincoln, who could put deep things in simple words for backwoodsmen, gave two definitions of freedom. He observed that when the North and South, the Rich and Poor, the White and Black, used the word *freedom* they meant different things.

Let us look at freedom in the wolf's dictionary. What does it mean? To the wolf, freedom means the liberty to cut the throat of the sheep; tear the flesh from the sheep's bones; and fill his (the wolf's) belly with red meat.

Now, if the shepherd meddles with the wolf when he gets a lamb down, the wolf feels insulted. Yes, the wolf cries that the shepherd is taking away his freedom. Undoubtedly, from the wolf's viewpoint, the wolf is right.

The South is very much like the wolf. If the damned Yankee wants to abolish the poll tax or pass an anti-lynch law—the South yells, that the damned Yankee is interfering with States' Rights!

And the Yankee is. The South wants the freedom to jim crow Negroes; the freedom to disfranchise Negroes; the freedom to lynch Negroes when they get out of their place. The South has taken its definition of freedom from the dictionary of the wolf.

Now, the sheep has a definition for freedom. It comes from the sheep's dictionary. It's entirely different from the wolf's definition. So never expect a wolf and a sheep to agree on the definition of freedom. If they should agree, that means a dead sheep!

Old Abe Lincoln says: "The shepherd drives the wolf from the sheep's throat, for which the sheep thanks the shepherd as a liberator, while the wolf denounces him for the same act."

For the same reason, Bilbo calls Walter White a traitor and we call him a patriot! Bilbo says the Negro should be free to go to Africa; and I say the Negro should be free to stay in Mississippi. The wolf and the sheep can never agree on the word *freedom!*

Well, what shall we do? I agree here with Abe Lincoln and the little people. We must repudiate the wolf's dictionary.

What does repudiate mean? It means to reject, disown, discard, renounce, cast away! Yes, this is what we must do with the Dog-Eat-Dog Rule which is derived from the wolf's dictionary.

But I, for one, am ready to do more than discard the wolf's dictionary. I am ready to cast out the wolf himself!

V
Writers and Readings

The Biggest Event of 1938
in Black America
March 19, 1938

The events of 1938 are moving like the tat-tat-tat of a submachine gun, or like the actors in an old melodrama. If you miss your newspaper seven days in succession, you're as far behind as a turtle in a race with Jesse Owens at the end of a hundred yards. Therefore, a wise man opens his paper to the editorial page . . . and reads forward and backward.

What I'm trying to say is this: Richard Wright, a black boy from Natchez, Mississippi, of all the places that God and civilization forgot—furnished the biggest event of 1938 for men and women of color-struck Afro-America.

Richard Wright won the Federal Writers' Project Contest in New York City with a remarkable novel called fittingly *Uncle Tom's Children*. There's plenty of TNT in that title; and there's genius in the pen of this young storyteller who came out of the Delta bottoms, where Old Man River and the good white folk raise hell, when the Lord God Almighty has His back turned and the big senators are trying to decide if it's constitutional to have human bonfires on the lawn of the Courthouse Square.

Where Was the Negro Press?

Where was the cat when the mouse whipped the lion? Where was the Negro press when Richard Wright struck a harder blow at the white man's vaunted superiority than Joe Louis ever struck. Negroes say that the race doesn't get enough favorable publicity in the white papers. If a Negro janitor in a fashion store steals some negligee to doll up a high-yellow Venus, he makes the front page. No lie. Now, if the Borntraeger Press puts out a treatise on fertilization by Dr. Ernest Everett Just, nobody but the Zoological Institute at Griefswald, Prussia, will know anything about it. As a citizen in the sweet land of libertines, I am not surprised at this.

But tell me—please tell me, dark brothers—how did the Negro press overlook the signal achievement of Richard Wright, who won the novel contest sponsored by Uncle Sam and *Story Magazine,* the most distinguished fiction periodical in two hemispheres? The announcement was not carried in most of the leading weeklies, and in others it was tucked away in a graveyard corner.

One of our papers that boasts dramatically and everlastingly about Negro this and Negro that gave three puny lines to the WPA novel winner. The rest of the space was taken up by half-naked, hip-shaking showgirls and the Black Four Hundred posing at the annual Big Apple Breakdown. A worldwide white magazine carried Mr. Wright's picture and a thoughtful biographical sketch.

My God! What does a Negro genius have to do to get his picture on the front page of a Negro weekly beside the six-inch-square grin of Madame Alpha Devine, proprietress of the Kitchen Mechanics Beauty Parlor?

I like to know that Gabby Gay and his Red Hot Rhythm Boys, starring Snakehips Flippens and Chitterling Sue, played at the Parisian Theatre on Broadway Avenue in Rome, Texas. But I like to know also that Sinclair Lewis, the Nobel Prize winner; and Harry Scherman, president of the Book-of-the-Month Club; and Lewis Gannett, the famous book critic of the *New York Herald Tribune* gave a black man a famous prize in competition with some of the best brains of the white race.

A Race Is Judged by Its Geniuses

A race is not judged by its dollars. Its skyscrapers. Its big business. Its high-powered cars. If these things measured racial and national greatness, America would lead the world. Wise men judge a race by its geniuses. Its arts and sciences. Its Einsteins and Charles Darwins and Voltaires. In other words, a people is judged by its brains. The Royal Society of Arts of Great Britain will tell you that if you take George Washington Carver out of Alabama you may blot out the whole state and the world wouldn't miss it twenty-four hours later.

Who was the wealthiest man in Athens? In Rome? In the London of Shakespeare's time? Who knows? Who cares? But every school boy remembers old Socrates and Plato and Phidias and Sophocles. Every ignorant M.A. knows D'Annunzio and Papini. Every jackleg A.B. knows the Venerable Bede and Sir Thomas Malory.

Ever since old Alfred the Great made every Anglo-Saxon learn his ABCs with which the Anglo-Saxon conquered the world the white man has looked up to brains. If a white man gets a million dollars by hook or crook, he starts inviting artists to his country estate to increase his prestige. Sometimes he monopolizes a Negro artist. Read Clemont Wood's *Deep River.*

It's a Long, Hard Road for a Black Boy

Arnold Gingrich, famous editor of *Esquire,* said in an editorial on Simms Campbell, brilliant Negro artist, that the road to success is twice as long, twice as hard, for a negro genius as it is for a white man. Despite this handicap, Richard Wright defeated 600 white novelists. I take my hat off to him—not because he's a Negro but because he's a genius. Race is a biological myth and race prejudice a virulent form of insanity.

Richard Wright was born on a plantation near Natchez, Mississippi, a typical Nazareth in the Bible Belt. Can anything good come out of Nazareth? Yes. If it's good, it's got to come out . . . or die in the wilderness.

Little Richard's father deserted him. I wonder what Papa Wright thought when he saw the announcement that his discarded son—the rejected stone, you know—was being crowned by the American Nobel Prize winner, the famous Sinclair Lewis. Life is a funny thing. You ignore a guy today, and tomorrow his handshake will do you honor. You throw something down . . . and lo, it's a diamond in the rough.

Wright's mother was right: she took in washing and kept the little family from starvation until paralysis struck her down. Young Richard then entered an orphan asylum. But he's a genius, and I bet my plugged nickel he'll put that good mother in a novel and she'll be living when no man will know that a million other fine ladies lived in fine houses while Mother Wright was working in the white folks' kitchen.

Wright has known bitter poverty. He's swept streets and washed dishes and portered. I wonder what his bosses will think when they see his pictures in the big papers. I've just finished reading one of Wright's stories—''Fire and Cloud,'' in the magazine *Story.* I've read his poems. That man can write. I told my students that last year, before he won the prize. He doesn't pull his punches. Thank God! Yes, the hated radicals picked him up when he was a nobody. Now, everybody will pick him up, including Fifth Avenue and the Big Negroes.

Richard Wright, if you see this, stay among the Delta Negroes and write—and you'll be all right.

A Giant Has Fallen in Israel Today
July 9, 1938

When James Weldon Johnson, novelist, poet, diplomat, professor, lawyer, translator, lecturer, librettist, crusader for Negro rights in our verbal democracy, was killed at a railroad crossing at Wiscasset, Maine, last Sunday afternoon, one of the cedars of Lebanon fell in the white man's wilderness.

I saw him only twice in my life, on dissimilar occasions, but you can tell a lot about him from one encounter. I've read all of his books since that time and done some research on his life and works; and I feel like paraphrasing Shakespeare. Yes, the elements were so mixed in him that all the world might take a square look at him and say: "Here was a man!" I think Sinclair Lewis, the Nobel Prize satirist, who doesn't give a plugged nickel what anybody thinks about his thinking, paid James Weldon Johnson a fine tribute when he said: "He is an ideal gentleman." Old Sinclair Lewis, a BIG WHITE MAN, never paid a compliment like that to a BIG WHITE MAN. I wonder what the little white men think about that at Waycross, Georgia, at Okay, Arkansas, and in Washington, D.C.

The Orator

I rate James Weldon Johnson as one of the great platform speakers of our day. Speaking is a great art used by great thinkers and psychologists. It has been much abused by tenth-rate windjammers, like all other arts. But Jesus did not disdain it. He was the greatest debater of all time, and it was said of Him: "Never a man spake like this man." Old Huxley, the noble scientist and often called "Darwin's Bulldog" because of his ability to defend the theory of Evolution on the platform, outmatched even the pulpit orator Bishop Wilberforce. Logic can be eloquent. Because a man is dealing with facts he doesn't have to put everybody to sleep with dullness. Facts are eloquent when the dynamite is let loose in them.

Witness, James Weldon Johnson. He could put the facts of lynching so powerfully that I have seen him hold 15,000 people of all walks of life breathless for two hours in the hot Convention Hall in Kansas City.

Mr. Johnson said in his autobiography, *Along the Way,* that the great orator sets up rhythms between himself and his hearers.

That's based on psychology and physics. The most powerful thing in the world is the WORD—the spoken or written WORD. Words contain ideas. An idea holds the vast British Empire together. The Big Boys fear the word-man. A radical word-man is more danger-ous than an army.

I saw Mr. Johnson again at the banquet of the Negro Press at Howard University. I was just an undergraduate then, but I can see him now, sitting at the next table, his chin on the palm of his hand. Speaker after speaker got up and said nothing—empty platitudes that wouldn't jar the brain of a bedbug. Mr. Johnson's eyes were fixed on space. Was he composing a poem then or was he thinking about some big issue before the people while those little Big Ne-groes said nothings? I'd like to know.

When Mr. Johnson spoke everybody listened, agreeing or dis-agreeing violently. A great speaker divides an audience. When you have heard a great speaker you don't come out saying: "Oh, what a wonderful speech!" You come out either wanting to murder him or make him king. I believe it was the immortal Plutarch who said that when people heard Cicero they talked about his fine rhetoric, but when they heard Demosthenes they looked around for their spears and cried: "Let us march against that tyrant Philip of Macedon!"

The great speaker jars you out of your snobbishness and smug-ness. You want to take up arms against WRONGS in the social order. When Mr. Johnson told he-men and she-women that a black man had been lynched in Georgia, indignation ran high. Poise disappeared. Sophistication was stripped off. You wanted AC-TION, ACTION, ACTION!

The Economic Basis of Prejudice

I am doubtful if Mr. Johnson ever really saw the economic basis of race prejudice. That interpretation of ethnic problems came after his intellectual maturity. He did a great work in his day. His faith lay in BIG WHITE MEN. Mr. Johnson believed in the Talented Tenth of his race; like Dr. Du Bois, he had no solution for the problems of the masses of Negroes. In fact, no Negro leader has ever had a solution for the masses of Negroes.

Here is a chain of reasoning that cannot be broken, and the facts of the Depression prove it as never before. The race problem is horizontal and not vertical. The Negro cannot get anywhere until the masses of poor whites get somewhere, and the masses of poor whites cannot get anywhere in the United States of 1938. Now take the dope of optimism if you want to.

Mr. Johnson made a heroic effort for the Dyer Anti-Lynch Bill, but no lynch bill will be passed until the economic causes of lynching are removed. No race problem will be solved as long as you have poor whites in competition with poor Negroes, and that competition will last as long as our civilization is a competitive civilization—all Congressmen Mitchells and Dean Kelly Millers to the contrary.

The race problem will be solved from the bottom up and not from the top down. What happens among the masses of Negroes in the Detroit factories, the Chicago packinghouses, and the New Orleans wharves is far more important that what happens in our colleges and exclusive circles. Read Carl Sandburg's "The Masses." He has the historical lowdown.

Of course the Negro must fight with the liberals and radicals on all cultural fronts. Langston Hughes, Richard Wright, Paul Robeson, James Weldon Johnson, and others have done that. But watch the Negroes in the unions. Watch the CIO. Watch the cotton fields and steel mills. The Black Moses of tomorrow will come out of yonder slum or cabin.

The great Negro leader will probably have on overalls instead of a tuxedo, a greasy cap rather than a top hat. He'll doubtless chew tobacco rather than smoke a fifty-cent cigar. His grammar will probably be so bad that I'll have to flunk him in English 6A.

That Black Moses of Tomorrow will scare Mr. Roosevelt's Black Cabinet to death. He will come to Washington with demands rather than pleas. He won't know how to grin. He'll frighten the little ladies in the drawing rooms. He'll have brass buttons on his overalls rather than a fraternity pin. He won't know the difference between a Ph.D. and a lemur. But he will knows his RIGHTS AS A MAN. My good old friend Edwin Markham describes him in "The Man with the Hoe."

Negro American, What Now?

Dr. James Weldon Johnson has gone. We honor him. He did a great work. Negro American, what now? Well, we're waiting for these youths to answer that. We older Negroes are going to play safe and stand in the way of progress until death moves us out of the way. We're still trying to meet the problems of 1938 with the techniques of 1918. We've tried our best to be just like our master THE BIG WHITE MAN. Mr. Johnson asked a great question in this Depression when he said: "Negro American, what now?" But Mr. Johnson couldn't answer his own question.

Of Ants and Men
July 29, 1939

I like truth better than fiction—milk better than *skimmed* milk. And that brings me to John Steinbeck, whose proletarian *Grapes of Wrath* is the best-selling book in America at this moment. A few years ago Mr. Steinbeck wrote a horrifying short novel called *Of Mice and Men*. It was the hair-raising melodrama of a feeble-minded giant who got a big kick out of squeezing mice to death in his great paw.

The giant with the baby brain wandered through California with his peewee pal, a wise guy. The peewee pal could not keep the big half-wit from stroking soft things, especially mice. It was inevitable that he should stroke the soft tresses of a woman and then choke her to death.

Of Mice and Men appealed to thousands when it appeared on the New York stage. It was a thriller—with all the stage props and artificiality of the thriller, as pointed out by critic V. F. Calverton in an issue of *The Modern Quarterly*.

Of Mice and Men is fiction. *Of Ants and Men* is truth, a more thrilling book, by the eminent Dr. Caryl P. Haskins, a research professor at Harvard and the Massachusetts Institute of Technology.

King Solomon's Wisest Proverb

Solomon spoke 5,000 proverbs. Some say he was the wisest man that ever lived. Orientals have always placed the sage above the rich man—wisdom above dollars, a Confucius above a Henry Ford. Oriental scholars write books on wise men; American pedants write books on "Captains of Industry." In Western civilization, greatness is the stamp of the guinea or the image of a dollar.

King Solomon, taking time out from his hundreds of wives and concubines, uttered a wise saying: "Go to the ant, thou sluggard, and learn of his ways."

Now, I don't know what kind of sluggard Solomon had in mind—Lazy Bones or Senator Bilbo or Sambo Doolittle. There are two kinds of sluggards: the physical sluggard and the intellectual.

I have met some admirable sluggards who refused to do manual labor. They had logical reasons. These gentlemen of leisure argued that in our civilization it was not the man who worked who got ahead, but it was the man who worked others.

Examples? Why, there are plenty of them! On the plantation the

Negro farmers raise the chickens, but eat sow's belly; the white planters who toil not eat the chickens. The captains of industry loaf at Palm Beach and Saratoga while their underpaid factory hands do the dirty work. Did you ever hear Paul Robeson sing "Old Man River"?

> Black folks work on de Mississippi,
> Black folks work while white folks play,
> Pullin' dat boat from dawn till sunset,
> Gittin' no rest through de livelong day.

1757 versus 1937

One day I was riding past a plantation in Louisiana. The Negroes were out there working in the field, and a big red-faced planter was sitting on the veranda of the Big House. I heard an old black man singing:

> Black folks work from kin to cain't,
> White man's restin' in de shade.

In 1757, old Benjamin Franklin published a collection of proverbs called "The Way to Wealth." It told the little fellow how to get ahead.

"Plough deep, while sluggards sleep, and you shall have corn to sell and to keep," said the Dale Carnegie of 1757.

But in 1937, Mr. Roosevelt gave a contradictory proverb to the little boys: "Plow the corn under, if you want the prices to go up yonder."

So today, the farmer, who is the backbone of the nation, is lying on his back, dreaming about the pie he'll eat in the sky, by and by. Negro leaders who have more mouth than brains tell the little Negro to stay on the farm. Of course, these black saviors stay in the city. Leaders seldom practice what they preach, just as doctors seldom take their own medicine.

Those who think Negroes should go to the farms should get the hard facts from *Seven Lean Years,* by T. J. Woofter and Ellen Winston, a treatise published by the University of North Carolina, the only university in the South.

These authorities say: "But today, those who have tilled and sown the fields decay in shanties which would not pass any decent housing standards, or else like nomads, wander from State to State, in search of jobs."

Negro leaders are overworked making speeches. Many of them would live longer if they did not suffer from plethora of words. I recommend, instead of the hot baths at Hot Springs, a good dose of facts like *Seven Lean Years.*

Intellectual Sluggards

Our machine civilization breeds idlers who scorn manual labor. Our society sneers at the men with horny hands. Even our churches prefer a school mistress to a scrubwoman and a physician to a hodcarrier.

"He's too lazy to work," says the snob. This is a statement used to damn a fellow who refuses to be a hewer of wood and drawer of water. Yet common labor is held in contempt. The upper classes have a sentimental attachment for the Man with the Hoe, so long as he remains in the field with a hoe.

If King Solomon was talking about physical sluggards, I can see why he told them to go to the ant. How can a king be a king in a land of sluggards? An empire of Stepin Fetchits would erect no palaces for a king to live in—to enjoy his wine, women, and song.

A king needs workers so the king can sit down and take it easy. But there is one kind of sluggard that the Big Boys like: he is the intellectual sluggard. The South admires Negroes who are physically active but mentally asleep. They make good peons, Uncle Toms, and race-traitors. Captains of industry like intellectual sluggards. They slave for nothing and die, without asking the reason WHY? A wise question is the beginning of wisdom.

Colleges Turn Out Intellectual Sluggards

Our colleges and universities turn out A.B.s and A.M.s and Ph.D.s who are intellectual sluggards. If an original thought should enter the brain of one of these machine-made scholars, he would cry like a baby with a bellyache. Dr. Harold Laski of London University will bear me out in this.

Sometime ago Langston Hughes said that our colleges were grinding out cowards. This observation stuck like a leech to the soft brains of some of our "scholars," and they let out angry protests.

What makes the intellectual sluggard? Is it not true that students in some institutions cram multitudes of facts? Do they not sit at the feet of learned scholars? But they fail to digest their facts. They fail to apply their facts to life. They suffer from mental indigestion.

At this point we circle back to the ants. The ants have a more sensible culture than ours. Go to the ant, thou intellectual sluggard, and learn of his ways. Perhaps you'll pick up something better than Big Business, better than the New Deal. Perhaps!

Ants Have Higher Social Development Than Men!

Man is always boasting about his concepts of justice and charity. He is the only animal with a conscience—and the only animal that needs a conscience. In moments of self-condemnation, he wails that he was conceived in iniquity and born in sin. Most of the lower animals will say: "Amen" to this.

He is the only animal that needs a "Savior" to die for him on a cross. Man boasts that he is the only animal that can think; and the other animals are doubtlessly delighted that he is. Man says that God made the earth for his benefit; and Man does his best to mess up the earth. Once an idiot smashed up a car to prove that the car belonged to him.

Look at the most highly developed species of ants. Then look at Man's jungle of civilization. The baby ants are tended by the State instead of by the parent. Therefore, you don't find any "spoiled ants." Human mothers, with their ignorant "mother-love," ruin more children than Hitler and Mussolini. Dr. Watson, the eminent behaviorist, can tell you all about that.

The ants are like the early Christians whom the mouth-Christians of today don't know anything about. The ants share their food on a communal basis. They practice the Golden Rule. The ants have too much sense to have millionaires. I started to say that the ants have too much Christian charity to have Henry Fords and J. P. Morgans.

The ants hold all property in common. Sometime ago I wrote an article on fences. Well, ants don't build fences. They are too intelligent, charitable, and self-respecting. Man and the hog, whom man resembles very much, need fences. Ants hold property for the common good, just as Man, in a bright moment, developed the postal service for the common good. How much would you pay for a stamp if Mr. Rockefeller owned the mail service?

Ants care for the sick and disabled. Savages do the same thing. Civilized man thinks a poor fellow should make hay while the sun shines; that he should prepare for a rainy day. How many heartless people do you meet who oppose old age pensions?

Dr. Haskins's *Of Ants and Men* was written for men. The ants don't need it. Dr. Haskins hints that this animal "made in the image of God" may learn something from the ants. Man—thou intellectual sluggard! Stop bragging! The proper study of mankind is ants.

If I had to be born again, I would say: "Oh, Lord, make me an ant."

But since I cannot become an ant, I shall try to give my fellow-men the social wisdom of ants.

A Chance for Every Negro to Understand
August 23, 1939

The golden opportunity has come for every Negro. Sometimes a man comes along with a master key. John Steinbeck is that man. With all my heart and mind, I ask Negro readers to get that challenging book, *Grapes of Wrath*. Not because it is the best-selling book in America today, but because it is the eye-opener of two decades. It is about white folk. There isn't a Negro character in it. But Negroes will learn more about the Negro's conditions from this book than from a thousand offered by chicken-fed Negro leaders.

John Steinbeck sees things. Black Boy, this white man sees more things than John saw on the Isle of Patmos. Indeed, this is the "Book of American Revelations." And John Steinbeck opens the "Book of the Seven Seals." No lie!

I have talked with intellectual white men and black men about this book in Memphis, Baltimore, and New York. I even heard it discussed in a jim-crow car. If the poor white man and the poor Negro understood this book, there would be no jim-crow cars. They would say:

> There is no black,
> There is no white;
> There's only man,
> There's only right.

Grapes of Wrath tells the heartbreaking story of the uprooted farmers of Texas and Oklahoma. It tells the tragedy of the Dust Bowl and the 300,000 families that migrate to California, seeking jobs in an imaginary paradise. It is the story of man's quest for bread.

These are white Americans. They are not "bums" or "vagrants" or "ne'er-do-wells." They are haggard men and life-starved women and hunger-ravaged children in a land where all men are created and made unequal.

The Week Inherit Contempt

Negroes can understand the contempt in the word "n———r." Jews know the scorn of "kike." These white Americans suffer equally from the contempt of the words "rubber tramp," "Oakies" and "Arkies." All underprivileged groups suffer from stigmatizing nicknames, whether they are white or black, yellow or brown. The weak inherit contempt.

The droughts of nature and the tractors of culture sent these tens of thousands on their terrible journey. The tractor business boomed between 1930 and 1937.

But an increase in Big Business does not mean an increase in the prosperity of the people. Some Negro economists haven't discovered that yet. Often an increase in Big Business means a decrease in jobs. Here is the story in a nutshell by the eminent Dr. William H. Harrison:

"Between 1930 and 1937 tractor sales jumped 90 percent in the ten cotton states, hard-pressed owners merged tenant-operated farms, evicted the tenants, and cultivated the enlarged land units with highly efficient labor-saving machinery."

Grapes of Wrath is the *Uncle Tom's Cabin* of 1939. It lays bare the economic basis of society. It reveals with X-ray delineation the crisscrossing forces that move men and women in the flux of society.

Ma is a memorable character—with the strength, foresight, shrewdness, and forbearance of every man's mother. The Rev. Mr. Casey got me. I think in him we have the best character analysis of the duality of man, the striving between the body and the spirit. Then there is Tom, the ex-jailbird looking for the Utopia of a job.

This book gives the lurid contradiction between the Constitution and the lives that Americans live. How can white Americans denounce dictatorships across the Atlantic Ocean while the Dictatorship of the Dollar rules the United States? There are half-cocked critics of the New Deal who say people don't want to work. Well, this book shows the eagerness of the average man for a job. Several facts stand out in regard to these migrants.

From the Dust Bowl

First, most of them come from the Dust Bowl of Texas and Oklahoma.

Second, half of them had lived at least twenty years in their original home before becoming migrants.

Third, the typical family consists of man and wife, with one child less than five years old.

Fourth, three-quarters of the men range in ages between 24 and 44.

Fifth, about 90 percent are white.

Sixth, the heads of the families have completed an average of eight years' schooling.

Those who are interested in getting the solid facts behind Steinbeck's *Grapes of Wrath* may read *Factories in the Field,* by Carey McWilliams.

One thing is true: the really great novels of today are social studies as well as dramatic stories. The modern novelist is a scientist as well as an artist. He has bridged the gap between fact and fiction.

Black Slavery and White Slavery in America—or a Great White Scholar Lets the Cat out of the Bag
November 25, 1939

These are the times that try men's souls—and also their pocketbooks. That eminent scholar, V. F. Calverton, in his head-shocking history, *The Awakening of America,* proves that American democracy has always tried the souls and pocketbooks of whites and blacks alike.

No wonder Dr. George S. Counts of Columbia University declared: "This book is required reading for all friends of American democracy!"

Thinking Negroes are particularly interested in Calverton because of his interest in them. Through the pages of the chief French, English, and American magazines he has fought an unceasing battle for Negro intellectuals and the Negro masses.

Mr. Calverton's *Anthology of Negro American Literature* is required reading. It is significant that when Harold E. Stearns asked thirty-six outstanding Americans to contribute articles to his famous book, *America Now,* an inquiry into civilization in the United States, Mr. Calverton wrote a masterly essay on the Negro and his culture. As one of America's outstanding lecturers, Mr. Calverton has defended the rights and abilities of black men, right in the heart of the South, before mixed audiences.

Like Being a Prisoner in Jail

In speaking of the Negro in American civilization, Mr. Calverton says: "Being a Negro in the United States today is like being a prisoner in a jail which has several corridors and squares in which it is possible occasionally to see the sun and walk amid the flowers and fields that belong to the unimprisoned elements of humanity. . . . In fact, when lynching is included in the picture, the Negro's plight is far worse than that of the German Jew or Communist."

These are the challenging words of the man who wrote *The Awakening of America,* the man who has stripped American history of its hypocrisies, shams, platitudes, and lies. In truth it is a rewriting of history from the viewpoint of the Underman.

Mr. Calverton spent five years collecting the evidence, facts, and tangential data for this brainshocking volume. He has gone back to the original sources. Therefore many will be surprised by this American Apocalypse. Let us look at some of Mr. Calverton's uncovered facts:

White men have talked a great deal about the exalted position of white womanhood. Yet, during the Colonial Period, the Indian squaws "possessed a higher and more independent status than the women of England, France, or Spain." The white man in his egotism said that God created Man first; the Indian contended that God created Woman first. Among the Iroquois all family property was in the name of the woman. Mistreated squaws could leave their brutal husbands; white women of that period were doomed to matrimonial servitude.

Were First Slaves at Jamestown

In fact, the first slaves sold at Jamestown were not black men—but white women? They were sold for tobacco.

The Indians did not have jails. Justice among the Indians was impartial. Just the opposite was true among white men. The Indian was not treacherous and cruel in the beginning. He learned that from the white men. At Plymouth, in 1620, the Rev. Mr. Cushman pleaded with the white "Christians" to be as kind and sincere as the red men.

Mr. Calverton does not pull his punches when he summarizes the history of Indian habits: "It was not the Indians but the Europeans who were the betrayers, the disrupters, the destroyers of the friendship which had sprung up between the two peoples."

Now the Founders of America were hard on women. A man could have his wife publicly whipped. In case of an illegitimate child the man had only to confess his sin: but the church elders thought the woman should have "a public lashing."

The attitude toward white women, then, was similar to the attitude toward Negroes in the present-day South: woman was viewed as "a more evil creature than man . . . definitely inferior in economic, social, and psychological status."

Maryland was so full of bigamy, sodomy, and bastardy that an English minister called that state: "A Sodom of uncleanness, and a pest house of iniquity."

And, too, the good Baptists in that State did not permit "women to pray in public." Negro women were forbidden to marry, but they were "seduced by their masters. Such seduction had already become an old Southern custom." A fine comment indeed on white chivalry.

Harder On White Slaves

Mr. Calverton gives us a vivid picture of White Slavery and Black Slavery. In the beginning the masters were harder on the white slaves. One historical document says that there were "continual whippings, and extraordinary punishments such as hanging, shooting, breaking on the wheel, and even burning alive."

When the popular historians tell us that America was settled by the lovers of religious freedom, then go to Calverton's documented *The Awakening of America* and get the tragic truth. Here are the firsthand facts. And they are shocking. But nothing educates us like a shock.

Massachusetts as well as Virginia sold slaves, both white and black. And the hellish practice was justified by quoting the Bible! Deacons and preachers as well as cutthroats sold slaves. Announcements and advertisements of slaves, black and white, appeared in the Boston newspapers.

The England that is always talking about democracy comes in for severe condemnation. Court ladies and noblemen made profitable investments by kidnapping and selling children, white children, into slavery. In one instance one hundred small children were torn from their mothers and sent over by the rich London Company.

Mr. Calverton quotes the historical documents that picture the slave traffic, white and black—the misery, diseases, and terrible stench. "These slave ships were literal prisons in which men, women, and children grew sick, suffered, and died. There were no doctors on most of the ships."

Ours a Dollar Democracy

Mr. Calverton has done for American democracy what Dr. Beard of Columbia University has done for the Constitution— stripped it of its pious platitudes and revealed its stark nakedness. Out of this overwhelming multitude of facts, one theme and indictment stands forth: our democracy has a dollar democracy; our government has been a government of the Big Boys, by the Big Boys, and for the Big Boys.

Every black American should read this book. It is a history that is different. It will rid every Negro of his inferiority complex. It will enable him to understand America Now.

This is the history of the masses and not of the classes, of the oppressed and not the oppressors, of the underdogs and not the topdogs. Here we see with our own eyes and hear with our own ears the savage crucifixion of black slaves and white slaves on Crosses of Gold.

Men of good will in America and England look forward anxiously to Mr. Calverton's succeeding two volumes of his monumental History of America.

In the meantime you may secure Mr. Calverton's *The Awakening of America* through the magazine, *The Modern Quarterly,* published at 16 St. Luke's Place, New York City, New York. Mr. Calverton is particularly interested in the comments and criticisms of his readers, and you may be assured of his immediate correspondence.

Gone with the Wind Is More Dangerous than *Birth of a Nation* March 23, 1940

The acting in *Gone with the Wind* is excellent. The photography is marvelous. Miss Hattie McDaniel registered the nuances of emotion, from tragedy to comedy, with the sincerity and artistry of a great actor. Some of my friends declare that the picture is fine entertainment. So were the tricks of Houdini. So is a circus for children.

But *Gone with the Wind* was announced in the movie magazines, in billboard advertisements, and in the film itself as more than entertainment. It was billed as the story of the Old South—not a story of the Old South. That difference is important for us truth-seekers. Remember—the novel is a historical picture. Both the novelist and the producer say that.

Therefore, the first question is this: Does *Gone with the Wind* falsify history?

Take other historical pictures that came out of Hollywood. *A Tale of Two Cities, Zola, Abe Lincoln in Illinois, Juarez, Henry VIII, The Life of Louis Pasteur.* Historians were consulted and libraries ransacked to get the HISTORICAL truth for these pictures. A HISTORICAL picture is more than entertainment. Let us get that straight.

The Point of View in a Picture

The Birth of a Nation was such a barefaced lie that a moron could see through it. *Gone with the Wind* is such a subtle lie that it will be swallowed as the truth by millions of whites and blacks alike. Dr. Stephenson Smith calls the moving picture the greatest molder of public opinion. And the Chinese say a picture is worth a thousand words. I believe it after listening to the comments of some of my friends on this movie, *Gone with the Wind*.

The fact that this movie caused a red-letter day in the South should have warned Negroes. The fact that it was acclaimed by Confederate veterans who fought to keep Negroes enslaved should have warned us. From Key West, Fla., to El Paso, Texas, the White South rejoiced. Margaret Mitchell, who wrote the novel, is the Joan of Arc of Dixie.

Why? Why? Because she told the story from the viewpoint of the South. The picture was praised extravagantly in Darkest Mississippi where Negro children are not permitted to read the Constitution in school. The commendation of the White South means the condemnation of the Negro.

The story of the Old South can be told from the viewpoint of the poor whites, the Negro slaves, the Yankees, or the white masters. Miss Mitchell took the viewpoint of the white masters. That's the reason the White South rejoices over the picture. Be not deceived, if you love your race. I am sure you would not ask an enemy to recommend you for a position.

What Fooled Negro Moviegoers

If you put poison in certain kinds of foods, you can't tell it. If you beat a man long enough with your fists, you can slap him and he'll appreciate the slap.

The poor Negro has been kicked so often that he considers a slap a bit of white courtesy. Since *Gone with the Wind* didn't have a big black brute raping a white virgin in a flowing white gown, most Negroes went into ecstasies. Poor Sambo!

Negroes are like the poor husband who caught his wife in the bedroom necking the iceman and sighed, "Well, it might've been worse!"

I must give that Southern novelist and the white producer credit for one thing: they certainly fooled the Negro and at the same time put over their anti-Negro, anti-Yankee, KKK propaganda.

The tragedy is this: Negroes went to see one thing; whites went to see another. Negroes asked: "Were there any direct insults to the race?'' The white folk wanted to know: ''Was the North justified in freeing black men?''

Both questions were answered in this picture. Negroes were not directly insulted. The North was wrong in freeing the Negroes. For seventy years Negro-hating white men have tried to prove with arguments and lynchings that the North was wrong in freeing the Negroes. And some Negro fools have agreed with the white Negro-haters. If the North was wrong, then old Frederick Douglass and the Abolitionists were idiots.

Lies in the Picture

Gone with the Wind pretends to show historically the Old South. It fails to do this. It falsifies by leaving out important facts. *Gone with the Wind* is what a description of Washington would be like without the Capitol, the White House, the Federal buildings, Howard University, and other landmarks.

Half of the picture deals with the Civil War. But the Civil War comes like a spontaneous combustion. It appears like a rabbit out of a magician's hat. Every critic in America will tell you that a truthful work of art must have motivation—causation. *Gone with the Wind* shows not a single economic or social or political cause that led to the Civil War. How could a civilization be "gone with the wind" unless there was something to MAKE it go?

According to the picture, slavery was a blessed institution. (Stick to the picture.) The Negroes were well fed and happy. Last summer I stood in the slave market of Charleston. In the picture there were no slave markets tearing husbands and wives, mothers and children apart. As a young man, Abe Lincoln saw a slave market and cried: ''If the chance comes, I'll hit this thing a hard blow.''

Read Tourgée's historical accounts of his trips through the South. Read Dr. Frank's historical documents on the Old South. See Dr. Reddick's documents on slavery in the famous Schomburg Collection. Read what Thomas Jefferson said about the South. The Civil War was the inevitable culmination of economic, social, political, and psychological events spreading over a period of two hundred years.

It was like water piled up behind a dam finally breaking through. In dealing with history, leave the ''if's'' out.

The picture, then, lacked the motivation of historical truth, although it was supposed to be a historical picture. The Civil War was inevitable. It had to come because of definite economic causes. Slavery was a bloody institution. Of course, there were good masters. But the institution was built on the rape of Negro women, the hellish exploitation of black men, the brutalities of overseers, and bloodhounds that tore human beings to pieces. Read the documents of Dr. Frank, a white Southerner, in his book, *Americans*.

These are the reasons why the Old South is "gone with the wind." The picture does not show that. Therefore, millions of white men, women, and children will believe that the North was wrong in freeing the Negro.

Propagandistic Tricks in the Picture

The picture aims to create sympathy for the white South. We see thousands of dying and dead Confederate soldiers. The only Yankee who dies (in the picture) is a blue-coated soldier trying to rob and rape a Southern white woman. Yet General Sherman ordered the Yankees to protect women and children! When they didn't he had them shot. Atlanta burns. But the picture does not tell us that the Confederates set it afire! We get the impression that the damned Yankees did it.

We see a Union shell crash through a window of a church containing a painting of Christ; wounded Confederate soldiers are in the church. We are not told that white churches defended slavery in the South. These tricks will hoodwink millions of people.

Even the Ku Klux Klan is idolized. We see white gentlemen of the KKK returning home at night, while a big burly Yankee officer questions the innocent white ladies. Nothing is said about the brutalities of the KKK that stank to high heaven. Hitler's persecution of the Jews is nothing compared to the KKK's hellish treatment of our black forefathers!

The happy Negroes (in the picture, of course) go out to dig trenches for the Confederates, to keep themselves and their wives and children in slavery! The historical truth is this: When the Yankees marched through Georgia, the slaves, like sensible people, deserted the plantations by the tens of thousands. Some fell upon their knees and kissed the feet of their Yankee deliverers. General Sherman had to make thousands of them go back to their good (?) masters.

When old Abe Lincoln entered Savannah, he had to chastise the mammy slaves for kissing his boots.

"You should bow to no one but God," said the Great Emancipator.

The picture did not show the poor crackers, who outnumbered

the white masters ten to one. These poor white men were degraded by pellagra, illiteracy, and the opium of poverty. That was a lie of omission in the picture.

Plato said 2,000 years ago that aristocracy is built on either chattel slavery or wage slavery. *Gone with the Wind* did not show that Southern aristocracy was built on both. I sat for four long hours waiting for that gigantic historical truth to appear—and all I saw was the heartless action of Scarlett O'Hara.

The South Won the Civil War!

I am not bothered much with what Negroes think about *Gone with the Wind*. Most of them won't think. They have bridge, and the Strutters' Ball, and the fraternity powwow, and church politics, and fornications to think about.

What, then, will be the effect on millions and millions of whites from the Atlantic to the Pacific? What will be the effect when the picture is shown in South America, France, England, Germany, and the islands of the sea?

It will be this: The North was wrong in fighting to free black men. The grand old Abolitionists were lunatics. Negroes didn't want to be free anyway. Slaves were happy. The greatest pleasure of the slave was to serve massa.

Southern whites understand Negroes; that's the reason they treat them as they do. You need the Ku Klux Klan to keep Negroes in their place. All slaves were black; no white men had any mulatto children. There were no slave markets. Yankee soldiers went through Georgia raping white virgins. Negroes loved (with an undying love) the white masters, and hated the poor whites because they didn't own Negroes. Dixie was a heaven on earth until the damned Yankees and carpetbaggers came.

The Negroes were so dumb that they hated the very Yankees who wanted to free them. All masters were gentlemen—without high-yellah mistresses. Southern gentlemen were so honorable that they didn't yield to temptation when hussies, like Scarlett, threw their passionate bodies at them.

These are the untruthful things white people, all over the world, will believe when they see *Gone with the Wind*. Yes, some Negroes will believe these lies also.

And now, dear readers, to see what I have seen, you will have to put yourself in the place of a white man. Can you do that? I hope you can.

Richard Wright, the Negro Emancipator:
His Tribute to the *Washington Tribune*
April 6, 1940

Richard Wright is like the NBC System. His name reaches from coast to coast. All over America, literary critics are singing his praises. The *Dallas Morning News,* the outstanding newspaper in Dixie, gave more space to Dick Wright than it has ever given to any other novelist in its history. A button on my vest popped off as I read the tribute. No lie.

I see that the *Washington Tribune* is taking orders for *Native Son.* I say HERE and NOW that the *Tribune* has a better right to do this than any other Negro paper. Why? Well, permit me to play upon the harp of your memory.

In 1938 Richard Wright won the WPA Novel Contest against nearly 600 white writers. The judges were Sinclair Lewis, Nobel Prize winner; Harry Scherman, president of the Book-of-the-Month Club; and Lewis Gannett, book critic of the *New York Herald Tribune.*

That week your Caviar-and-Cabbage columnist carried two columns on this achievement. That week your columnist lamented the tragic fact that Negro newspapers buried this achievement beneath a mountain of photographed high-yellah mamas and I'll-get-the-kinks-out beauticians.

Your columnist asked the question: "What does a Negro genius have to do to get his picture on the front page of a Negro weekly beside the six-inch grin of Madame Diana Devine, proprietress of the Kitchen Mechanics' Beauty Parlor?"

The Richard Wright Chorus

Negroes have a song named "Too Late, Too Late." The white intelligensia discovered Dick Wright some years ago. Before me lies a letter from Jack Conroy, the novelist and editor of *The Anvil.* Back in the twenties, Jack Conroy published the stories of this Negro genius. What were we doing then?

My point is this: As Negroes we are always kicking off the white man; yet we do little for unrecognized black genius. After the whites have made a Negro famous, we break our necks to get upon the bandwagon. We are good at singing the chorus, after the white man has sung the "lead." When Marian Anderson was unknown, we couldn't squeeze out two bits to hear her. But now that she is famous, we'll pay $2.50 to sit in a peanut gallery to hear her.

Since Fifth Avenue is now calling for Dick Wright, every sassiety matron in the Capital will want to invite him to dinner. Dick Wright, the black ex-hobo, will be fawned over by the high-yellah wives of overworked dark Babbitts. I know when I see Dick Wright again I'll have to crawl through forests of silk-stockinged legs.

Jews, Irishmen, Scots, Mexicans, Czechs, Slavs—all racial and national groups recognize their geniuses first. The Negro lets other racial groups discover Negro genius. Why? Well, for centuries the Big White Man taught us that a Negro was a nobody until a white man said he was somebody. We suffer from a Caucasian Complex. We do all we can to prove our inferiority. A black scholar will quote a white scholar, as if the white scholar were the Lord God Almighty!

Back in 1938, Dick Wright expressed his appreciation for the tribute paid this work by the *Washington Tribune*. He said that he was going to do something bigger. He wrote a letter to this column saying that he was putting the final touches on *Native Son*. He said he was packing in it "all the sinews of his body and soul." What-a-man!

Every Negro Should Read This Book

The hardest job facing a Negro is trying to break into print as a novelist or poet. Literature marks the high-water mark of any civilization. A hundred years from now the only thing that will be known about the contemporary Negro is this: In 1940, Richard Wright, Countee Cullen, Langston Hughes, Sterling Brown, and Zora Hurston wrote in America. Time may salvage a few other Negro writers. I don't know.

I am trying to say that a writer has the greatest chance at immortality. Books are our greatest social legacy. The true attribute of a cultivated man is his love of good books. I am not talking about the books of specialists, either. Every teacher has to read books in his field in order to hold his job. I am talking about the MUST BOOKS of CULTURE.

Now, Mr. Wright's book is such a book. It is not only a work of art; it is a work of education. It has an advanced point of view. It contains all that is scientific in sociology, economics, and psychology. It is radical. It is as radical as truth itself. It takes Bigger Thomas, a "bad nigger," and shows WHY he is bad.

It is an emancipation proclamation in the Negro world of today. It will do more to improve interracial relations than a billion interracial dinners and a thousand Negro choirs broadcasting Negro spirituals.

The Solution of the Race Problem

When you read the speeches and books by our Big Negro leaders and experts, you feel like sentencing these gentlemen to fifty years of study at the feet of Richard Wright. They don't know what it's all about. They have a microscope looking at the pimple on an elephant's ask-me-no-questions.

Mr. Wright gets at the CAUSES of racial prejudices and poverty. He is a bitter enemy of Capitalism, like the recent John Steinbeck in *The Grapes of Wrath*. When a white man reads *Native Son*, he hangs his head in shame. He knows the race problem cannot be solved by interracial dinners and ping-pong charities.

For two years in this column, I have thundered the economic basis of racial prejudice. I have said that the Big White Man is the Negro's worst enemy. Mr. Wright has proved that. Thousands of whites all over the country have said "Amen." Not a single critic has said "nay." That is remarkable, indeed.

I shall never forget what Mr. Wright said two years ago: "A Negro writer must see the connection between a black woman picking cotton in Alabama and a cotton broker in his swivel chair on Wall Street."

Mr. Wright has pointed the way to Negro freedom. Millions of black men and women will have to about face. It took guts to do what he said. It took also supreme art.

Mr. Wright has faith in the Negro underdog. He does not scorn Sambo and Aunt Hagar. His attitude is antipodally different from that of our 2x4 upper-class Negro snobs. Mr. Wright is not interested in "The Talented Tenth." He is concerned with black humanity. There is a sermon in *Native Son* for every Negro preacher in America. There is a lesson in it for every Negro teacher. I hope they see it. Of course, most of them won't.

The Philosophy of the Big House
September 21, 1940

You saw the picture *Gone with the Wind*. I wonder if you saw the most significant thing in that melodramatic movie. Some people were held by the thrilling plot. Others, by interesting characters. And others, by the breathtaking photography.

But those were not the significant things in the picture. They were on the surface—could be easily seen by any casual eye. Strange to say, only after the lapse of months did I really see the big thing in the picture. And I saw it with the eye of the mind rather than with the eye of the body.

Now, everything in *Gone with the Wind* could've been left out of both the novel and the picture but one thing. The movie could've had other characters, other settings, other happenings. Indeed, its author might've used another plot. But there was one thing Margaret Mitchell had to use to create *Gone with the Wind*.This novelist had to put into the book the Big House. The director of the movie had to use the Big House. Southern aristocracy could not be pictured without the Big House. The Big House is the most significant thing in the history of Dixie.

The Men and Women Who Write about the South

Every civilization has its symbol, its cornerstone, its label, its trademark. The pyramid represents ancient Egypt; the Via Appia, ancient Rome; the bombing plane, Nazi Germany; the $ sign, the United States.

The symbol of the South is the Big House. When economists, sociologists, historians, educators, New Dealers, and novelists write about the South, their collective volumes may be called *The Big House*.

When Booker T. Washington gave his famous address at the Atlanta Exposition, his theme grew out of the Big House. When T. S. Stribling wrote his famous three-volume novel which won the Pulitzer Prize, his stories revolved around the Big House. When old Senator Bilbo advocated sending the Negro back to Africa, his speeches came from the Big House. Mr. Caldwell's conscience-shaking *Tobacco Road,* Mr. Basso's realistic novel *Courthouse Square,* Mr. Faulkner's shocking *Sanctuary*—all of these writings develop, in some way, the history and tragedy of the Big House.

You have read Langston Hughes's powerful poem, *Mulatto.* You have seen the play that bears the same name. Perhaps you know about Randolph Edmonds's one-act play, *The Breeders,* which was given this year as a high spot on the program of the drama meeting at Chapel Hill, at the University of North Carolina. Mr. Hughes and Mr. Edmonds develop the theme of the Big House.

What the Big House Means

Most of the Negroes and few of the whites who saw the Big

House in *Gone with the Wind* realized what the Big House means. I admit there is a veneer of glamor about the Big House, with its sweeping green lawns, its magnolia blossoms, its high-ceilinged rooms, its magnificent staircases, its waltzing couples, its mellow aristocracy, and the stables of fine horses.

But look *below* the Big House, as it sits majestically on its overlording hill. What do you see? You see the poverty of the cabins, the half-fed and ragged slaves and serfs. The Big House rests on the blood and sweat of the white masses and the black masses. The Big House is built on corpses. Through the wide windows of the Big House floats the stench of the cabins.

It makes me think of my youth. I used to work in the wealthy country-club district of Kansas City, Mo. Many times, as I cleaned the drawing room, through the open windows came the stench of the packinghouses in the river bottoms.

Plato said, a long time ago in ancient Greece, there could not be an aristocracy without slavery. An aristocracy must have either wage-slaves or chattel-slaves. Senator Calhoun, defender of the Big House in antebellum times, said that. Northern Senators could not answer him on this point. I thought of this as I stood beneath the statue of the great slave-advocate in Charleston last summer.

The Big House represents exploitation, jim crowism, disfranchisement, chauvinistic superiority. The Big House represents the spirit of the Ku Klux Klan. People who admire the Big House fail very often to look at the human misery on which the Big House is built. Those without conscience see the human misery—and close their eyes.

The Negro and the Big House

The biggest tragedy of the Big House is this: its hellish philosophy has trapped the minds of so many Negroes. The black mammy in *Gone with the Wind* loved the Big House, for she received the crumbs that fell from the Big House table. There are Negro teachers and politicians who love the Big House for the same degraded reason. A man's body may have to accept crumbs, but a man's soul can demand his share of the dinner. A man may be as poor as a church mouse; but he doesn't have to accept, without a struggle, this picture of desolation:

> Ill fares the land, to hastening ills a prey,
> Where wealth accumulates, and men decay.

This is the way Oliver Goldsmith pictured England. It is well to remember that England has her Big House—Buckingham Palace, surrounded by the slums of London. Wherever there is a Big House, wealth accumulates and men decay. Yes, the Big House theory means starvation in a land of plenty.

But most people see nothing wrong with the Big House. Now, the Big House scorns the cabins. When a Big House falls, there is weeping and wailing and gnashing of teeth. Nobody weeps when a cabin is gone with the wind. Nobody wants Sambo to come to the front door of the Big House. Don't highfalutin' Negroes object to ignorant Negroes who "embarrass" them in public places?

We should like to clean up the cabins about the Big House. Yea, whitewash the cabins. But don't tear down the Big House and produce a democracy of clean cottages! You see, our talk about democracy is bunk. We want a democracy with Big Houses. That is impossible. A democracy cannot have a Big House with its cabins of wage-slaves. In an American democracy, all the people would live in clean cottages. But we don't want that.

A White American Asks Negroes to Kick Him in the Pants
November 2, 1940

A strange request lies before me. It comes from a white American—a gentleman and scholar. It's the kind of letter that makes a Negro sing hymns of joy instead of the blues. It inspires my soul to say to my body: "Keep your hand on the plow. Hold on!" In a world of racial conflicts, it is a shot in the arm of the mind.

But let me tell you briefly about the man who blames Negroes for not kicking white Americans in the pants. Mr. William Blake is a historian, an economist, and a novelist. As a white-collar worker, he has studied international banking, behind the scenes, in the capitals of Europe and America. He knows, therefore, by theory and practice, what makes the wheels go 'round in high finance. His eyes *saw*, and his ears *heard*.

He has written two best-selling novels—*The World of Mine* and *The Painter and the Lady*. He is now at work on another novel dealing with the Civil War. It will not be a perversion and distortion of history like *Gone with the Wind*. You may rest assured that William Blake will not paint a Big House with slavery-loving slaves.

His Ancestors Demanded Emancipation before Lincoln

We often say: "He is a chip off the old block." This makes me hot in the heart. Most people—including [misguided Negroes—make this statement proudly]. A truer statement would be: "Environment will tell." That's the reason we ask a man: "Where are you from?" If a White man is from Onward, Miss., I know what to expect.

Sensible people are more interested nowadays in ideas than in blood. Theories of heredity and blood superiority belong to the "Ratzis" and Fascists. Hitler and Senator Bilbo believe "blood will tell." However, their barbarian beliefs and savage motives prove "ideas will tell." As a man thinketh, so is he! That goes for genius, too—which is as rare as a white black bird.

I hate to hear a Negro snob boast about his family tree. A man should never shake his family tree in public. If you do, you may be shocked to death. Why? Because an idiot or a murderer may fall out.

Now, Mr. William Blake tells me about his ancestors in this letter. But he says nothing about heredity. He writes about the ideas of his ancestors. I respect him for this.

Mr. Blake says: "My ancestors were in the Home Guard that knocked out the quality in St. Louis in '61, and demanded the emancipation months before Lincoln saw its widsom. He thought you kept the Border states in line by caution, whereas we knew liberty was the solvent. We also followed the earlier and wiser Carl Schurz on the necessary distribution of land and credits and agricultural education to the freedman."

Mr. Blake is proud of the freedom-loving ideas of his ancestors—not their biological heredity. In this sense, he is a chip off the old block. I like that kind of chip. Today, Mr. Blake is fighting for manhood rights.

A Stubborn Mule and the Ozark Men

Again, Mr. Blake writes revealingly: "I am as stubborn as a mule, and as incredulous as the Ozark men."

Have you ever watched a mule? His hardheadedness takes him in a straight line. Hold this point a minute. I want to say a word about Mr. Blake's being "as incredulous as the Ozark men." I've lived in the Ozarks. Those folk are incredulous, skeptical, inquisitive, disbelieving.

Plato says a wise mind is an interrogating mind. It wants to know why. It doesn't accept a thing because the Big Boys say it's right. It doesn't get on the bandwagon. A wise man thinks for himself. He questions everything. That's the only way to find truth.

You can see that Mr. Blake questioned economic theories and racial standards. He has not accepted the popular prejudices against the Negro. Beware of the man who says *Yes* to the status quo. Shun the man who is out to win friends and influence people in spite of Justice, Truth, and Democracy. I like a man who is as stubborn as a mule, after he has discovered what is right. Be sure you're right, then go ahead like an Ozark mule!

> A pussyfooter is worth
> A ball of lead:
> A middle-of-the-roader
> Is better off dead.

His Only Objection to Negroes!

When it comes to my people, Mr. Blake is brutally frank. What he says will shock many whites—and some Negroes. But we Americans need educating. And Dr. Will Durant says: "Nothing educates us like a shock."

Now, Mr. Blake has a peculiar objection to Negroes—as a whole. His attitude is challenging. Both Senator Bilbo and Uncle Tom won't like this. It is steak—to be chewed and digested. Many whites object to Negroes in different ways. So do many Negroes.

Mr. Blake says: "The only objection I have to Negroes is that they don't kick us in the pants enough, and make us pay them compound interest for all the rottenness we have shown to them and theirs."

It's almost miraculous to have a white man say that Negroes should kick whites in the pants! Yet, God knows that's exactly what they need. I've kicked whites on the shins. But I never thought of kicking them in the pants.

A man should face the world standing up. Prejudice keeps a man down. Too long has the white man sat down on the Negro to keep him in his place. The white American has sat down on Democracy and Justice. All my life I've searched for Democracy and Justice; and, lo, the white man has been sitting on them! His pants have worn the Constitution to tatters. The Bill of Rights is so crumpled and messed up that you can't read it with a powerful microscope.

Mr. Blake, we thank you for your invitation. We shall remove your objection to the Negro by kicking the white man in the pants. We shall kick and kick until the white man stands erect and looks the world in the face as a man should. Then, as man to man, the Negro will shake hands with his white brother!

Negro Heroes of the Oar, Track, Diamond, Court, Gridiron, and Ring
November 9, 1940

> To set the cause above renown,
> To love the game beyond the prize,
> To honor as you strike him down,
> The foe that comes with fearless eyes,
> To count the life of battle good,
> And dear the land that gave you birth,
> But dearer yet the Brotherhood,
> That binds the brave of all the earth.

With these sports-inspired lines from Sir Henry Newbolt, Mr. Edwin B. Henderson, the dean of Negro track and football officials, opens his drama-packed book, *The Negro in Sports*. This is a two-fisted, pioneering volume produced by its champion of Negro youth through the urgency of that father of Negro historians, Dr. Carter G. Woodson.

From Herodotus of Greece to H. G. Wells of Great Britain, historians have painted the march of Man. Perhaps tomorrow some scholar unburdened by academic degrees will give us a profound history of Man revealed through the pageantry of sports. The sports of a people are socially significant. Mr. Henderson is vitally alive to this fact. Therefore his study of Negro athletes gains added depth and scope.

The Timeliness of the Book

Man is both animal and human being—Body and Mind. That's the reason great scholars, both ancient and modern, have declared that education is the developing of a sound mind in a sound body. Mr. Henderson points out that Rome was conquered by a race "physically fit and mentally alert." That is the story of the decline and fall of all nations. Luxurious living and effeminate manners have always sealed the doom of peoples. It is the barbarian, ancient or modern, with his emphasis on physical culture, who crushes effete civilizations.

Therefore, Mr. Henderson's *The Negro in Sports* makes illuminating drama against the background of contemporary events. The totalitarian dictatorships, where fascist or communist, have gone in for mass athletics. Their young men and women are physically fit.

226

Mr. Henderson observes: "The decline of Rome was coincident with the professionalism of her athletics and games."

This is something for our educators to ponder in this period of national crisis and international chaos. The culture of the Dark Ages produced consumptive monks, but not athletes of Phi Beta Kappa distinction.

The Duke of Wellington used to say: "The battle of Waterloo was won on the field of Eton."

That is another way of saying with Aristotle: "On the education of the youth rests the safety of the State."

Yes, the ideal in education is a sound mind in a sound body. While *The Negro in Sports* displays a glittering galaxy of Negro athletes, it also reveals the writer as a staunch advocate of high-principled manhood and womanhood. This stands out especially in his emphasis on eligibility rules in the CIAA, the MAAA, the SAAC, and the SWAC. Mr. Henderson goes back continually to the ancient Greeks and Romans to signalize the ideals of good sportsmanship.

Negro Pioneers in Sports

Emphatically, this is a pioneering work. While we may be familiar with contemporary Negro athletes like Joe Louis, Henry Armstrong, Kenny Washington, and Wilmeth Sidat-Singh, we may be unaware of the existence of such early heroes as Bill Richmond and the "Morocco Prince."

It is interesting to observe that the first college director of physical education was a Negro, Professor A. Molineaux Hewlitt. I wonder how many Negroes are taught this when they take their degrees in physical culture at Harvard and Columbia. The gentleman was described by T. W. Higginson in the Harvard Book published in 1875 as a "respectable estimable character." Professor Molineaux—a full-fledged professor, by the way—taught Harvard gentlemen the manly sports in 1859, while members of his race were being sold along the Potomac!

There were giants in those days. As I read the thrilling pages of *The Negro in Sports* I thought of the great Joe Louis and Jack Dempsey. How would they have stacked up with those ancients? Today we have three-minute rounds; then a man fought until he was knocked down. A fighter rested thirty seconds instead of a minute. He could use the pivot blow, the rabbit hook, and the kidney punch. At that, fights went sixty and seventy rounds! Now, at the end of forty-five minutes, fighters are winded like two marathon runners. In that day the Negro, "Morocco Prince," battled, with bare knuckles, Tom Cribb for four hours and seven minutes!

The Social Significance of the Book

Negro athletes, professional and amateur, of Today and Yesterday—boxers, football stars, baseball players, golfers, basketball artists, tennis stars, sprinters, hurdlers, jumpers, weight lifters, fencers, marathon runners, marble champions, soccer players, bicyclists, lacrosse players—Negro masters of sports move through this volume in a glorious pageantry of verve and color.

Mr. Henderson has discussed impartially the problems that face Negro athletes in both Negro and Caucasian colleges. Evils are pointed out; but solutions are also explained. Away back in the 18th century Negro fighters, sometimes slaves, were gentlemen, in and out of the ring, long before Gene Tunney established respectability for fighters in our day, by lecturing on Shakespeare. For example, Bill Richmond hobnobbed with the poet, Lord Byron, two hundred years before Gene Tunney was a boon companion of Professor Phelps.

Many times along the road of sports the Negro athlete has battled hydra-headed racial prejudice. But I conclude from Mr. Henderson's research study that there is a greater spirit of brotherhood among white and Negro athletes, on a whole, than among the mouth-Christian public. Perhaps it's a case of Kipling's strong men who "stand face to face." White football and baseball players have delighted in competition with Negro athletes.

Social Significance: While Mr. Henderson's *The Negro in Sports* received brilliant notices and reviews in metropolitan papers all over the country, the white press of democratic Washington gave it 19 words—"incidentally." Giving birth to that solitary sentence must have caused sportswriter Francis E. Stan a Caesarean operation.

The Squarest Man on the Negro Problem,
I've Ever Known
June 14, 1941

Be sure to get your copy of *The Modern Quarterly*—the Memorial Issue, dedicated to the memory of V. F. Calverton. It is published by Nina Melville, at 16 St. Luke's Place, New York City. You won't regret that thirty-five cents.

When V. F. Calverton died, even the *New York Times* wrote an editorial on this super-intellectual. I remember that *The Saturday Review of Literature* called his house at 16 St. Luke's Place, "the cultural crossroads of the world." There, at his parties, you were sure to meet *anybody* who was *somebody*. Men and women of every race and creed mingled there.

VF was the squarest white man, on the Negro problem, that I've ever known. And that covers plenty of ground. He and I were closer than brothers. He could eat and talk, work and drink, harder than any other man in America. He was at home in a dozen fields of knowledge. Big-shot scholars say he was a walking encyclopedia. He knew about everybody who'd ever done anything in science, history, philosophy, music, art, and literature. I've seen him talk from midnight to dawn, and nobody got sleepy.

"A Man against the Idols of the Tribe"

This is the title of the article that I wrote about VF for *The Modern Quarterly*. Naturally, I want you to read it. It was not written for you, like "Caviar and Cabbage." It was written about you. It speaks to those super-intellectuals who whoop it up for Democracy. I'm told it created quite a stir.

When you realize how a certain big-shot magazine cut an article by Walter White, you'll understand this case better. The editors of *The Modern Quarterly* did something that white editors don't do for a Negro writer: they let me say what I wanted to say. And, Sambo, I said plenty! No lie. I said things I've wanted to say to white intellectuals for twenty-five years. I hit so hard that I felt sorry for the white Democracy-whoopers.

If VF read the article somewhere in eternity, I just know he bellylaughed so hard the angels put him in the hospital. Almost every time VF wrote me, he ended by saying: "More power to you!" And we wrote each other about every week—for years.

VF could certainly throw verbal brickbats. He could give it and take it. I learned from him how to do the same. He used to say: "When you get in the ring to battle for truth, don't be a sissy!" He and I used to argue until we both fell across the bed, exhausted, and went to sleep. He made me read books I'd never heard of in the University. He'd write me a twelve-page letter discussing, perhaps, a literary technicality. If I happened to beat him out on some point, I could tell that, in spite of all his swearing, he was delighted. He always called me MB and I called him George.

Incidents and Places and People

Whenever I went to Baltimore or to New York City, he dragged me into high places among strangers. I had to go wherever he went. As a Negro, in a jim-crow country, this was something new under the sun. Money meant nothing to VF.

I wonder if he ever spent a quiet evening at home. Sometimes he would say he was going to bed; then he'd call me up, in Harlem, at midnight. Didn't I know about the big party at 16 St. Luke's Place? Well, the distinguished guests were tired as hell waiting for me! I was acting just like a Texas dumbbell! Get a taxi right away. So I'd get up and catch the Subway. VF would meet me anxiously at the door, slap me on the back, denounce me as a stumbling block to social progress, and then introduce me solemnly to the forty-odd guests as "one of the most promising discoveries in our Republic of Letters."

I remember once we were dining in a famous Japanese restaurant. It was deep down in Greenwich Village. The walls were papered with the pictured covers of books. Each cover was autographed by a celebrated poet, novelist, or playwright who'd dined there before he became famous. The Japanese hovered over VF Calverton like a guardian angel, waiting for his bidding. Things weren't going so well with me, and I had the blues.

I told VF about some of my schoolmates—ordinary fellows, then—who'd played the game and now had big jobs. I told VF that if I, instead of following my social conscience, had played ball with the Big Boys, I'd been away upstairs by now. VF turned chalk-white, choked on his food, banged the table with his fist, and let out an oath. That was the only time I ever made VF really angry with me.

A Lesson I'll Never Forget

He shouted across the table: "MB, how can you harbor a filthy thing like that in your mind? I'm ashamed of you! That's the trouble with the Negroes now. They have too many Uncle Toms and bootlickers. Success! Success! Now, listen, MB, if you had a million lousy bucks and the Crown jewels of England, I wouldn't walk out of my way six steps to eat with you. I'm expecting you to do SOMETHING in the world.''

We walked out and left a scared Japanese cleaning off the table. That was years ago. But I remember it today, vividly. We must have walked a block before VF said anything. He was in deep thought.

Then he seemed to be talking to himself: ''Well, MB, I flew off the handle, didn't I? You see, so many two-bit successful men have said that same thing to me, VF, why don't you get in Wall Street? Why don't you write the kind of books that'll become best-sellers? With your mind, you could be a world-beater.''

The Voice of Conscience

The voice of conscience. Yes, VF was a man of conscience. I don't doubt that men will be reading his books 500 years from today. By the time he was forty he'd written seventeen important volumes. He was a trailblazer in American thought and life.

He turned his back on $$$s, the American god. In my article I tell some of the things he did for black folk. The last article he wrote was a defense of the Negro. The Negro-phobes hated this man of stupendous intellect. He had many Negro friends: Alain Locke, Abraham Harris, George Schuyler, Walter White, Sterling Brown. He was a man-to-man democrat. He never pulled his punches. He fought for the Negro in the North and in the South. He was threatened but still he fought for black men. I shall review his last book.

Dr. Alain Locke and the New World
December 5, 1941

Every now and then—with a wide desert between the now and then—some Negro scholar comes out of his ivory tower to do something for his people. So often a Ph.D. becomes the graveyard of a Negro scholar. A Ph.D. should be the Alpha of Scholarship and not its Omega. I have shed many bitter tears over the graves of colored Ph.D.s and A.M.s.

Mr. Alain Locke is not one of these. Seventeen years ago he edited a special issue of the *Survey Graphic* called *Harlem: Mecca of the New Negro*. I still remember its inspiration, its illumination.

Today Mr. Locke, in the same magazine, gives us a survey of *Color: Unfinished Business of Democracy*. I ask my readers to secure a copy of this special Negro number, at 112 East 19th Street, New York City. It is a bargain at 50 cents.

The most powerful blitz in the world is the Word. The South won the Civil War with the Word. If the United States needs the Word to win this war, we lowly Negroes need it a thousandfold. Our salvation lies in the propaganda of our just cause.

The Conspiracy of Silence

The Negro has suffered more from the conspiracy of silence than any other minority group. A Negro criminal can make the front page. A Negro achievement goes unmentioned in the White press. All the American public knows is what it reads in the newspapers.

A race must toot its own horn. Negroes waste too much time grumbling among themselves about their injustice. The Bilbos use the radio, the press, the pulpit, the classroom, and the Congress to spread the poison of race hate. If a lie is uttered often enough and loud enough, it becomes a truth to the public. That's the reason other races and nations and pressure groups propagandize. In the last election Big Business used $25,000,000 for propaganda.

We Negroes seem to think if we say nothing, we'll wake up some morning with the race problem solved. Agitation is the price of liberty. It took 150 years of agitation against human slavery to build Howard University. The master talks; the slave remains silent.

The first thing a tyrant does is to muzzle the press. Caesar did it. Hitler does it. The South does it. Napoleon was asked why he destroyed the freedom of the press.

He replied: "If I granted freedom of the press, I wouldn't last three days."

The Unfinished Business of Democracy

So in the November issue of the *Survey Graphic*, Mr. Locke takes up the unfinished business of democracy. He breaks the conspiracy of silence. And he is ably assisted by both White and Negro writers.

I cannot give you a picture of this fine banquet of facts and inspiration. Herbert Agar is here with "The Quest for Equality." Elmer Carter with "Shadows of the Slave Tradition." Walter White with "The Right to Fight for Democracy." John A. Davis with "The Negro Outlook Today." A. Philip Randolph with "Why We Should March?" Sterling Brown with "Out of Their Mouths."

Black America and White America speak from these pages with tongues of fire. They burn through the conspiracy of silence.

Yes, Color is an outstanding example of the unfinished business of democracy. Now, my readers, how can you help finish this business? Yes, you have a weapon—the greatest weapon in the world. It is called the Word.

I mean a letter to the editor. Read newspapers. Read magazines. When some writer defends the race, write the editor a letter. Use the Word. It is a two-edged sword for democracy and justice.

As the heirs of slaves, we have been taught not to use the Word. It was a crime in slavery times to teach a Negro the Word. If we are ever to be free, we must do what Mr. Locke has done in the *Survey Graphic*. We must place our cause before the bar of public opinion. We must toot our own horn.

A Negro Can Buy a Declaration of Independence for 10 Cents
May 1, 1943

Of course, the greatest document for human freedom in the history of America is the Declaration of Independence. Out of that document came the Emancipation Proclamation. The Fourth of July is the red-letter day!

I am sure that some of you Sambos and Aunt Hagars are wondering why I gave this column such a peculiar title. But when I get through explaining, I am sure all of you will say Amen.

All of you know about that hell-damned article on the Negro press, which was written by Dr. Warren Brown, and was reproduced in the *Reader's Digest*. It certainly hit the Negro below the belt. Remember, always, that the blow was delivered by a black Uncle Tom.

Remember, also, that the Negro newspapers are standing like the Rock of Ages for human rights. Never has the Negro had a more manly journalism. Old William Garrison and Fred Douglass would be proud to see Negro editors in action.

The Man Who Pays the Fiddler

When Judas started carrying the money bag, he started on the road of betrayal! It's hard to be true to your principles when you have the root of evil in your pocket. No lie.

So get a load of this—and watch out. The so-called League of Democracy, which Dr. Brown works for, has issued an invitation to Negro editors "to come up and see me sometime." These good white folk want to tell Negro editors how they can get some big advertisers!

Every dumbbell knows that he who pays the fiddler calls the tune. George Seldes, the editor of *In Fact,* calls the big white papers "the Harlot Press." Read his book, *The Brass Chalk.* Newspapers make their money out of advertising. Therefore, the editors print what the Big Boys want printed.

I have said many times that the Negro press is the only Free Press in the United States. Take me, for example. I have more freedom on the *Tribune* than any columnist on the *New York Times.* That is true for every Negro writer for Negro newspapers.

Why is this true? Well, the Negro paper doesn't have any big advertisers that it must cater to. Therein lies the freedom of the Negro press. Negro readers keep Negro newspapers going. Therefore, the Negro press is responsible to the Negro readers alone.

What 10¢ Will Do for Freedom

In other words, the Negro newspaper is a Declaration of Independence. And it costs only 10¢. Today the Negro newspaper is feared by the enemies of Democracy. Nobody can tell Negro editors what to print or what not to print. This means the truth comes out. That hurts.

Negroes, big and little, ought to buy all the newspapers they can from Negro editors. It was the Negro press that fought the cases of Judge Hastie, Mrs. Bethune, and Dean Pickens. It was the Negro press that scared Peg Leg Pegler to death when he attacked Negroes.

Every Negro city, town, and hamlet should have a Negro newspaper to fight things locally. This need not shut out the patronage of the big weeklies. Most white people buy a big daily and the local paper.

What is two bits a week for freedom of the Negro? I am a poor Sambo. But I buy six Negro newspapers weekly to keep up with freedom.

Yes, the Negro editor has a hard time keeping his little sheet going. I have seen them here and there collecting news, setting type, writing editorials, and being cussed out by Sambos and Aunt Hagars.

But if I had a medal to give for unselfish loyalty to the Race, I would give it to the Negro press—the only Free Press in America. I have never met a Negro editor who sold his Race out for thirty pieces of silver. So I say: Let the Negro editor starve on dimes and nickels; and let the Big Advertisers go to Hell!

Some Flashes from an Old Copy of *Flash*
May 15, 1943

Before me lies a copy of *Flash,* dated May 15, 1939. That seems to be a far-off century, indeed. *Flash* flashed and died, but I remember it was a wonderful adventure in the field of the illustrated weekly. I wish it had continued. We need such a magazine.

The Chinese say: "A picture is worth a thousand words."

That is especially true of a race only a short distance removed from slavery. Shall I ever forget my first pictures of Dunbar, Senator Bruce, Booker T. Washington, and Toussaint L'Ouverture? I should not. They were burning stars in my young life.

I glance at the board of editors: Joe Sewall, Mortimer Smith, and William Forsythe. I remember that chilly day when I visited their offices in that far-away time. Their enthusiasm filled me up!

Some Pictures

Here is a large picture of Senator Bilbo's Back-to-Africa Sambos and Aunt Hagars, three hundred strong, in the shadow of the Capitol. Brother Bilbo slobbered for four hours in the U.S. Senate. You remember that was the summer when the Nazis were being appeased. Ethiopia was already in the doghouse of fascism.

Yet Brother Bilbo was slobbering about sending the Negroes back to Africa. Well, the Negroes did go back. But not in the manner planned by the two-bit Demosthenes from the Yazoo Bottoms. Negroes went back to liberate Africa from Nazi exploitation!

Another picture is called "The Forgotten Men"—afflicted soldiers of World War I, at Castle Point. I look long at this picture. Here are black men, like you and me, who gave legs and arms for Democracy.

We see the veterans whiling away their time at cards. There is every modern facility for these men. Everything is spick and span. Yet they are forgotten! And by whom. By the ones who are not at Castle Point.

This must not happen again. We mustn't be traitors to the crippled in this World War II. By adopting a World Charter of the Four Freedoms, we can show our love and respect. And that is the only way we can show it. Therefore, we must give every Fifth Columnist hell who opposed a true Parliament of Man.

Some More Pictures

The next picture that attracts me is called "On the March with the Illinois National Guard." Here we see the old regiment getting ready for war. No, most of them didn't know war was coming. Sometimes we prepare for a thing unaware of its existence.

Today, tens of thousands of Negro soldiers are in Africa, Australia, the Solomons, India, and the islands of many seas. Here is a picture of the chef. He is a fat, stocky man, with a big belly. Every chef I ever saw was fat. That shows his food is good. You may follow him.

This makes me think of Mr. Roosevelt's *Freedom from Want*. After this war we shall have to help feed the starving peoples of the world. That's the best way in the world to bring Democracy and Friendship. Jesus fed the people!

The next picture shows the poet, Sterling Brown, sitting on a stool. Beside him on a chair is a black man playing a guitar. His name is "Big Boy." He inspired the poet to write that famous ballad in *Southern Road*. Nobody in our America can beat Sterling Brown writing ballads.

The Negro has been on the *Southern Road* a long time. In this World War II, I hope he meets Democracy on the Southern Road!

Missing over Germany
May 6, 1944

The air warfare over Europe came to me with a terrific shock today. Missing in action is a phrase that does not get beyond the eye of most Americans. Then, the words are connected with the name of a husband, a brother, a friend. What a fear, what a tragedy, enters the life of the person-behind-the-lines!

From London comes the story about Sergt. Eric Walrond, the West Indian writer. As a member of the Royal Air Force, he attacked over Germany and was reported missing. For sometime he had lived in London. Before that in Harlem and Paris.

I shall always treasure the memory of his last night in Harlem. But more about that later. I want to say a few things about his place in The Harlem Renaissance, back in the 1920's—the Era of the Lost Generation.

The New Negro

It was in the '20s that the New Negro came upon the scene. Most of you have read Dr. Alain Locke's famous book by that name. Well, Eric Walrond was one of the writers who ushered in that rebirth of Negro art and literature. Maybe it was a birth instead of a rebirth.

V. F. Calverton said once, in the *Saturday Review of Literature,* that in the 1920's if a white publisher failed to get a Negro writer on his list, he wept like a drunk at the funeral of a friend. Do you remember? Jim Europe had taken the capitals of Europe captive with Harlem jazz imported from New Orleans, St. Louis, and Kansas City, via Chicago.

In the midst of Harlem's literary bedlam, Walrond arrived with his *Tropic Death,* a vivid volume of short stories breathing the exotic air and color of the West Indies and Central America. He united with Marcus Garvey, as editor of the *Blackman.*

In 1931–32, at Columbia College, I made a study of the Harlem Renaissance. Among other things I came across the two magazines put out by the Harlem intellectuals: *Fire* and *Harlem,* edited by Wallace Thurman. I may say, parenthetically, that Dr. Locke, the "angel" of the Renaissance editors, lost many bucks in the Cause of Negro Letters.

How I Met Walrond

It was my duty to interview the poets and novelists of the Harlem rebirth. This was indeed a high adventure. For the first time I started knocking around with celebrities. And of course I collected a lot that I didn't put into my study.

For a long time I looked for Walrond. Nobody seemed to know where he was. Then one night I went to a big dance at the Rockland Palace in Harlem. I had never seen so many Negroes dancing at the same time; and high, in spite of prohibition. That was in the spring of 1932.

Well, in the middle of the dance, the woman with me let out a squawk and ran into the arms of another woman who had deserted her partner. We two men grinned at each other, and introduced ourselves. You're right. The man was Eric Walrond! That was the first time and the last time I ever saw him.

The next morning he was sailing for Paris. A count had turned over his chateau to the Negro writer for the summer. Walrond begged me to come with him. He'd show me Paris, and my board and lodging wouldn't cost me a franc!

Well, Walrond is missing over Europe. He was a wireless operator and air gunner in a Sterling bomber. He had joined the RAF when England was desperately in need of airmen after the fall of

France. He took part in the decisive battle which saved Britain from Nazi invasion. This is a story that black mothers may tell their children when Bilbo talks about his Back-to-Africa Movement!

VI
Reminiscences

Caviar and Cabbage
November 20, 1937

Bessie Smith, Queen of the Blues singers, has made her last record and sung her last ballad. I remember an autumn night in 1918, when our company was swinging along a lonesome road in Tennessee. A Victrola in a dim cabin was playing one of Bessie Smith's records, "When Uncle Sam Calls Out Yo' Man." A sudden hush fell upon the boys, and all you could hear was the steady tramp, tramp, tramp.

> To hold him back
> Might make him slack,
> Just say you got them
> Draftin' Blues.

That was the first time I'd ever heard Bessie Smith, and I went to bed in the barracks that night with the blues all about my head. Bessie's husky voice made you remember and made you forget. She was the sobbing scop of aristocrats and common people. Carl Van Vechten wrote a great article about her years ago in *Vanity Fair* when the golden coin flowed into her lap. I've heard her records played in San Francisco's Chinatown and in a log cabin at Onward, Mississippi, and in an elegant apartment on Fifth Avenue. The last time I heard her was in a crowded theater on a Saturday night in Houston, Texas. She had returned to the stage after an unsuccessful marriage.

She stopped the show as she did in New York's Apollo. Selma, Alabama, ought to give her most famous daughter a monument. She was a true artist with a heart as big as charity itself. The blues came from the common folk, like the airs of Old Ireland, and like them they touch the universal heart. They have humor and pathos and artistry. It took some highfalutin Negroes a long time to see that.

No more will Bessie sing:

All day long I'm worried;
All day long I'm blue;
I'm so awfully lonesome,
I doan know what to do;
So I ask yo', doctor,
See if you can fin'
Somethin' in yo' satchel
To pacify my min'

Bessie Smith made several fortunes and spent them, on herself and on unfortunate friends. Like the Persian poet-philosopher, Omar Khayyám, Bessie had a here-and-now philosophy: "Eat, drink, and be merry, for tomorrow we die."

Judgment Day
March 26, 1938

The administration didn't have anybody else to take the job; so I was made coach of the Wiley College debating team. I've traveled about 75,000 miles since that happened, and in the days of my denser ignorance I used to boast of the number of Negro and Caucasian colleges and universities my "system" defeated. Like good Congressman "I" Mitchell and other bourgeois black men, I was "Exhibit A" of the rugged individualist. That wise old bird Emerson said there's a crack in everything God made, and I was able to find the crack in the debate systems of other coaches. But I'll tell you about that at some other time.

It was after the great debate with the University of Southern California three years ago. Then I had become aware that there's more to life than winning personal victories. I was training my boys to go after the ugly truth and let the judges and respectable audiences go hang. That's not so easy as you think. It endangers one's job. I am happy now, for I know the jobs were here before I was born, and they'll be here when I shall be covered with the dust of oblivion.

Well, after the debate before some 2,000 people in Bovard Auditorium in Los Angeles, I attended a little dinner given in our honor by a few of the intelligentsia. No bridge, no dancing, thank God! Just a little heart-to-heart talk among a few blacks and whites concerning the mess our civilization is in. There was a blonde artist from Prague and a Negro doctor from the University of London, who'd been born in Central America. An interesting group, indeed. The host was a well-known literary critic and editor.

A cultivated mulatto woman said: "I have been in social work now for two years. I'm about ready to call it quits. I don't see that we're getting anywhere. Poverty! poverty! hungry, dirty children, overworked mothers, broken-down men tramping the streets month after month looking for work. When, oh, when will our leaders wake up?"

Her beautiful face, in the light of the floor lamp, was dark with despair. I shall never forget it. If I had been a Leonardo, I would have painted her thus.

"When will our leaders wake up?"

The doctor from Central America stirred in his chair and answered: "In the judgment day!"

His voice sounded like a bomb. I don't know what he was thinking; perhaps about the hellish oppressions of his own people by the modern Pharaohs. You could hear nothing in the room but the breathing of those present.

The learned physician who had been much in the slums of Lambeth, in London, continued: "History has no record of leaders or rulers who, however much the common people suffered, gave up their property without a struggle. In your own country, did England give the Colonies their freedom on a gold platter? In the South, did the South graciously give up her human property? Leaders and rulers guard what they consider their rights jealously. In your own glorious land of the free and home of the brave, do not thugs shoot down women and children who beg for bread? If I am not betrayed by a faulty memory, you've had thousands and thousands of strikes in this land of opportunity. Employers have used thugs to beat up workers living in shacks. Employers have used innocent Negroes to break strikes and then left them defenseless before angry mobs. Do not Southern leaders and editors inflame ignorant whites every day? No, the leaders and rulers never give up the exploitation of the underdogs until judgment day!"

Judgment Day in Paris and Haiti and Babylon

I've often thought about that distinguished Central American doctor. I wonder where he is tonight. I remember riding through the streets of the great city with him about 2 A.M. Our car slowly drove by a palatial home, with a wonderful iron fence. The place was beautifully lighted. Across the lawn came the rich music of a

waltz. The curtains were up and you could see the elegantly dressed men and women dancing. The doctor looked at it thoughtfully
for a while.

"That's the way they danced in the courts of Louis XVI before
the underdogs of Paris brought on the judgment day. That's the
way the big planters danced in Haiti before Toussaint L'Ouverture
and the black underdogs of Haiti decided that they'd taken enough.
Leaders and rulers never wake up. Do you remember the biblical
story of the Babylonian feast? Was not Belshazzar forewarned,
before Daniel deciphered the mysterious handwriting on the wall?
Hadn't Belshazzar heard the prophecy? Wasn't George III forewarned by Edmund Burke? Wasn't Caesar forewarned? Was not
Napoleon forewarned? Wasn't your own South forewarned by
Thomas Jefferson and countless others?"

Will Judgment Day Come to the United States?

The doctor settled back in the car and puffed on his cigar. I was
thinking about the contradictory things I'd read. We glided over
the smooth pavement. The beautiful mulatto woman whose face
was Madonna-like leaned forward and touched the Central American, who was riding in the front seat. Her voice was just a whisper.

"Doctor," she said, "then you think judgment day will come in
the United States?"

The doctor drew slowly on his cigar, and blew the smoke into the
night.

"Are Americans with empty stomachs any different from Span-
iards or Frenchmen with empty stomachs?" inquired the physician. "I have operated on men in London and Panama and West
Africa; and, madame, I have found no difference. Human beings
are fundamentally human beings the world over, whether they are
black or white, yellow or brown. Madame, empty stomachs mean
judgment day in all ages and in all countries."

Into the eyes of the beautiful mulatto woman came a light that a
man sees in a woman's eyes once in a lifetime.

"Judgment day!" she said. "I hope I'll be here to see it!"

I Get the Jitters
April 16, 1938

Sometimes I get the jitters when I think about the things that have happened to me—things that I cannot explain. I pass these mysteries on to you, dear reader. Perhaps you can illuminate that which is dark. Yes, there are more things in heaven and earth than are dreamed of in my philosophy! Shakespeare hit the nail on the head.

A Night in Arkansas

I was en route some years ago with a debating team which was to meet Fisk University in Nashville, Tenn. It was about 2 o'clock in the morning. The river was up, smashing levees and sweeping cabins toward the sea. In places the angry waters rushed over the roads. We were in a weary land, a weary land. Cattle and horses and hogs stumbled through marshy undergrowth, filling the night with unearthly sounds. The fog covered everything—everything. Our choking, coughing car moved along at a miserable rate of speed.

Suddenly we came to a huge sign which informed us: "Railroad Crossing Ahead." We rode on and on. The young man at the wheel, who was inexperienced as a driver, kept looking for the crossing; then someone cracked a joke about the slow train through Arkansas. Unexpectedly we came upon the railroad. I looked to the left and saw the headlight of a train, barely visible. I thought nothing of this, for the train was so far away. I simply dropped the remark, "A train."

The young driver stopped the car. At that split second the Memphis Express thundered by, filling the night with the sound of some prehistoric monster. Nobody spoke for at least five minutes. The driver's hands were paralyzed on the steering wheel.

I had said, "A train." I had not intended to warn the driver. It was just a casual remark, a passing observation. The driver and the others in the car had not seen or heard the approach of the lightning Memphis Express. And the curious thing is this: the old car had stalled at that very instant and the driver had not intended to stop. He was trying to go ahead!

We learned later that the Memphis Express was making a trial run to secure the right of carrying the United States mail. At that particular crossing the train was averaging 69 miles an hour. It had missed us by ten feet. A choking Ford that should have been on the junk pile had saved us! Or was it an inexperienced driver who had saved us? I get the jitters when I think of this. I sit here writing this column. Perhaps hundreds will read it, read my thoughts. Perhaps I shall make friends and enemies. Perhaps the world will be better off for my having lived in it. And all because of a battered Ford and an inexperienced driver. I speculate. Logicians say: "A good car and a good driver for the road." But a bad car and a bad driver saved my life! Figure it out for yourself.

The Same Night in Arkansas

Troubles come not singly, but in multitudes. We crossed the railroad that night and ran into a mob looking for two Negroes. But that's another story.

On, on, through the fog. There was a big football player in our car, who had been sleeping all night. We had to wake him up and tell him about our narrow escape. He sighed and went to sleep again. About 4 A.M. we climbed a steep hill several miles South of Memphis. The angry Mississippi was on each side of us. The night was black as the pit. The fog hugged the ground. Slowly we moved along a high bluff until we came to a fork in the road. One branch led down to the blackness of the river; the other continued along the high bluff. Of course we took the latter.

Then a curious thing happened. The big football player started screaming in the car.

"Let me out! Let me out!"

"He's having a nightmare," somebody laughed, and the car kept going.

Then the football player flung open the door. This caused the driver to stop the car. The football player got out and walked ahead, mumbling to himself. We sat there cracking jokes on him. In a few seconds he returned and his eyes were as large as saucers. Saying nothing, he took me by the arm and led me forward, the flashlight in his hand playing on the ground before us. Suddenly below me yawned a broken levee, with the angry waters of the Mississippi lashing like a wounded animal. We had stopped the car twenty yards from death! We were on a road that plunged into an abyss. I was in a cold sweat and my knees buckled.

Now, this football player had never made the debating team, but he had tried to do so for four years. Over the protests of the other boys who'd said the car was too crowded, I had brought Aldridge with me . . . and he had saved the lives of four debaters of Wiley College! He has never been able to explain why he knew—knew—

death was lying ahead. But he was as sure of it as I am sure that I composed this article on a typewriter.

Where Do We Go from Here?

A fool is a man who is certain in a world of uncertainty. The best laid plans of mice and men go wrong. The Book says: "Put not thy trust in things." Then you won't be disappointed. A genius like Napoleon lays the plan for a great battle, and loses the battle because of a bellyache that keeps him from carrying out the details. A brilliant student in an Eastern university works his way through two institutions of higher learning and then drops dead on his way to receive his coveted degree in medicine. A hunter in the Northwest sets a trap for a bear, takes sick and forgets about the trap, and later walks into the trap himself. Where do we go from here? Well, you boys with the lowdown on things and the inside dope, answer the question. I am just a poor black boy inching along in a world of unreason—a poor black boy trying to practice the Golden Rule.

I'm writing this article because a neighbor across the street died in a wreck. The car turned over on a level road and the experts don't know how it happened. They are burying my neighbor this afternoon. From my window I see her son whom I taught in college. He is leaning against a pillar of the porch. As his teacher, what can I say to him? Alfred Tennyson was right: "I would that my tongue could utter the thoughts that arise in me." My neighbor died in a car wreck. How will her son die? How will I die? How will you die? You wise birds tell me! Where do we go from here?

I Am an Unprejudiced Negro
August 26, 1939

My hair is kinky and my skin is brown. I am a racial accident, an ethnic missing link, an undifferentiated amalgam. Those who don't know what a Negro *is* call me a Negro, without the sanction of science or the benefit of democracy. It is easy for conscience to pigeonhole that which is perplexing. But like Banquo's ghost, it will not down!

It is hazardous to shake a family tree. One never knows what will fall out. Undesirable birds have an impish way of roosting among the finest genealogical branches. Several aristocratic families in a proud Southern State were sorely embarrassed by lineal investigations when the commonwealth, with more prejudice than wisdom, introduced its Pure Race Laws.

And recent dispatches from Europe graphically indicate the mortification of certain high-placed Italian and German families when the official toadies shook their genealogical stems and branches.

Americans ought to be glad that we don't have a horde of bureaucratic ancestor-worshipers invading the privacy of our homes. In our democracy, a man's house is still his castle. No minion of the law tries to tree a non-Aryan. One may talk about one's family, talk to one's family, talk for one's family, or talk to one's lawyer. I shall now exercise my constitutional right.

What is a Negro?

In my boyhood I discovered that something was amazingly wrong with my family tree. That was twenty years before Mr. Hitler started shaking non-Aryan skeletons out of everybody's genealogical tree but his own. I have a vivid memory of the time when my little walnut-hued mother took me for a visit to the old Mark Twain country, which was the Promised Land of my ancestors and relatives.

Puzzled and Shocked

The clan which had produced so many gun-toting preachers and God-fearing badmen gathered to meet us. I was puzzled and shocked. I saw a variety of racial stocks: whites, half-whites, dark yellows, walnut browns, golden browns, reddish blacks, pot blacks, and some indescribable colors. They ranged in size from a 200-pounder who stood six feet and seven inches to a runty backwoods circuit rider.

I saw blonds with wooly hair, blacks with silky hair, and browns with curly hair. I saw eyes that were black, blue, brown, and gray. My Aunt Hilda's rich black tresses were so long that she could sit on them; and my Aunt Sarah's kinks were so short and tightly woven that she had to use a comb with long wide teeth.

Aunt Sarah's husband said: "I ain't never got nothin' because Sarah keeps wearin' out so many combs."

Add to these diversities a confusion of dialects, and you can imagine how difficult it was for my boy's mind to grasp the amazing fact that these were my "kin folks." And these were also Negroes! Would a man from Mars believe it? What is a Negro? It is obvious that only a prejudice-blinded person would attempt to use scientifically the term *Negro* to include Walter White, the blond secretary of the NAACP, and Paul Robeson, the Sudanese-featured baritone and actor. What is a Negro? It took me twenty-five years to find out. I was then making a study for a department in an Eastern university.

Negro Is an Amalgam

Dr. Melville J. Herskovits, one of our foremost ethnologists, explains the term in this manner: "We speak of Negroes in this country, but plainly this is nonsense if we are employing the word 'Negro' in a biological sense. The American Negro is an amalgam, and the application of the term 'Negro' is purely sociological."

This explained the diversities in my family that had puzzled. It also gave me a new approach to the problems of race and the democracy of culture. Francis Bacon said that if we want to find truth we must get rid of the idols of the tribe. And a man is a traitor to a democracy if he is not a cool, dispassionate truth-seeker!

For many years I was mired in the bog of race prejudice. Yes, a Negro can be as biased as a white man, but of course for different reasons. I have encountered prejudices in a hundred varied forms and disguises. It is easy for a man of good will to sympathize with the lynched or the relatives of the lynched; but it is not so easy to understand the poignant tragedies that Negroes endure day by day on the job, in the street, on the trolley car, and in the theater.

I know what it is to feel the stabbing glances of white fellow-passengers as they read the headline glaring some alleged crime committed by a member of a sociological race. Since this is true, a man of good will can appreciate my terrific struggle to become an unprejudiced person.

It is a long, hard road to intellectual freedom; but every individual must travel this road if our Constitution is to be more than sounding brass and tinkling cymbal. I am optimistic. A man is not born with any kind of prejudice. He is not even born a human being.

> Nature conceives him, and nurture shapes him. Like a mirror his mind reflects his environment. Change is the Immutable law of life. The mouths of those who voice prejudice are stopped with dust. The race—the human race moves on.

Men of good will are rising everywhere in the South. They realize that Booker T. Washington was right when he said: "You can't keep a man in the ditch unless you stay in the ditch with him."

Color of Mind Important

Meanwhile, in our colleges and universities we are studying the Negro more and talking about him less. We are learning that the color of a man's mind is more important than the color of his skin. Magazines are publishing articles and pictures that show the diversities of Negro life.

Negro poets and novelists and scholars are securing a wider

hearing. Archeologists are excavating the ruins of lost African civilizations. Anthropologists, like the eminent Boas and Radin and Jean Finot, are pointing out the ridiculosities of pseudo-racial superiorities.

Difference Is Not Inferiority

We men and women of good will know now that differentness does not mean inferiority. Civilization is a mighty river with many ethnic tributaries. Mongolian, African, Indian, and Caucasian races have all made their contributions.

It is foolish to stigmatize any race as being criminal, lazy, cowardly, thievish, unintellectual, and happy-go-lucky. It shows that one is not cultivated and well-traveled. There are greater differences within a racial group than there are between racial groups; and advanced scholars have gone so far as to declare that race is a myth!

When I meet a Continental I do not feel inferior because my beloved America has not produced a Shakespeare, a Beethoven, a Michelangelo, a Voltaire. Neither do I feel inferior because the sociological Negro cannot point to a Walt Whitman, a Thomas Jefferson, or a Theodore Dreiser.

In my days of darkness I used to boast of the fact that Alexander Dumas, Alexander Pushkin, Robert Browning, and Antar had Negro blood in their veins. I paraded the fact that Toussaint L'Ouverture defeated the legions of Bonaparte; that a black man led the Americans in the Boston Massacre; that Napoleon's bravest general was black; and that the black rebel, Nat Turner, caused the Governor of Virginia to crawl under his bed.

A hostile white civilization was the initiator of this defense mechanism.

A Southern White Sees the Truth

Once I read this sentence in a book by a white Southerner who had returned from a trip around the world: "I have met black men who were my superiors, black men who were my equals, and black men who were my inferiors."

I think this expresses the sentiments of most unprejudiced men and women who have had extensive contacts with the members of another race. Men differ quantitatively and not qualitatively. In every man is the blood of saint and blackguard, genius and idiot.

It is hazardous to shake a family tree. One never knows what will fall out. Biologically, the Negro does not exist. Sociologically, he is the amalgam of the good and bad, the gay and the sad, in

America. One of his poets sang: "What is Africa to me?" And another, thinking of the deep secrets of his people, turned the phrase: "We wear the mask."

America is bone of my bone, blood of my blood, and flesh of my flesh. No Negro has ever betrayed the Stars and Stripes. I know of no black Benedict Arnold or Aaron Burr. I was born an American. I shall die an American.

Jim-crow laws, rope and faggot—nothing can take from me those imperishable words: "We hold these truths to be self-evident, that all men are created equal, that they are endowed by the Creator with certain unalienable Rights, that among these are Life, Liberty, and the pursuit of Happiness."

Fellow Travelers in Dixie
September 2, 1939

It's a long hard way from Texas to Georgia, and from Georgia to Washington. It's a long hard way in a jim-crow car. The car is a car. But the jim crow is a Negro in a white democracy.

I soon get tired of riding, though I like to see strange places and alien faces. Nothing thrills me like a train—if you leave out old wines, soulful women, rare books, boon companions, crafty enemies, exquisite music, baked chicken, football games, and boxing matches. Of course, I would walk a mile for a good cigar. I cannot conceive of a heaven without good cigars.

Trains. Trains. Trains! How I used to watch them as a boy! They were the symbols of adventure. You have read that marvelous book, *Of Time and the River,* by Tom Wolfe, now dead. I am writing this article two hundred miles from Asheville, where Tom Wolfe lived. This is my first time in this section of the Bible Belt. I'd like to go to Tom Wolfe's hometown. But I can't. So near—and so far.

Well, Wolfe is one of the men whose life and work keep me from committing suicide. No man has pictured so vividly an iron steed thundering across a continent, moving through the illimitable reaches of Time. As I rode I thought of Time. I thought of *Of Time and the River.*

The Tribune in a Jim-Crow Car

Memphis. A Saturday night. The train clipped off the miles, like a ticket machine. I had left Beale Street. In a room overlooking Beale Street I had talked with George Lee, the Negro novelist, and argued about Life. George Lee, who wrote *Beale Street* and *River*

George. I had read the letter from Mae West—the cablegram from the British Broadcasting Company. George Lee had told me about Beale Street—about Tree-Top Tall and Coal Oil Johnny. But now I was on a jim-crow Car thundering toward Atlanta. I thought of Angelo Herndon and the chain gang.

A little bald-headed man sat across the aisle. I hate a bald head. Every morning when I get up I look into the mirror to see if I have as many hairs as I had when I went to bed. I like hairy men. Hair is a sign of manly vigor. Or, is that a lie?

Anyway, I felt better toward the little bald-headed man when I saw that he was reading the *Tribune*. Yes, he was from Washington. He had visited his daughter in Memphis. He had found a great deal in common between Beale Street and U Street. In fact, he didn't see much difference between one Negro street and another, whether North or South.

I was very much flattered when I saw that the little man was reading "Caviar and Cabbage." Really, I liked him a lot in spite of his bald head.

Suddenly the little man said: "Do you know anything about this guy?" He pointed at my angelic profile above the column.

"Yeah," I said. "Do I know him? Mister, I know that guy like a book."

The little man looked up surprised. "What kinda fella is he?"

"Well," I hesitated, "his character is better than his writing."

The little stranger grunted: "I hope so." After a lengthy pause, he continued: "He's got funny ideas."

"Yes," I said. "People have said that about him before."

The little man bit off the end of his stubby cigar and said: "How do guys get like that?"

"It's a long story," I said. "Now I've known this particular guy from the day he was born."

My companion looked up in surprise. "Who gave 'im that middle name—'Beaunorus'? That's a hulluva name, ain't it?"

I said solemnly: "It sure is. They tell me his godmother gave 'im that name. She's dead now. So the guy just carries it around, I guess. Sort of a momento, I guess."

The little man shook his head. "Well," he said, "the guy is nuts."

"Why do you say that?" I inquired.

The little man grimaced: "He wants to change the world. Only a guy that's nuts will try to change the world."

"Then Jesus was nuts," I suggested.

The little man threw up his hands in terror. "Say," he squawked, "you talk nutty just like that guy in this *Tribune*.

"I told you I'd known him for a long time," I laughed. "Association begets assimilation."

"Sez you!"

"Why do you read the guy?" I asked.

The little man was silent for a long time, as our iron steed raced across a sun-dried landscape. "Perhaps I'm getting nutty, too," he sighed.

"That's good," I said. "When we get to Atlanta, I shall introduce you to this nutty guy."

"You will!" exclaimed the little man. "I'd like to meet 'im. But please don't tell 'im what I said."

"I shall let you do that."

"Good Lord!" said the little man.

"He won't mind it," I explained. "As long as you read his column, he'll let you call him a nut."

"He's a regular, then."

"As regular as a jigsaw puzzle," I said. "He'll probably call you a nut."

"What?"

"Yes," I said. "A nut knows that only a nut will read a nut."

The little bald-headed man laughed until the tears came into his eyes.

A Colored Ex-Brakeman

It was eight miles out of Anniston Junction, Alabama. The Limited on the L. & N. gave three sharp whistles and initiated the race with our Southern Express. The two huge iron steeds thundered down the rails on parallel tracks, their breaths white and steaming in the afternoon. Everybody on the train was excited. Some pressed their faces against the windowpane. A little black boy let out a yelp of delight.

An old Negro began telling me about his episodes on the Southern. He had been a brakeman. He had retired after forty years' service. Now he spent his time riding in day coaches from one end of the country to the other. He said the L. & N. and the Southern were great rivals. They always raced when they reached that level stretch outside of Anniston Junction. When he was a bold young man he used to leap from the top of one boxcar to the other as the freights raced over the flat land. I asked him if he wasn't afraid of falling between the trains.

"Naw," said the ex-brakeman. "I was all he-man in them days. I wasn't scared of nothing on earth or in hell."

The old man's laughter filled the coach. He got up. He strutted up and down the aisle. A big yellow woman wearing a tiny red hat guffawed.

"You're like my husband," she said. "You're always boastin' about what ain't now."

More dark laughter in a jim-crow coach. Laughter is the savior of black folk. When the train stopped at the little station, I saw many white faces—pale, drawn, perturbed. I thought of the white man's burden. Later, we sped toward Atlanta. The Negro passengers were giving their various destinations.

But I knew they were wrong. All men are passengers. All have a common destination. It is called Death.

Black Brutes and a White Woman— a True Story
February 17, 1940

It is 3:55 A.M. The house is asleep. The town is asleep. I hear the lonesome whistle of a North-bound train. My only companion is a mouse that listens to the familiar peck, peck, peck of my typewriter and rubs his nose meditatively. Now, I couldn't sleep. Yesterday I read the old familiar story, in a Southern daily—the story that justifies lynching as a defense of white womanhood. Economists and sociologists have proved this a lie time after time. Nevertheless, this lie elevates many a Southern gentleman to Congress.

So I count such men as enemies of democracy. And this lie about black brutes, which stigmatizes the manhood of a race, makes me want to get out the shotgun of old Reverend Alonzo Tolson.

Now this is a leaf from my autobiography, which will be published on the day of my death. I haven't done much myself. But I've seen and heard a lot. In high places and in low places. If I started talking, there'd be suicides and murders. Of course, I'd be the first among the missing. You know what happens to those who know . . . but don't know How to keep what they know.

The autobiographies written by Big Negroes are the worst in the world. They seldom tell the truth. And that's the only reason for writing the story of your life.

In fact, that's the only reason for writing anything!

II

In the heyday of Al Capone and the President of the United States who had Negro blood in his veins, I was waiting tables in a beachfront hotel, in Atlantic City. I wanted to be a writer. But my A's in English ruined me.

Today, when I read *Grand Hotel,* by Viki Baum, I know that she doesn't know anything about hotels from the inside. Theodore Dreiser comes closer to life in those passages in *An American Tragedy.* Arnold Bennett does a good job in his *Imperial Palace.* Sinclair Lewis romanticizes the hotel in his *Work of Art.*

Dreiser views the hotel from the point of the bellhop. Sinclair Lewis, from the position of the hotel keeper. I saw it from the viewpoint of the waiter. Bellhops and waiters know what goes on. If you want to know what kind of woman Mrs. Superior is, talk with the maid or cook. The parlor is a poor place to get your knowledge of a house. I didn't know, in the Roaring Twenties, that I had a ringside seat from which to view Life and write stories.

III

Now this is the story of an Irish girl who came to the Play Ground of America. Love had brought her there—love of a white gentleman who stood high in a Southern city. He left her, big with child, and she came to our hotel to keep from starving. She was the salad girl.

As the weeks of the summer months went by, her feet began to drag in the pantry and her face had a look that stabbed you to the heart with pity for her. All the waiters and cooks were colored. She was terribly afraid of the white manager. When he came into the kitchen, you could see the poor girl drawing on all her strength to keep the manager from knowing the condition she was in.

Now, waiters and cooks are rough men in the kitchen. I've worked on a dining car and in six hotels. The heat is terrific. The jam is inhuman. The guests are often subhuman. Sitting in the cool serenity of the dining room, they wonder why the waiter is so slow. The waiter is after tips. He must have tips to live. So the guests lash the waiters and the waiters lash the cooks—since they're scared to lash the guests. I'm glad the waiters and cooks are getting a union. It is hell in a hotel kitchen!

If you educators want to study the effect of environment on human beings, get a job in a kitchen. The fellows I worked with cursed themselves, cursed each other, cursed the guests . . . in the kitchen. Between meals the boys rested or gambled or told dirty stories downstairs. When I was off duty, I ran from the place as if pursued by the Black Plague.

That was a mistake. I should've stayed there. I should've put down what I saw and heard. I'm doing that NOW. Years later.

I've told you these things to make you see the kitchen; make you feel what that poor Irish girl must have felt. Every day the strain on her grew more severe. She was staggering now and holding her stomach and head. But she had to go on.

A change came over the kitchen. The fellows no longer cursed. Different ones would slip into the pantry, when the white manager wasn't around, and make the salads for her. Somebody made her a comfortable seat. There she sat behind the rows of salads, with the most grateful expression on her face that I've seen on a human being's.

In the basement of the hotel were several rooms. Also, some old mattresses where the fellows rested between meals. Two of the waiters would help her downstairs. The boys gambled in one of the rooms but they didn't make any noise.

One afternoon I was lying asleep in the basement. I came to myself, aroused by the most terrifying scream I had ever heard. Again and again it filled the basement. I heard running footsteps. When I arrived on the scene, two coatless waiters had lifted the woman. She was writhing in agony. The men carried her upstairs.

In the kitchen, we were met by the white manager. A waiter explained the woman's condition. The white manager turned red in the face, and began cursing the woman for disgracing his hotel. The woman whimpered and whimpered, like a dog that is beaten so badly it can not move.

"Get out of here!" shouted the white manager.

Now, Bob, a silent mulatto, was a captain of waiters. He had graduated in medicine, but he'd never practiced. He ran the gambling games downstairs. When the boss ordered the poor woman out, Bob cursed the boss as a yellow coward. The boss started toward Bob, and Bob knocked him down and out. The chef poured some ice water on the boss's face.

Now, I don't know what became of that Irish girl who followed a Southern white gentleman to Atlantic City, for love.

But you see, everytime I hear a white man talking about black brutes and white womanhood I see the mulatto Bob knocking down that white manager, in order to protect a white woman who was about to give birth to a white child.

Candid Camera Shots of
Negro Intellectuals
June 29, 1940

It is a chilly, star-studded night in the late spring. Hundreds sit expectantly in the college chapel. Having finished my introduction of the famous scholar, I take my seat. After a long pause, the distinguished-looking gentleman gets to his feet, hesitates a moment, then steps forward briskly. He has the aspect of a dusky Parisian.

For an hour he talks quietly on the evolution of modern society. He pictures the tremendous changes in the economic order. He shows how the American frontier developed rugged individualism and the democratic idea. The audience see the young American Republic striding in seven-league boots to the shore of the far-flung Pacific. Then come the seven lean years of the Great Depression. The frontier has vanished from the geography of the nation; but the frontier spirit still exists in the American mind. Starvation in a land of plenty.

What now? The audience leans forward for the answer. The learned scholar quietly takes his seat. He folds his soft velvety hands. The meeting ends quietly. We leave the chapel quietly. We cross the campus quietly.

Dr. W. E. B. Du Bois looks up at the heavens. Then he says in an awed voice: "How beautiful are the stars!"

A Negro Poet and a Taxicab in the Rain—1932

It is an elegant parlor on Sugar Hill in Harlem. I am talking with an elderly gentleman. His fashionable wife is talking with the Poet. I do not hear the gentleman. The Poet is explaining to the lady his proposed lecture tour through the South. The lady is telling the Poet the kind of attire he must wear before the distinguished audiences. They expect celebrities to be just so! The Poet listens like a child whose mother is telling him where to find the cookies.

Suddenly the Poet grows serious. He's almost forgot something. He names a prominent Harlem church. Yes, there is to be a huge rally to collect money for the Scottsboro boys. The lady insists that it is raining too hard. He'll get soaking wet!

There is a tenseness, an agony, in the Poet's face. It seems that his life depends on getting to that meeting in time. We hasten downstairs and catch a taxicab. The rain is now torrential. The Poet leans forward, tells the driver to put on speed. The Poet talks passionately about the Scottsboro boys. They are innocent. They must go free. It'll take money.

The car stops. It skids. Before us looms the great, aristocratic church. It is dark. In front of the church is a milling multitude. We learn that the church would not let the rally be held in the house of God. People said it was just Communist propaganda. The Poet asks me to come with him. I tell him I have a previous engagement.

Langston Hughes looks at me with a sad half-smile. He says good night. I see him pushing through the crowd in the rain. His face looks tired and old and pain-ridden. I start to get out. Then I tell the driver to step on the gas. But I'm to feel a hundred times that I double-crossed the Scottsboro boys!

The Brocaded Parlor on Seventh Avenue

It is in 1932. I am in Harlem making a study of the Harlem Renaissance. It is in the late afternoon, and I am sitting in the brocade parlor of the novelist who delights in writing about the dusky aristocrats. I am seated on the brocaded settee. The room has atmosphere. The elegance of the room bespeaks the personality of the lady novelist. Her Husband sits across from me.

The Husband informs me in awesome whispers that the lady cannot see me this afternoon. She is going to Philadelphia to see her brother. I can hear now and then the delicate voice of the lady in the kitchen. She seems to be preparing something for her brother.

The Husband gives me the impression of one overwhelmed by the greatness of another. He talks about the lady in hushed tones. I ask him questions about her work, her distinguished friends, her latest literary dinner. He replies in the same subdued manner.

I begin to get the jitters. The atmosphere of the room with its brocaded silks, its brittle delicacy, its overawed husband—well, I feel cramped and want to get out into the freedom of Seventh Avenue.

I leave apologetically and tell the Husband to tell the lady novelist I shall see her at her earliest convenience. But I know I'm lying. I shall write my study of Jessie Fauset without interviewing her. In fact, I know now all that I need know about her. I see now why the characters in her books are so stilted and unreal. She is always trying to prove that Negroes know Emily Post.

The Best Logician I Ever Saw

It is the night after the interracial debate between the debaters of Wiley College and those of the University of Southern California, national champions at that time. We have gathered at the home of Loren Miller, lawyer, critic, and newspaper editor. It is a mixed group. Loren Miller has missed the debate because he says he doesn't like conventional academic arguments. The surgeon from Guiana and London remarks that the debate was different.

Loren Miller says: "I'm sorry I missed it then." He sits on the floor with his back against an Ottoman stool and his hands clasped behind his head.

The argument starts about ten o'clock and ends at two in the morning. It involved the whole question of genius and environment.

You have seen a smooth-muscled wrestler use all the subtle tricks of his trade. You have seen a master boxer display the cunning tactics of his game. You have watched the expert fencer at work. Well, these will give you some idea of the mental gymnastics of Loren Miller. Nothing is so beautiful as a logician, a dialectician, in action. You see his strategic retreats and advances, his thrusts and parries.

Biography, history, science, art, literature, and every aspect of human culture pass in review. New angles of knowledge are presented. Popular beliefs are ripped open. The arguers ask no quarters and give none. At the end of his intellectual game, Loren Miller is slumped against the Ottoman stool, tired out. The surgeon from Guiana and London walks with me into the silence of a Los Angeles street.

Keep Your Hand on the Plow
October 5, 1940

I knew a man, an ordinary man to most people, who was a great hero to me. He was a Missouri farmer. His family of six grubbed out an existence on a few acres. Sometimes the drought came with armies of grasshoppers. Disease struck down his wife and two children.

As a man of some imagination, I could sympathize with that unfortunate father. Although a boy, I could see tragedy in the lives of ordinary folk. Lincoln could do that. So could my hero, Frederick Douglass, the man the Negro has given to a thousand ages.

When dumbbells see tragedy, they bury their heads in the sands of ignorance and say: "It ain't there!"

A wise man looks at tragedy and studies its causes and effects. As a boy, I tried to do that. So I looked at that old farmer and listened to his philosophy. I learned a great lesson which I'm passing on to you. After I'd looked at the old man for a while, I was able to look *into* his life. I guess you see what I'm driving at.

The Song the Old Man Sang

One day I saw the old man plowing in his field. He was trying to whip Nature. Now, the poets, in most cases, have painted Nature as something beautiful. But I have seen Nature in her ugly moments. So had that old farmer. He had to fight Nature all day. Nature was bent on the destruction of the crop that would feed his children. While he slept, Nature tried to choke the corn and wheat, with evil weeds. During the day Nature scorched the old farmer's acres and burnt his crops.

I heard the old farmer sing—to himself:

Hold on, hold on!
Keep your hand on the plow,
Hold on!

The stubborn earth made the going tough. Hard times in the field and hard times in the old farmer's house. Perhaps he said to himself: "What's the use?" The mule was hardheaded, like some people I know. The plow jerked and revolted. The old farmer sweated and tugged.

Then the old farmer's Soul said to his Body: "Keep your hand on the plow. Hold on!"

The White Man with the Hoe

You've seen Millet's famous painting of the Man with the Hoe. My deceased friend, Edwin Markham, saw it and wrote a poem with the same name. We'll not go into that now. It's another story. The Man with the Hoe was brutalized by the Big Boys. He sank so low that he became a brother to the ox. That's the way he looked to the genius of Edwin Markham.

I regret that Edwin Markham and Jean François Millet didn't see that old black farmer in Missouri. He was worthy of both a picture and a poem. If I had the genius of either Millet or Markham, I would give the world a masterpiece called "The Man with the Plow."

Now, you will remember that the Man with the Hoe was so

brutalized that he became a "monstrous thing distorted and soul-quencht," a brute, an ox, a dumb Terror. Poverty does that to men. Lynch mobs do that to men.

I can see now that every day the Man with the Plow was being dragged down toward the level of the Man with the Hoe. But the old farmer had not reached the depths at that time. As I sit here hunting and missing the keys on this typewriter, I wonder if that old farmer lost his soul in the misery of the soil. I wonder.

Now, a man killed in an automobile wreck is never so tragic as a man killed, by slow degrees, on a job from which he is trying to wring enough to keep soul and body together. There are more heroes on the farm than on the battlefield. You see what I mean.

The Black Man with the Plow

I wish Edwin Markham had written a poem called "The Man with the Plow." You can leave off the word "black." Humanity is bigger than race. Hitler and some white Americans have not seen that yet. This poem about the Man with the plow would've had a knockout climax. It would've revealed the unconquerable nature of universal Man. The Big Boys can crush a man, but they can't crush Man. That's the reason all tyrants, whether in Germany or Georgia, are doomed to failure. No power on earth can crush Man.

The newspapers talk unending about the *morale* of the English people. Unthinking Negroes join the chorus—as usual. Now, *morale* is that spirit in a people which keeps it from cracking up when "the heat is turned on." Sambo, listen to me. I tell you that the Negro has greater *morale* than the proud Anglo-Saxon. Now, the English have ruled the world for centuries; so they ought to have *morale*. On the other hand, the Negro has been enslaved and whipped and lynched for centuries; but he can still sing, with that old black farmer:

> Hold on, hold on!
> Keep your hand on the plow,
> Hold on!

The Negro can take it—when he doesn't have a chance to give it. The English have bombing planes, tanks, and the greatest navy in the world. The English have 400,000,000 dark men and women to fall back upon. The English own one-fourth of the world. The English have Uncle Sam behind them. Therefore, the English should have *morale*.

Put King George VI in the place of Sambo, with nothing but a two-bit razor blade as protection; then you'd have a chance to test the *morale* of King George. Sambo isn't so bad when you consider the fact that Sambo was conceived in ignorance and born in illiteracy. King George was born with a golden spoon in his mouth. Sambo was born with the white man's foot in his ask-me-no-questions.

So, Black America, in these dark times, remember the heroic words of the Black Man with the Plow: "Keep your hand on the plow. Hold on!"

Thanksgiving Day—
Leaves from My Autobiography
November 23, 1940

Thanksgiving Day: Mason City, Iowa, 1917. It was a blustery afternoon. The barber shop where I shined shoes was closed. It was located on Main Street and catered to whites. My Father was the pastor of the only Negro church in Mason City. The white "Christians" had built the church so that they wouldn't have to worship with their dark brothers and sisters!

I was sitting at a small table in the barber shop, writing a poem for the Sunday edition of the white daily. I heard a sudden noise. I looked up and saw a blonde woman in a fur coat enter and slam the door.

"Don't tell him I'm here," she said breathlessly, and ran into the small room at the rear.

About two or three minutes later a white man rushed in, hatless and excited. Curses against the woman roared from his lips. I saw the revolver in his hand.

"Did you see her?" he yelled. "Did she come in here?"

"All of our customers are men," I said.

He cursed again, hesitated a moment, and stormed out into the blustery street. In about ten minutes the woman reappeared.

"Kid," she said, "you saved my hide."

She pulled her fur coat together at the throat and walked to the table where I sat. She tossed a crumpled bill upon the sheet containing my poem. It was a five-spot. And the first money I ever received from writing.

Thanksgiving Day: Harlem, 1931

It was about 11:00 p.m. A mixed racial group of artists, writers, and actors were in the apartment of Wayland Rudd, then a star at the Provincetown Theatre in Greenwich Village. The play was

Marriage in Cana. A Jewish woman, the director of the Harlem Players, was there. Also the late Dewey Jones, the brilliant journalist.

Now, if you want to see some *real* entertainment, get with a group of actors at a party. But more of that later. That night Wayland Rudd did two scenes from Eugene O'Neill's *The Emperor Jones,* the role made famous by Gilpin and Paul Robeson. It's funny how each one of these great actors gave O'Neill's black monarch a different interpretation; yet all three were great in the role. Wayland had done it first at a theater in Philadelphia.

That night I was sitting next to a playwright from London, who was sipping a cocktail. Remember *that.* But we all forgot that we were in a Harlem apartment as Wayland staggered through an imaginary jungle pursued by ghosts of his past. The Emperor Jones took off his boots to rest his feet. He was scared and terror-stricken. He prayed. We could hear the tomtoms of the natives talking in the midnight jungle.

When I tell you that Wayland was at times a more sinister Emperor Jones than even Charles Gilpin, you know that he outdid anything of its kind in the American theater. The English playwright was so enthralled by the acting that he gripped my arm and dropped his cocktail glass.

The scene ended. Wayland stretched out on the floor. His audience remained speechless for a moment, then clapped their hands violently. Then I think I saw two of the most beautiful gestures ever made to an artist. The English playwright put on Wayland's shoes, which he had taken off as the Emperor's boots. The Jewish woman put her arm under Wayland's head and placed a cocktail glass to his lips . . .

Wayland Rudd, the Negro, could not get enough roles in New York to make a living. He is now with the Moscow Theatre. You saw him in the picture of Marian Anderson which was taken in Moscow. Wayland Rudd went to Russia on the toss of a coin. I was with him when he tossed the coin in an Italian delicatessen shop on Seventh Avenue.

Thanksgiving Day: Superior, Wisconsin, 1932

I was traveling with a college quartette in the Middle West. Winter caught us in Wisconsin. Holy smoke, is any place colder than Wisconsin? I've seen football teams playing in a foot of snow and players skidding on the ice.

We came into Superior about dusk. It was sleeting. Sambo, I've never seen such sleet. It got in your nose and ears and eyes and made you want to sing "Dear Old Southland," like a black mammy who'd never tasted freedom. We were to appear at a conference of ministers. We went to the parsonage, but the clergyman directed us to the YMCA. The Color Line. We went to the YMCA, and the gracious secretary directed us to the Salvation Army. The Color Line.

I thought I heard one of the boys curse to himself; but I guess I didn't. All the boys were "Christians." We had come four hundred miles across a land of sleet and snow and driving winds. We had come to sing for white "Christians." Trying to find a Negro in Superior was like trying to find snow in the Sahara.

At the Salvation Army we met a white gentleman. He was shocked because no accommodations had been prepared for us. I think my boys confronted destitution for the first time. Yes, they saw the dregs of humanity in the Land of the Free. It is easy enough to say what you'd do if you got down and out. I say no well-fed, well-clothed, well-housed person can realize the nth degree of hopelessness experienced by a down-and-outer. Perhaps some great artists can. But that's genius. The average person cannot.

The Salvation Army. Broken-down old men. Crippled middle-aged men. Young men ravaged by poverty and dissipation. A Salvation Army is the last station on the Road to Ruin. The place reeked with disinfectant. Desolate iron beds stood against the walls. Wrecks of men looked at our clothes with envy in bloodshot eyes.

The only thing human in the place was the young man who served those beaten souls and ruined bodies. Suddenly he went to the phone and called up the pastor of the church. The young man delivered a sermon on Christian charity over the phone. He denounced racial prejudice. As I looked, I saw not the young man but Jesus. The conscience-stricken pastor found us a comfortable home.

The Battle of Races
in the Missouri Bottoms
April 19, 1941

The United States had entered the First World War—to make the world safe for the Big Boys . . . I was a kid then, and I believed what the dollar-men and Uncle Toms and Sambo professors told me. My faith was the size of the Rocky Mountains. So I volunteered, after three years' training as a cadet officer.

The summer before I enlisted, I worked in a packinghouse in the Missouri Bottoms. I lived in one state and worked in another. Every morning I crossed the river into Kansas, with men of all nationalities and races. Wage slavery makes men hard; so I lost some of the softness of the poet.

First, I was a trucker. I pulled five times my weight. The 200-pounders laughed at me on the loading dock. But in three weeks I was leading the gang. I'd learned the physics of trucking. We went underground to get boxes of meat, where it was 18 degrees below zero. Then we came up on the docks, where it was as hot as a furnace. Some of the truckers died of TB. But I was lucky. I scoffed at the Abe Lincolns in the Labor movement who wanted to set Labor free. I thought the unionists racketeers. It took me years to find out that I was a fool. College economics taught me nothing about everyday economics. Yet the late Justice Brandeis commended me as a college debater. Something was wrong!

The Company That Ruled Our World

I hated the packinghouse world. I intended to escape through my college training. The men called me The Kid. They admired my toughness. The Boss boasted about me. He said The Company liked men like me. I usually ate my supper at midnight. You see, I was so tired when I got home that I went to sleep.

The Boss promoted me. I became a loader of refrigerator cars. I could heave a quarter-beef to a hook. I got time-and-a-half for overtime. I was coming up in The Company. Sometimes, when there was a rush, bosses from the Big Office in long white coats came down to the docks. I was the lightest loader and the fastest. Later, I would overhear the bosses cursing the bigger and older hands. I saw the reason for that ten years later.

"Hell," they would say, "can't you—keep up with The Kid?"

I felt big and hard. During the noon hour I'd put on the gloves with men outweighing me fifty pounds. I could dart into an opening and deliver a corkscrew punch like a blast of lightning. I felt prouder of my muscles than of my poetry.

The bosses sent me to The Tub. I worked under Old Man Jeff, the best souser among thousands of men in six packinghouses. I was an understudy. I was coming up in The Company. I could've learned a lot about economics and sociology. But I didn't. You see, my professors had me studying the wrong books. I was simply a rugged individualist getting ahead!

Nimrod, the laziest Sambo I ever saw, said I'd burn myself out. Then The Company wouldn't need me. Old Man Jeff wasn't old in years. He was just old on the job. Soon he'd be gone, and I'd take his place. Then I'd be gone—and somebody else would take my place. Nimrod knew the technique of loafing better than Shakespeare knew the drama. Nimrod told me that he worked two hours, in eight, for The Company—and still The Company beat him! Nimrod couldn't understand WHY a college man couldn't see through that. Nimrod said that when Old Man Jeff died, he'd have a tub for a tombstone. Nimrod married an oil heiress in Oklahoma!

The Dirty Radicals Started a Strike

We worked under miserable conditions. Men stood in water all day. They were always scared of losing their jobs. Most of them bowed under debts. We had the eight-hour day, but we were killing as many hogs in eight hours as we'd killed in ten. This was the SPEED UP. The men grumbled, cursed.

I was on The Tub. Five men set the pace for ten thousand workers in the packinghouse. First, there was the huge German downstairs who stuck the hogs as they passed on a long chain. In five minutes, he was covered with blood. He drank blood—and said nothing to anybody. Everybody feared him. Some said he'd cut a man's throat as soon as a hog's.

Second, there was the Negro dropper. He stood above The Tub and dropped hogs from a turntable into tons of boiling water. He sang blues as he set the killing pace. One day I tried to do his job. A mammoth hog, in its death agony, almost hurled me into The Tub.

Third, there was Old Man Jeff. Old-timers said he was slipping; yet he could souse hogs faster than a cat can lick its paw. Fourth, there was the little Mexican who hooked the hogs to the dehairing machine. His hands were faster than Joe Louis's punches. Fifth, there was the big black man who split the hogs. With one mighty blow, he could half a 600-pounder. Stripped to the waist, his huge muscles worked like big ebony snakes.

These five men who set the killing pace received big wages. The dirty radicals told the boys WHY. The Company used these five experts to speed up ten thousand men. So the strike came.

I Had Eyes and Saw Not

One morning, as I attempted to enter the plant, I discovered pickets outside. I didn't want to quit work. I had to make enough money to get to college. Fights started here and there. The workers argued with the five pacesetters. They didn't want to strike. The workers told them about the bad working conditions, the speed up, the poor wages, the women and kids at home without proper food and clothing. The black hog-splitter and the German sticker started in anyway. The angry crowd beat them up. Negroes beat up Negroes. Mexicans beat up Mexicans. Blacks and whites beat up whites.

I couldn't understand that. Negro misleaders hadn't told me anything about the class struggle. I'd thought that whites were always arrayed against blacks. I didn't know that the struggle between Capital and Labor breaks down racial barriers. Then years later I understood. But I didn't learn the lesson in either college or the university.

Now, I know WHY workers strike. They want to live. They want their wives and children to live. You can do without capitalists, but you can't do without workers. A servant is worthy of his hire. Poverty is an awful thing. It is hard to start a strike. Reds didn't start our strike. Bad working conditions start strikes. Capitalist newspapers try to smear unions, just as cracker newspapers try to smear Negroes.

Our union leaders were hardworking husbands and fathers who got disgusted with the money-grabbers of the First World War. The same is happening now, in spite of what the newspapers say. When I was in the packinghouse I never met a worker who knew Communism from *gogol*. Neither did I. I know now we didn't get what belonged to us. *Workers never do.*

Sights and Sounds—en Route to Tuskegee; "When the Choo Choo Leaves for Alabam" May 10, 1941

There's a big kick in the sights and sounds of a train. I have vivid memories of stations. When I was a boy, I worked for an old conductor. All his sons were trainmen. I wanted to be a railroading man. I did become a cook on the M & P. I know boys on the steel rails from the four corners of the little old USA. Railroading men are fine brothers.

> Gonna buy a ticket long as I am tall,
> Gonna buy a ticket long as I am tall,
> Gonna ride dat train until de engine stall!

I found myself in the jim-crow car, bound for New Orleans. It was night. The iron monster thundered toward the Gulf, across a low-lying region of antebellum plantations, with their dilapidated big houses and run-down cabins.

The small stations were ghosts in the night. The shadows of passengers passed. The rhythms of the rail made me think of George Gershwin's "Rhapsody in Blue." A friend in Greenwich Village told me Gershwin got his idea from a train ride.

The Hometown of a Negro Novelist

The iron monster stopped at Alexandria, Louisiana, its breath white and steaming in the chill night. I got out. Alexandria is the birthplace of Arna Bontemps, author of *God Sends Sunday* and *Black Thunder.*

This is the beginning of the Creole country. I remembered the stories Arna told about his native region, when I cooked him a breakfast of ham and eggs. He said he wasn't hungry—but!

I thought of Little Augie, the hero of *God Sends Sunday.* Arna is crazy about Little Augie. So am I. So was that old Negro jockey in Harlem whom I showed the novel in 1932. Little Augie went to St. Louis and became a bigshot on the tracks. But, everything that goes up must come down. So. Little Augie came down—down the Mississippi and down to poverty again. Is there a law of moral gravitation? Drummond thought so in a book I read as a boy.

I wondered why Arna left Alexandria. I wondered what his destiny would've been if he'd remained in Alexandria. That put me to thinking about O. Henry's *Roads of Destiny.* And then I thought about Robert Frost's magnificent poem "The Road Not Taken." Wasn't it funny? There I was in a jim-crow car thinking about the books white men had written. You can't jim-crow thoughts. What—if Arna had stayed in Alexandria? My mind took a trip to England. I recalled a stanza from Gray's "Elegy":

Full many a gem of purest ray serene
   The dark unfathomed caves of ocean bear;
Full many a flower is born to blush unseen,
   And waste its sweetness on the desert air.

I decided it was a good thing that a black boy like Arna Bontemps had got out of Alexandria. Thomas Gray, the English poet, had said, in 1751, that Alexandria was no place for a genius. And I add, especially, a black genius.

Crossing the River at New Orleans

The railroading men put our train, in three sections, on a huge boat. I got out. It was early in the morning. I walked forward to watch the vast expanse of yellow waters. Some un-American whites looked me up and down, as if I were a Nazi. Their heads went into a huddle.

If it weren't for the laughable ignorance of some white folk, I'd have to see more burlesque shows. I know they were discussing me, with profound deliberation. I felt my ego bursting with importance.

Isn't it funny how a black skin can send the white folk into a weighty conference? The author of *God Shakes Creation* says that the whites are scared of Negroes. They have an inferiority complex, I guess.

I am small in stature, as men go. Yet I was able to upset a half-dozen white men as large as Joe Louis or Jackson. Realizing how powerful I was, I struck the pose of being monarch of all I surveyed. I examined the lifeboat, I counted the lifesavers. I contemplated the ships at anchor. I meditated on the seagulls. I recited a stanza from Byron's poem, "Apostrophe to the Sea," and gestured at the waves!

The whites stood aghast. I made my English as the English. I've observed that whites are more baffled by a Sambo who uses the King's English than by bombs dropped upon their roofs. As I got back into the jim-crow car, a Redface drawled: "I thought I knowed n———rs, but that's the damnedest n———r I ever seen." At least, I'd broken a stereotype!

A Negro Sailor at Mobile

He'd just returned from Japan. He was a graduate of a famous State College. We had a long chat. He'd been in England, Germany, and France. He named mysterious islands. I asked him many questions about foreign lands, and he answered intelligently.

He said the whole world was in a hell of a fix. Everywhere he'd gone the Big Boys were fleecing the little ones. He was on the first American boat to leave England after the declaration of war. He told me about his experiences with a German submarine, which stopped and searched his ship.

He liked the sea. But a Negro didn't have a chance to go up in the navy. So he'd quit. He'd got tired of waiting on white folk.

He didn't understand how the German people had become such persecutors of weaker peoples. Perhaps Hitler had shot them the dope of racial prejudice, and they'd gone mad. He thought racial prejudice was the worst thing in the world. It made the human inhuman.

He liked the Chinese. He disliked the Japanese and English. He thought them snobs when it came to dark people. He said a cracker is a cracker, whether in Mobile or Paris. He said he'd received far better treatment as a man in foreign countries.

He thought the war would last a long time. He wanted to see

Africa—a free Africa, with no Englishmen and Italians and Germans and Frenchmen exploiting the natives. Wherever he went, dark people were talking about the freedom of Africa and India. He didn't think he'd live to see democracy in Alabama.

An Old White Man from Arkansas
January 16, 1943

A man is what life makes him. No more. No less. Change the place of a man's birth, and you change his life. Birth is a biological accident. It happened to all of us. A plant grows the way it is bent.

It was at the Dunbar Apartments in Harlem, about ten years ago. It was in the dead of winter. The colored YMCA was having a small interracial meeting in a reception room.

Each man present was asked to give an experience from his contacts with a member of another race. The value of the incident, of course, depended on the integrity of the storyteller. The chairman warned us concerning timidity. Yes, the stage was well prepared. It turned out to be one of the most interesting meetings I ever attended.

The Gentleman from Little Rock

In a front chair sat an aged white man. I supposed Negroes would call him a redneck. But a man is no more responsible for the redness of his neck than the blackness of his face. Selah!

I could see that the old gentleman was having the time of his life. His small figure was erect and tense. From time to time, he adjusted his glasses. Seemingly that enabled him to hear everything as well as see everything.

When the chairman sat down, the old man was the first to get to his feet. He drawled, as his face lighted with almost a holy light. He said he was in his first interracial meeting. Yes, that was also his first time North. He was staying at the white YMCA and he'd decided to make this meeting by all means.

Of course, he was a Southerner. He said it without apology. He had been brought up to think as the whites think down there. Like most men, he'd never stopped to question what everybody in his group said was right. Yes, that was the trouble. Men didn't question things. You could never get out of a mental rut unless you questioned the things you believed.

His Black Mammy had died recently. She was the best woman he'd ever met. He was at her deathbed. Her last words to God were not for herself but for him. He left the bedside weeping. As he talked, he wiped his eyes. He loved his Black Mammy, and he didn't care who knew it. Her death had started him on a new road. He was very old, but now he was going to find out things about Negroes.

A Negro from Yale

The old man was followed by a young Negro just out of Yale. The Black Mammy story had burned him up. He said every time a Southerner spoke to Negroes he told a mammy story. I saw the old white man look surprised; then he seemed to shrivel up. For ten minutes the young man from Yale poured it on.

When he sat down, I got up. I too was burning up. I went to the rescue of the white Southerner. I told the Yale scholar that Yale hadn't taught him anything about human nature.

I said, hell, there isn't anything wrong with loving a black mammy! Or a white mammy, for that matter. The wrong lies in not loving more black folk than the black mammy. Love is love, whether it's for a dog or a man. The emotion is a good one. It's not wrong to love your family. But it's wrong not to love the families of other men.

The old white man's face lighted up again. I told him he was on the right road. Yes, his Black Mammy had started him right. He must now learn to love Negro art and literature. I do not believe in pushing a man back into the darkness when he catches a glimpse of sunlight. I saw the Yale man seven years later. He said I was right. He had been to Russia with a white Southerner who was the best pal he's ever had.

Don't Pull Your Punches When You Get Upstairs!
April 24, 1943

Since I am full of mistakes, every now and then one happens. While I work night and day for This Cause and That Cause, I can't eliminate my sins of Commission and Omission. I write this to say: "By and by I'll answer the letters I receive from the dearest readers in the world." When I feel my punches are getting weak, I read the old letters that come from Here Yonder. Some from South Africa; others from Cuba; and still others from Bilbo-damned Mississippi.

It's really funny how far the *Washington Tribune* carries the old writings in other places. It seems that they just happened to stumble upon some of my stuff upstairs, or overheard some of the good dishes of cabbage and caviar. So thanks a million, for the letters.

Some of my readers damn me for not telling them about my white folk talking.

I was glad to discover that these friends of mine discovered that I didn't pull my punches upstairs. So I shall call attention to some of my stuff, for a writer writes to be read. If he has a conscience, he doesn't write to get the bucks. Although the bucks may buy some pork chops now and then!

Common Ground

The finest magazine published on the race questions in the United States is called *Common Ground*—222 Fourth Avenue, New York City. The present editor is Margaret Anderson, a modern Abolitionist. I'm told that the best writers of 50 different races write in these pages.

My first poem in *Common Ground* appeared last summer. It was called "Rendezvous with America." I tried to show that America was made by all races. Yes, I wanted to show that the Negro gives credit to whom credit is due. I think the Negro knows more about Democracy than anybody else. Why? Because the Negro knows what Democracy is not! A man suffering from a dreadful disease knows the value of good health!

Of course, I want you to read "Rendezvous with America." It is in nine sections, because I had a lot to say about America. It was broadcast twice last July 4. It was used to open the Drive for War Bonds at San Francisco. Archibald MacLeish, librarian of your Congressional Library, thought it exciting. Last month *Common Ground* brought out my "Woodcuts for Americana." Margaret Anderson says the letters are still coming in.

The Atlantic Monthly

I just received word that the *Atlantic Monthly* is bringing out my poem, "Babylon." Some of you read "Dark Symphony." Well, I hope you like this last piece. It has an interesting history.

Your Bible will tell you lots about Babylon, the enslaver of peoples. Babylon was the ancient tyrant. You know how Daniel read the handwriting on the wall. Well, your little Sambo poet brings Babylon up to date. Yes, this bit of stuff has enough TNT in it to sink all the Bilbo ships in the Black Belt. I'm talking about the TNT of truth!

I finished the poem last December, and sent it to Boston. Since that time two other artists have handled this tyrant, Babylon. Look them up.

First, there is Orozco, the famous painter of Mexico City. He painted Babylon in the Cathedral of Jesus. They tell me it's wonderful.

Second, the poet, William Benet—you know the Benets—wrote on the Babylon theme in the *Saturday Review of Literature,* February 13, 1943.

Some people say the language of my poetry is very different from the language of "Caviar and Cabbage." Well, when you go to a formal ball of the Big Boys, you have to put on evening clothes. No lie! When I'm at home, among friends, I go about the house in my patched pajamas. A woman doesn't cook cabbage in her Sunday best. In "Caviar and Cabbage" I try to be so simple that only a Howard professor can tell I am a professor.

The City by the Patapsco River
September 4, 1943

Baltimore, the city of contradictions, at the mouth of the Patapsco River, which old John Smith first gazed upon in June, 1608! Eleven years later the First Negro slaves landed at Jamestown. Remember that.

And 106 years later, after burning Washington, the British fleet sailed into Chesapeake Bay and fired on old Fort McHenry, day and night. Francis Scott Key peered into the dawn and saw the American flag still flying. On the back of an envelope he wrote the stirring song—the "Star Spangled Banner." The flag that waved over Fort McHenry was made by Mary Pickersgill, in the old Flag House in Baltimore.

I am a Negro American. I look at Fort McHenry. I look at Flag House. I look at Key Monument. I look at the famous Catholic Cathedral, the Mother Church of all Catholic churches in this country. Then I think of Jesus and the "Star Spangled Banner."

I am a Negro American in Baltimore. I add 2 and 2; and I get 5!

Memories of Baltimore

I remember my first night in Baltimore. I was just a boy, then, on my way to Lincoln University. I had traveled all the way from my hometown in Missouri. I was tired. So I fell asleep on a station bench. Yes, I was so tired I had sprawled out upon the bench. I woke up, dazed. The sole of my foot ached from a sudden blow. I looked into the red face of a frowning policeman. I've always wondered whether the cop struck me because I was a boy stretched upon a bench, or a *black* boy stretched upon a bench.

I remember that Countee Cullen, the Harlem Negro, wrote a poem on Baltimore. It tells the strange story of a white boy and black boy walking down the street, arm in arm. Such companionship puzzles both the white citizens and the black. The curtains raise stealthily. The whispers rise and scatter. It seems that a white-and-black friendship in the City of the "Star Spangled Banner" is a miracle.

Then, too, I remember my good friend, V. F. Calverton, the great defender of black men. His house at 2110 East Pratt Street was a rendezvous of the races. Here met Langston Hughes and Alain Locke and Abraham Harris.

The grave of Edgar Allan Poe is here. He died a wanderer in the underworld of Baltimore. This City by the Patapsco River, where Francis Key sang of the Land of the Free and the Home of the Brave has not always been a loving mother to her geniuses.

Out of Baltimore came the young H. L. Mencken, the editor of the *American Mercury,* to blast the prejudices of North and South, East and West. Richard Wright read Mencken's articles, became a free man, and wrote *Native Son.*

The Morgan Christian Center

I find myself on the campus of Morgan College for two weeks. Dr. Edgar A. Love brought me here from the Bible Belt. He is doing a marvelous work in the field of home missions.

At the Morgan Christian Center I encountered my old friend from Oklahoma, J. J. Seabrook, the Director of this up-and-coming institution. Dr. Seabrook and his lovely wife are putting in a social program which should be a tremendous aid in building the good life among Negroes of this section.

The purposes of the Morgan Christian Center have been set forth as follows: providing Christian education for students; conserving those values which students bring to college; developing personality; maintaining a wholesome social and cultural environment; meeting the constantly developing intellectual life of students.

Today I lectured to some one hundred ministers. It is indeed an interesting experience for me and for them. We are discussing social trends at home and abroad. Yes, we are having some hard-hitting debates. If any Negro is looking for Freedom of Thought and Freedom of Speech, he will find it here at the Morgan Christian Center. It is something like the old Town Hall meeting.

From Harlem to Moscow
September 25, 1943

Perhaps you have seen a copy of Marian Anderson's Souvenir Program, with the pictures of her cameo personality caught in various moods and poses. I like the one of her in Moscow, islanded by the worshipers of her race-eclipsing genius, while Wayland Rudd, the Harlem actor, watches her out of melancholy eyes.

It's a long, hard odyssey to the Moscow Theatre. It's no Glory Road for a beggarly black man on the cavernous stage of the Harlem Opera House. But the quest for the mysterious X is a prop to the spirit.

It was a wintry afternoon in the spring of 1932. Wayland Rudd and I sat at a table in Mr. Walburg's place on Seventh Avenue, and as usual the little Jew was playing a Negro spiritual on his ancient Victrola. It was always dusk in Mr. Walburg's store, and "Go Down, Moses" deepened the dusk.

"I have a chance to go to Moscow with Langston Hughes and the Negro actors," Wayland sighed. "The USSR is going to make a Negro movie."

"A grand idea!" I said.

Wayland was in one of his brooding seasons. "A relief from the boredom of Hollywood's black mammys and Uncle Toms," he gloomed, and tapped the saucer with the bottom of his false-silver spoon.

"I wonder how your name would look in Russian!"

Wayland stared beyond me, then pulled a billfold from his inside pocket. "Now, I have seventy-five bucks. Just enough to pay my rent, past and present."

Peg Leg Snelson used to sing the "Rocky Road Blues" in the Harlem Opera House, and dusky voices flowed into the chorus from the morgue of the balcony. Many a Negro actor kissed the Tree of Hope in front of the Lafayette and uttered a prayer to the goddess of luck. Langston's piano player thumped, thumped the blues until the sun blew out the night hours in the sky. Broadway critics praised Wayland Rudd's acting in *Blood Stream;* but the play shut itself like a horny turtle and left a perilous world outside, with the "Rocky Road Blues."

The door dragged open, and a ragged black woman shuffled in. On wintry afternoons, the only things warm in Mr. Walburg's place were the little Jew's heart and the Negro spirituals. I shivered at the table. Mr. Walburg got the snuff from a battered showcase, as the tottering woman extricated the coin from her knotted handkerchief.

Wayland watched the miniature drama out of the corner of his eye, and the shadows sank in his impressionable face. I thought of the odds and ends of races I had seen on the dead-gray streets of Harlem during the Great Depression.

"Hunger is hunger," said the actor, "whether in Harlem or Moscow."

He finished his ice cream. Like Joe Louis, Wayland Rudd

seemed never to get enough ice cream, in the summer or winter. Many Negroes are like that. Young Booker T. wanted to become a rich man so he could buy all the gingersnaps he could eat. Perhaps others are like that. I read a tale about a Chinese boy who dreamed a paradise of barns bursting with rice.

"Wayland," I said, "why not try Moscow?"

"But what about my landlord?" he puzzled.

I thought about the old miser in his great fur coat who owned the row of ancient apartment houses in the block where Wayland Rudd lived. Up and down the street, almost any day, one could hear the Negroes wrangling about the skyscraper rent. In the tomb of a basement bedroom the Black Moses of Harlem had nicknamed the landlord "Judas Pockets." His father had come from Georgia after Sherman had scorched the land to the sea. Only white folk lived in that section of Harlem then, and the legend said the Confederate colonel had willed that no Negro should ever rent one of his apartments. And now Honey Chile sings in her kitchenette, before going into her act at Big Blue's By-and-By:

> There's a change in the seasons
> And a change in the sea.
> There's a change in the times,
> And I don't mean maybe.

Finally I said to Wayland, "Can't you send the old skinflint his money from Moscow?"

The actor groaned, "I always heard that poet and idiot mean the same thing." On the impulse he gave his knee a resounding slap. "Say, Mr. Walburg, bring me that dime the old snuff-woman gave you."

As a man of the Harlem world, Mr. Walburg should expect the unexpected. But that afternoon he fumbled with his beard until the impatient actor repeated his request. Mr. Walburg shook the aged cash register, gently, as if it were an old man that had fallen asleep; then he came to the table, wagging his head.

Wayland thanked him and passed the shiny coin to me. "Flip it," he said.

I got to my feet then placed the dime between my thumb and the tip of my forefinger.

Wayland was as taut as a criminal eying the hangman's noose. "Let me flip it," he said. "You call it."

I knew that old trick. Entering with heartfelt joy into the spirit of the game, I said: "If chance is to decide, let chance have a chance."

"Go ahead," he said doggedly.

The acute quality in his voice jerked me bolt upright. I saw that he was suffering from a great fear, and realized that our tomfoolery had gone too far.

"Old man," I said, "let's call it off."

"Hell, no!"

I hesitated. Mr. Walburg's store was no longer chilly. I was aware that Wayland was pained by my dilemma.

"What's you waiting on?" His voice cracked.

I remembered dimly, in the far-off past, how Wayland Rudd had railed about an actor whose voice had cracked in the Lafayette Theatre. My flip of the coin was bad.

While it was still in the air, Wayland said: "Tails . . . I stay in Harlem."

The dime hit the dingy floor, rolled a short distance, and lay still. Wayland and I stood foolishly looking at each other. Mr. Walburg hobbled to the coin, pulled at his iron-gray beard, and bent almost double.

"What is it?" said Wayland, with an awful quietness in his voice and manner.

After a decade of silence, Mr. Walburg said, "Heads, gentlemen."

O Lord, I'm Writing This in Mississippi!
May 13, 1944

If the toothless Bilbo could see me now, your little columnist's jig would be up! I am writing these words in the Asylum of Illiteracy and Ignorance. Here and there, I have come across the footsteps of Jackass Bilbo. I have talked with men who know him. Yes, Sambo, I have many tales to tell, when I get back!

I remember vividly the last time I was in Mississippi—away back in 1929. At the time I was traveling in a car that I expected to fall to pieces at every mile.

I was en route to Nashville, where my debaters were to meet Fisk University. All day we had passed through the swamps and undergrowth of the Delta country. I don't know when I have ever suffered from the blues as I did that day.

Forward, Miss.

Have you ever heard of that village? I have asked many that question. Nobody has said "Yes." It was no more than a boxcar with a general store in the middle of a plantation. The river was up, and we had to detour many miles.

Late in the afternoon we saw the biggest sign I have ever seen above a station. It read ON-WARD. Eddie Hines, my ace debater who was a devout Christian, said: "See, Prof., even in a desolate spot like this, Man aspires to God. These poor people have named their village Onward. That means progress."

A cynic in the car sneered. I said nothing. I was just taking in the scene. At last we came to the general store. Some Negroes were sitting on the porch, with their shoes off, airing their toes.

Our car was leaking badly. We needed some water. We asked an ancient citizen of ONWARD where we could get some water. He told us to drive to the rear of the store. There was a well.

The driver got out to get the water. In about two minutes the longest, tallest, meanest white man I ever saw came to the door. His eyes were bloodshot. He was so drunk he could barely stand.

"What do you —— —— N——rs want?" he shouted.

"Just a little water," I said.

The boss of ONWARD yelled like Bilbo in Congress: "Onward, or I'll burn you N——rs up!"

We obeyed.

A Winchester Speaks to Us

As our car raced into the road, I looked back. The "Cracker" had staggered upon the front porch. I saw him put the Winchester to his shoulder. The Negroes had scattered like children before a mad bull. I saw the heels of one going across the yellow furrows. The Winchester barked. The ball whizzed past our windshield.

We ran the car until it was smoking like a furnace. About one mile down the road we stopped. Two old black citizens of ON-WARD came out of a cottonfield. We told them about the "Crackers." Their eyes got as big as saucers. It seemed that they thought us ghosts.

Their eyes seemed to say: "How did you get away alive?"

Then a funny thing happened. Most people will defend their hometown and the people in it—no matter how bad things are.

Finally, I said: "My God, that's a bad man—shooting at us just because we wanted some water."

One of the old men scratched his wooly head, his eyes still big with fear. Then his cracked voice came to me from a great distance:

"He ain't bad, only when he's drunk . . . and he's always drunk."

Index